A Curious
Discovery

A Curious Discovery

An Entrepreneur's Story

Founder and Chairman
of Discovery Communications

John Hendricks

HARPER
BUSINESS

An Imprint of HarperCollins*Publishers*
www.harpercollins.com

HarperCollins books may be purchased for educational, business, or sales promotional use. For information, please e-mail the Special Markets Department at SPsales@harpercollins.com.

FIRST EDITION

Designed by William Ruoto

Library of Congress Cataloging-in-Publication Data has been applied for.

ISBN: 978-0-06-212855-3

13 14 15 16 17   OV/RRD   10 9 8 7 6 5 4 3 2 1

To Maureen, Elizabeth, and Andrew

Contents

A Curious
Discovery

An Irresistible Notion

My life changed forever on a Sunday morning in February 1982.

There comes a time when every prospective entrepreneur must first share his or her big idea with another person. It is a perilous, even terrifying moment. What has been boiling in your brain for months, the obsession that has consumed your every waking moment and wrecked your sleep, suddenly demands to get out of your head, to be told to another human being—if only as a reality check to make sure that you aren't crazy.

And in those last seconds before you finally speak, you realize that all of the certainty you've felt for so long can now evaporate with a single laugh or stunned look. How many promising new business ideas are nipped in the bud simply because the first listener made the wrong response? I had built this immense logical fortress in my mind—and yet a single amused look from my wife could have brought down the entire structure into a pile of rubble.

We were in the kitchen of our crowded little town house in Greenbelt, Maryland, having a late breakfast. I tried to be as casual as possible, as if the notion had just come to me on a whim: "Hey," I said, "what would you think about a new cable channel that just showed great documentary series like *Cosmos*, *The Ascent of Man*, and Walter Cronkite's *Universe* series? You know, informative but entertaining shows about science, nature, history, and medicine?"

So there it was; it was out. The fate of endless hours of plotting and scheming had now been tossed into the hands of someone with no experience in the field, who had no idea of the magnitude of what I was suggesting, who had just seconds to correctly respond to the most simplified presentation possible, and who would be biased by the deepest conflict of interest imaginable. It was both unfair and unjust—and yet, looking back, it was the perfect practice for every "elevator" pitch I made to investors in the months that followed.

Why did this notion of a new enterprise matter so much to me, and why did it seem like such an opportunity? I'm not sure that any entrepreneur can give you a precise answer. Only now, looking back, do I realize that all of the great turning points in my career have been less the product of some stunning insight or epiphany than they have been the convergence of numerous threads in my life, some going back to my earliest childhood. At that nexus, which can occur at the most unexpected times, often when you have other plans, everything comes together into an idea so stunning that it captures your imagination and won't let go until you do something about it. In so many ways, since I was a child I had been on a journey that had brought me to this moment in 1982.

On this morning, that irresistible notion of a new cable television channel devoted to documentaries—the product of my first experiences of television as a child in West Virginia, of witnessing rocketry and scientific research as a boy in Alabama, of watching cable TV as a young man in Greenbelt, and examining media at the beginning of my professional career—was now about to make its public debut.

Maureen listened to my words, looked at me for a moment that seemed an eternity, then announced with surprising vehemence: "That would be awesome!"

Redemption. I wasn't crazy after all.

But then, after another moment of reflection, Maureen asked: "But if this is such a good idea, why didn't Ted Turner do it?"

It was a very good question. A question that I hadn't dared to ask myself. In those days, cable programming may have still been in its infancy, but future giants like CNN and ESPN and HBO were already up and running. So, if my idea for a nonfiction documentary channel was such a winner, then why weren't the established players—with all of their smart, veteran content people—already working on their own versions of that same idea?

Almost instantly, my excitement at having my idea validated as brilliant faded into self-doubt. After all, I was just twenty-nine years old and I had no background in television. Maureen and I had little money and, at that point, no wealthy investors to whom to turn. How could I be so delusional as to think I could take on not only the well-funded new cable channels, but also those three giants of network television: NBC, ABC, and CBS?

But it's *my* vision, I told myself. I've checked it and rechecked it. I've challenged every part of it and not found a single fatal flaw. I've read everything I can get my hands on about cable television, satellite communications, content sourcing, sponsorship prospects, and business plan development. I *know* I'm right—and if the Big Boys haven't seen it, then it is their mistake, not mine.

Looking back over three decades, I'm astounded at both my presumptuousness and my confidence. But I also now recognize that it is just this kind of bravado, mixed with a healthy dose of passion, that every entrepreneur needs in order to tackle the nearly impossible task of getting a new enterprise off the ground. And to keep it flying—to weather the hardships and challenges of the months and years ahead—that confidence and passion has to evolve into something very close to obsession. Entrepreneurs have always known this. I was about to learn it.

The Soul of an Entrepreneur

The idea I first shared with Maureen that morning for a cable channel devoted to nonfiction programming has, over the last thirty years, been transformed into the global media empire known as Discovery Communications—an enterprise that now reaches more households on the planet with more television programming than any other company or government.

That is the magic of entrepreneurship—a miracle I don't think we celebrate often enough. In my case, what began as a mere germ of an idea now encompasses fourteen networks in the United States—including Discovery Channel, Animal Planet, TLC, and the Science Channel. As of this writing, we also now deliver more than 150 television networks to more than 1.8 billion cumulative subscribers in more than 215 countries and territories. And those numbers continue to grow as subscription TV services take hold in emerging markets around the world. We transmit our networks in more than 45 languages and use 30 transponders on 18 different satellites. Discovery is now a major public company with more than 4,000 employees working in 50 global offices, one that brings in more than $4.2 billion in revenue each year. And with its public market value exceeding $23 billion, Discovery Communications is, as I write this in October 2012, worth more than any of the big four U.S. broadcasting networks (ABC, CBS, NBC, and Fox).

Did I know that morning in 1982 that Discovery Communications would become all of this? Yes and no. Like every entrepreneur, my passion for my new idea had no bounds. I was absolutely convinced that I had the recipe for a world-class company. But at that moment, did I have a road map for getting there? Not a chance. I didn't even have a plan for what I was going to do the next day.

It is precisely that vast chasm between vision and reality, between the big picture and the secret, private dream that makes entrepreneurship one of the most exciting, and important, of all life endeavors—and in my mind puts great entrepreneurs on the same plane as those scientists, artists, and political leaders we celebrate on Discovery television. And yet, just like the stories of musical geniuses and mathematical prodigies, the inner workings of great entrepreneurs are almost opaque to us.

What makes a Sam Walton, a Bill Gates, or a Steve Jobs? I don't have the complete answer. There are just too many variables of personality, life experiences, and context. But having traveled the same path of these remarkable individuals—as well as millions of other entrepreneurs who have built big enterprises and small—I do know by heart the map of the path that we all take. And to that basic knowledge, I can at least provide the inside details of my own path to entrepreneurial success.

That may not be everything you need to understand the soul of an entrepreneur, but it is a lot. And, by remaining as honest as I can be through this book—that is, by looking at both my successes and failures with a cold and objective eye—I hope to provide some of the insights and answers that are typically lacking from books like this one.

I want to intimately explore the motivations and behavioral traits that underlie entrepreneurship. For example, what do the entrepreneurs of today have in common with inventors and creators of the past? To what degree do curiosity, vision, passion, and purpose contribute to the creation of something new in the world? How are entrepreneurial ideas incubated to a point where a driving passion becomes an obsession?

I also want to examine and describe the practical realities of creating a business—too many books about entrepreneurs cover the early struggles and then jump to the great success without really looking at the all-important middle period, the quotidian reality of actually building a real company.

Thus: How does the entrepreneur learn where to find investors and capital? How does that kitchen table dream actually get converted into products and offices and employees? What role does government play in facilitating or thwarting the success of business formation and operation? How do you spot technology trends and consumer forces that are shaping the evolving landscape of a competitive marketplace—without getting there too late to compete? This is what real entrepreneurship is about: the garage may be the great mythical beginning, but it's what happens in those months *after* you leave the garage that makes or breaks most companies.

Finally, and certainly not least, I intend to tell you the history of Discovery Communications, one of the most unlikely business tales in recent memory. So far, at least, it has a very happy ending.

Perhaps like me, you have read a number of books on "how" particular companies were created and "how" they operate. These comprehensive studies are very helpful in understanding corporate strategies and management systems.

I have taken a different approach in this book. I want to explore "why" businesses are created. Why do entrepreneurs do what they do? Why do they devote such enormous time, with a very high risk of failure, to create something new in the world? Why don't they give up in the face of enormous obstacles? Why can they see things that others do not? Why are entrepreneurs so passionate about what they do? Why do they spend so much time daydreaming? And why are they so darn optimistic?

It all begins, I've come to believe, with an overpowering sense of curiosity. Hence the title of this book. I believe that if you scratch any entrepreneur you will find a little boy or girl who was intensely curious about the world: how bees flew, what mommy and daddy did at work each day, how clocks worked, how automobiles were built, how sugar, water, and lemon juice could be turned into money and then into candy.

I was certainly one of those curious children. And I suspect that, because you've picked up this book, you were one as well. No doubt, like me, that child is still inside you, forever curious, asking questions and searching for answers—and every once in a while that child asks a question that is so compelling that it can't be simply set aside as unanswerable. Rather, it has to be *lived*.

That is the story of my life—and the story of Discovery Communications. I now humbly offer it to you in the hope that you will be entertained as you gain insights to help you write your own story of curiosity and discovery.

Part One

Incubation

Chapter 1

Four O'Clocks

I think, at a child's birth, if a mother could ask a fairy godmother to endow it with the most useful gift, that gift should be curiosity.

—Eleanor Roosevelt

I remember the cool stone against my back.

I was four years old, shirtless, sitting up against the foundation of my house, waiting for the sun. My mother had told me about "four o'clock" flowers—the ones that open late in the afternoon—and I wanted to see it happen. So I had crawled through what must have been a little hedge of them and now sat facing west and under a canopy of the closed buds.

I waited and watched for what seemed forever . . . and then the sun dropped just enough for the light to stream through the leaves. Suddenly, everything became bright and vivid. The green leaves became nearly transparent but for the veins that crisscrossed them. I was puzzled and entranced by those strange lines. What was this presence I'd never noticed before?

I heard my mother calling "John Samuel," but I stayed under the flowers, silent. I was seeing this structure where there wasn't any before, and a powerful feeling welled up in me: I just had to know why there were lines in the four o'clock leaves.

As far as I can tell, this was my first memory. It came at a comparatively late age, but also with an almost supernatural force. I wanted so much to understand something—everything—about those lines.

I don't know what finally got me to leave the four o'clocks, but I do recall finding my dad and asking him about the lines. He was an older father, fifty-two at the time, and so he had veins on the back of his hands that stood out. He pointed to them and said they were like the lines on the leaves—part of the system that carries the blood and nutrients that life needs.

I can remember the power that surged through me at the thought that I now owned that piece of knowledge—and at the same time, the wave of mental, even physical, relief that came with no longer having to live with an unanswered question. Those kinds of questions, I realized, made me anxious and unfulfilled; their answers made me calm and complete. A half century later, I'm still driven by that same compulsion.

Even years later my dad still talked about that incident with the four o'clock flowers and all the other questions I had as a kid. Because he was so well-read, he was a good target for my constant inquiries. Looking back, I realize that his recognition of the power of that moment in my life suggests that he had lived his life with the same unbounded curiosity. He was never able to give that curiosity full rein; I'm sure he'd be happy that I have.

Bottom and Hollow

My early years were spent in the little Appalachian town of Matewan, West Virginia—a village famous for all of the wrong reasons, from labor strife to America's most notorious feud.

We lived just outside of town at Hatfield Bottom, which was

along a railroad line and the Tug Fork of the Big Sandy River. The Tug Fork River served as the border between West Virginia and Kentucky. If the valley had been a little narrower, it would have been a "hollow" like so many others, and not a "bottom."

On our side of the Tug Fork River were the railroad tracks, a road, and then a hill; to the west were the hills of Kentucky. From the front of my house, I could look out and see perhaps four or five houses in our little bottom. The rest was woods and open land.

I would often walk around these wild areas with my father, continuously asking: "What's this?" "What's that?" I can remember once becoming endlessly fascinated with a pebble—and wearing out my father by pestering him with questions about how old it was, where it came from, and what it was made of.

I also became fascinated with cars at an early age, adding those man-made marvels to my boundless curiosity about the natural world. By the time I was five, I could name all of the cars that we encountered along the highway. Soon, whenever my dad had a friend or relative in the car with us, he would bet that I'd be the first person to name the make and model year of an oncoming car. He almost always won.

But, as the reader no doubt knows, curiosity can also get you into trouble. I was with my parents visiting my mother's father, James Marion Daugherty. My grandfather was of Irish Protestant stock. Losing his wife early and being left with three young children during the Depression—and sending them out to his two older, married daughters because he couldn't take care of them—had made him a hard man, quick to anger.

My mother, Pauline Daugherty Hendricks, was just eight years old when her mother, Ellen Hatfield Daugherty, died in 1929. As her name suggests, she was part of the Hatfield clan of West Virginia, the family that tangled with the Kentucky McCoys in

America's most famous feud. After her mother died, my mom was sent to live with her older sister, Edith.

In the late 1950s, when we went to see him, Grandpa Jim still lived up in one of the hollows near a place called Red Jacket. While the adults were talking and eating, I went outside to his flower garden and began exploring wherever my curiosity led me. I must have done something Grandpa Jim didn't like, because he came running out of the house, yelling at me. I took off.

"If I see you in there again," he shouted after me, "I'll come after you with my shillelagh!" I didn't know then that a shillelagh was a walking stick—one that doubles as a club—but I could tell it was not something I wanted to meet.

Grandpa Jim was just one of my "interesting" relatives. I happen to be a descendant of a rather long line of independent-thinking and self-reliant Virginians and West Virginians. This may, or may not, have anything to do with the course of my life. But it certainly made my childhood unusual.

Family records and genealogical records on my father's side indicate that I am the ninth-generation descendant of Hance Hendrick, who settled in Virginia about three decades before the time that Thomas Jefferson's father, Peter, was born.

According to research by Robert Baird in his narrative genealogy, *The Pamunkey Hendrick Family*, it was in the early 1680s that Hance Hendrick arrived with his wife, Jane, and ten other persons to claim 594 acres of land on the south bank of the Mattaponi River in the Virginia Colony. The land had been acquired from Richard Yarborough, who had managed to buy a large tract of property from the Pamunkey Indians—the Pamunkeys themselves having received official title to their land from King William III as part of a 1677 peace treaty.

Remarkably, no historian or genealogist has yet been able to confirm Hance's country of origin—although the leading candidates are England, Germany, Holland, or Sweden. My daughter, Elizabeth Hendricks North, a Princeton history graduate, believes that Hance Hendrick was likely of Swedish descent, since he named one of his sons Adolphus, perhaps in tribute to the legendary King Gustavus Adolphus of Sweden. The spelling of the name Hendrick also fits with the Swedish spelling of the surname.

My family descended through the line of Benjamin Hendrick, one of Hance's four sons, and the one who in his late eighties signed a petition urging religious tolerance that was submitted to Virginia's first House of Delegates in the fall of 1776. Benjamin's grandson, Daniel, like most patriotic Virginians of his time, fought in the Revolutionary War, after which he moved to Charlotte County, Virginia. In Charlotte County, his son, Daniel H. Hendrick Jr., married Eliza Ann Cary, who gave birth in 1844 to my great-great-grandfather Richard D. Hendrick. Richard was just sixteen years old when the Civil War began. At some point an *s* was added to his last name, most likely during the registration process for his military service.

After the Civil War, Richard moved to Patrick County, Virginia, and married Mary Victoria Deatherage. Soon after, in November 1867, my grandfather Sampson Octavius "Sam" Hendricks was born. Sam Hendricks married Nannie Belle Lewis and by the time my father, John Gilbert Hendricks, was born in 1904, the family had moved to West Virginia.

My paternal ancestors in America were modest plantation owners in the very beginning but as the initial land wealth of Hance and his sons became divided through inheritance, their ever-poorer descendants took up farming and craftsmanship throughout the eighteenth and nineteenth centuries. Carpentry and construction had become the family business for my grandfather Sam Hendricks.

Together with his sons, he built many of the homes, schools, and commercial buildings for the new mining communities that were springing up along the railroad tracks in West Virginia in the early twentieth century.

Orbit

The great postwar changes of the 1950s eventually reached even a little hamlet like Hatfield Bottom. As a kid who had never left West Virginia, I found my mind opened as wide as the skies by news of the Soviet Union's launch of Sputnik. The idea of a satellite orbiting the planet was so exciting to me; it was like a doorway to a huge new world beyond earth. I was stunned to learn that the satellite was traveling an amazing 18,000 miles per hour—I couldn't imagine anything moving so fast. And lots of people—including our little Hendricks family in West Virginia—listened to Sputnik's "beep, beep, beep" on the radio as it circled our side of the world. We sensed, even if we didn't know how, that Sputnik would change our lives.

Even in my earliest West Virginia years I loved thinking about space travel. My favorite book was a little Wonder Book titled *Tom Corbett: A Trip to the Moon*. It told the story of a space explorer who journeyed with a boy and girl named Johnnie and Janie in the spaceship Polaris. This was an era when space travel seemed almost within our reach—*Tom Corbett: A Trip to the Moon* allowed me to dream about my impending life far beyond the hills of West Virginia. The space race was on, and almost every kid my age dreamed of somehow being a part of it. I felt privileged and lucky to have been born into one of the great Ages of Discovery.

Chapter 2

Wired to the World

Where a new invention promises to be useful, it ought to be tried.
—Thomas Jefferson

We tried to receive a television signal in Hatfield Bottom but got only static—the hills and mountains were in the way. The great invention of television that had begun to sweep the nation in the late 1940s and early 1950s was literally passing over us in the air above the mountaintops.

Then, in 1957, my uncle Ralph Daugherty came to the rescue. He had been a radio operator in the Pacific during World War II, and so he knew a lot about the burgeoning world of electronics—including television.

Uncle Ralph had an idea: he would plant an antenna on a nearby hilltop and run a cable wire down to our house. He would then split the signal and feed additional wires to other neighbors who also wanted to watch TV. He didn't know it, but he was firing one of the first shots in what would soon be a media revolution.

It was a cold fall day and all the leaves had dropped when Uncle Ralph, my father, and my older brother, Kenneth, began their TV project. They climbed up the hillside with a clamshell digger and dug a hole for the antenna, then poured in a bucket of concrete to secure it in place. This wasn't a fancy antenna—just a rooftop-style one, but larger. Once the antenna was secured, they unspooled about four hundred feet of wire down the hillside and ran a connection through our living room wall to our brand-new television set, which, as was typical in those days, looked more like furniture—an oak laminate cabinet with a small black-and-white tube screen in the middle.

Looking back, I figure that Uncle Ralph must have rigged some type of an amplifier to boost the signal down the hill. But what I did know, even at age five, was that the antenna had to be pointed in just the right direction, toward Charleston or Huntington, or we would get nothing but static. And the first day, that's all we got. My dad or my brother would run up the hill and turn the antenna in one direction and then run down to see if there was a signal. I went up a couple times too, without luck.

Uncle Ralph eventually provided clunky two-way radios, which saved a lot of time and energy. The antenna was turned slightly this way or slightly that way—fuzzy, fuzzy, fuzzy, and then finally we got a signal . . . a clear signal. It was a variety show, and at that moment the distant world of New York City miraculously appeared in my living room. For days thereafter I sat in front of the TV set, mesmerized.

Magic Signals

Without knowing it, Uncle Ralph had just created a tiny, make-shift cable TV operation. And, indeed, that is exactly how cable TV actually started around the United States, beginning in the late 1940s. It was called community antenna television, and it was typically used in places that couldn't get reception because of significant distance from transmitters or because of hilly terrain. Cable wouldn't have its own programming for decades; it was simply a way to bring broadcast television to outlying small towns and communities far from the larger cities where the signals originated.

These days cable systems take pride in their high reliability. But back then it took constant work to keep our little system up and running—what with the wind blowing and snow pulling down on the tree branches above the cable line that first winter. And then in the spring, when the leaves came out, we realized that the antenna was too deep in the hilltop foliage to receive a good signal. The antenna had to be repositioned to a better clearing on the hilltop. Finally it worked again, and Hatfield Bottom once more had its lifeline to the outside world.

As a newborn in 1952, I did not come home from the hospital to a household that had flickering television images. Because television did not arrive in my home until I was five, I have long suspected that it had a much bigger and more profound impact on me than it had on my baby boomer counterparts who experienced the sights and sounds of television almost literally from the crib onward. At age five, I was old enough to appreciate the sheer amazement of seeing moving images from a distant place and, in the case of movies, from a different time.

I was also old enough to be puzzled by the magic and curious enough to ask a million questions. My ever-patient father struggled to explain invisible radio waves to me and how pulses of these waves could be used to transmit sound to radios and moving pictures to television sets. He had already taught me a little bit about electricity . . . in particular that there were small, invisible, and dangerously "shocking" things called electrons running through those wires and cords in our home. My father now tried to explain that in the TV tube these same electrons painted pictures real fast, so fast that my eyes could not see the individual still pictures. And that all of these pictures blurred together to create smooth motion.

It was all way too much for a five-year-old to understand. I finally gave up until I was much older and found myself in eighth-grade science class. At that point I began to understand about the enormous spectrum of visible and invisible electromagnetic waves that permeates the universe, how our human eyes evolved to detect only part of that spectrum, and how humans could manipulate the electromagnetic spectrum to transmit and receive codes for audio, video, and other data.

I didn't know it at the time my uncle was setting up our antenna, but cable television had been born nine years earlier just north of Matewan, in Mahanoy City, Pennsylvania. Mahanoy City is also a place surrounded by mountains and hills that effectively blocked the new broadcast signals coming from Philadelphia and Pittsburgh.

John Walson owned an appliance store in Mahanoy City and was anxious to sell television sets to local residents. But no one could get a clear signal. So, in 1948, Walson erected a mountaintop antenna and strung "twin lead" or "ladder" cable to the valley community below, like my uncle Ralph would do for us almost a decade later. John Walson charged $100 per hookup and $2 per month for his community antenna television (CATV) service. That was a considerable sum in those days, but the locals, anxious to participate in this new media phenomenon sweeping the country, quickly signed up by the score.

In nearby Lansford, Pennsylvania, Robert Tarlton organized a group of fellow TV set retailers in 1950 and together financed a community antenna system that offered Philadelphia broadcast signals for a fee. This particular CATV system was featured in *Newsweek*, the *New York Times*, and the *Wall Street Journal*—and the resulting publicity sparked an explosion of cable system construction across the country. Robert Tarlton soon became a valuable consultant to many of these systems—and his equipment supplier, a new company called Jerrold Electronics, emerged as a leading provider of amplifiers, converter boxes, and "head-end" (the master facility for receiving and distributing signals) equipment for the new industry.

So, like me, cable television was born in the Appalachian Mountains. Although cable and I had roots in coal country, we were both bound for other places.

Chapter 3

Rocket City, USA

Space travel will free man from his remaining chains, the chains of gravity which still tie him to this planet. It will open to him the gates of heaven.

—Wernher von Braun

In June 1958, I was six years old and ready to enter the first grade. It was at this time that my parents sat me down to explain that we were moving from Matewan to Huntsville, Alabama, a growing city in the South.

My older sister, Linda, had already moved to Huntsville to take her first job. And I knew from the telephone calls with my sister that she lived in the place where they built space rockets. Other kids might have been sad about leaving their childhood home—but not me: I felt like the luckiest kid in the world. *Rockets!*

Redstone Renaissance

In 1950, Huntsville, Alabama, was a sleepy little southern town with a population of just fifteen thousand. Many of the town's buildings and residences had survived the ravages of the Civil War. Beautiful antebellum homes, some with their former slave quarters still intact, lined streets named after U.S. presidents such as Adams, Monroe, and Jefferson. During World War II the U.S. Army had constructed army ordnance facilities on land adjoining Huntsville—designated as Redstone Arsenal in 1945.

The destiny of Huntsville was forever changed when, in 1950, the U.S. Army transferred its top missile engineers, led by Wernher von Braun and his team of German scientists, from Fort Bliss, Texas, to the Redstone Arsenal. In 1956, the Army Ballistic Missile Agency was formed at the arsenal. This agency was tapped to develop, under von Braun's engineering leadership, the Jupiter C missile that on January 31, 1958, launched America's first satellite, Explorer I, into orbit.

Huntsville soon became the engineering and technology center for America's new space program—a fact cemented on September 8, 1960, when President Eisenhower visited Huntsville to dedicate the formation of the George C. Marshall Space Flight Center.

In the spring of 1958, fresh from her graduation from secretarial school, my sister, Linda, left West Virginia for job interviews in Huntsville. Just nineteen, she had decided to look for a job in Huntsville at the suggestion of my father's nephew, John Howell, who had earlier moved down to the bustling Alabama town from Norton, Virginia, to work in the local telephone company. Linda quickly landed a job at Brown Engineering, a contractor with the Army Ballistic Missile Agency. It wasn't long before Linda began to telephone us in Matewan to convince my father, a home builder and master wood craftsman, to move the family down to Huntsville to take advantage of the building boom there. Recognizing the dismal outlook for construction in West Virginia, my father and mother soon agreed—and headed for Huntsville with me and my fifteen-year-old brother, Kenneth, in tow.

I could not believe that I was going to move to the actual place where they built the Jupiter C missile. Over the phone my sister said she could even hear the rocket engines being tested at Redstone Arsenal from where she worked at Brown Engineering.

It would only be a few months until a new president would take office and declare a bold new goal for America. Before a joint session of Congress on May 25, 1961, President John F. Kennedy issued his famous challenge: "I believe that this nation should commit itself to achieving the goal, before this decade is out, of landing a man on the moon and returning him safely to the earth."

Huntsville had a job to do. Not only would its engineers have to design and build rockets large enough to get small satellites and a manned capsule into orbit, but within the decade they would also have to build a giant rocket, the Saturn V, that could lift a heavy manned payload bound for the moon. Before long, I knew the statistics of this mighty rocket by heart: at 363 feet high, the Saturn V stood taller than a 36-story building . . . 58 feet taller than the Statue of Liberty from the ground to the tip of the torch. When fully fueled it would have a total mass of 6.5 million pounds. The Saturn V would be able to propel an enormous 262,000 pounds to earth's orbit and a 100,000-pound payload to the moon. It would be—and it still remains—the tallest, heaviest, and most powerful rocket ever built.

I grew up in the house of a home builder, so construction blueprints were always around. But now, just a few miles from my house, I knew there were engineers who were poring over blueprints of all the components of the mission to the moon: the Saturn V Rocket, the Command Module, the Service Module, and the Lunar Excursion Module (the LEM).

That was thrilling enough for a teenager. But I was fortunate enough to be directly exposed to the planning of one of the key engineering marvels on board the Apollo missions: the Lunar Rover.

Starstruck

Here's how it happened. My sister Linda married James M. Sisson, a bright young aerospace engineer who had earned his aeronautical engineering degree from the University of Oklahoma in 1958. One of Jim's summer jobs had been in Dallas, where he worked on studies of wind tunnel testing for the Chance Vought Corporation, which had developed the F8U Crusader, the first Navy/Marine Corps aircraft capable of sustained supersonic flight, and of exceeding 1,000 mph in level flight.

On the morning of July 16, 1957, Marine Corps Major John Glenn took off in an F8U Crusader from Los Alamitos Naval Air Station in California bound for Floyd Bennett Field in Brooklyn, New York—and in the process set a transcontinental speed record of 725.55 mph and completed the historic flight in 3 hours, 23 minutes, and 8.4 seconds.

Jim Sisson received his U.S. Army draft notice two weeks prior to his graduation from the University of Oklahoma. Taking note of his aeronautical engineering degree, the U.S. Army assigned Jim to the Redstone Arsenal in Huntsville, Alabama. There Jim worked in the wind tunnel testing program, a role that he continued, after his two-year service in the Army, with Chrysler Corporation, at the time a NASA contractor. It was in 1958, while working on the wind tunnel testing program, that Jim met Linda (Brown Engineering was also working on wind tunnel tests). They were married in 1960.

Suddenly, to my infinite joy, the space program was part of my life.

For example, the phone rang in my house on Warner Street on a weekend morning in early January 1966. The city was digging out from under an unusual twelve-inch snowfall. My mother answered the call. She told me to be ready to join Jim, when he pulled up in his Jeep, for a ride to the airport. She added that we would be picking up a "special friend" of Jim's on the way.

I put on my coat and waited by the living room window. When Jim finally arrived and I hopped in, he had a little smile on his face. He didn't answer my questions as he navigated his blue Jeep through the snow-covered streets bound for the Carriage Inn Hotel.

Jim may not have been talking, but I was already guessing. He had told me in the past about his trips taking astronauts to the airport. And if it was to be an astronaut, I was certain to know who it was. I had a scrapbook full of newspaper and magazine clippings about all the NASA astronauts, from the original Mercury 7 to those slated to fly in the Gemini and Apollo programs.

I also knew that there had been a recent space mission, Gemini 7, that was the twelfth American manned flight. The flight had launched on December 4, 1965, and had returned to earth fourteen days later—the record flight duration to date. The crew of Gemini 7 had also rendezvoused with the crew of Gemini 6A, another space first for NASA. Astronauts Jim Lovell and Frank Borman were aboard the Gemini 7 capsule and the Gemini 6A capsule was crewed by Astronauts Wally Schirra and Tom Stafford. I had followed the mission every day through the CBS coverage anchored by Walter Cronkite.

I waited in the back of the Jeep as Jim walked into the hotel lobby. He returned with a man whose face I knew well. My heart raced as it hit me that I would be spending the next twenty minutes in a vehicle with Astronaut Jim Lovell. I was starstruck the entire ride. I barely managed to speak . . . but I did at least manage to shake his hand and say hello.

I was thirteen years old and I had actually touched someone who had been in space.

Rumblings

As the plans for the later Apollo missions came together in 1969, Jim was appointed by NASA to be its chief engineer in charge of the development of the Lunar Rover. Rovers were planned to be on board the Apollo 15, 16, and 17 missions. And that meant the blueprints for one of the most exciting machines of the NASA program were now going to be in our family.

Now seventeen years old, I used every chance I got to spend time at Jim and Linda's house on Delta Avenue. Most weekends they could count on me to babysit my young nephews, Martin and Alan, ages seven and six. I loved being with my nephews and I was captivated by Jim's NASA work. There were always so many interesting items from the space program in Jim's home office, such as photos from space, rocket models, Apollo design plans, astronaut correspondence, and construction drawings of the Lunar Rover.

Early on, Jim detected my keen interest in the space program and he took the time to go over details of the challenges his team was facing in building the little battery-powered electric vehicle that would transport two astronauts across the lunar surface. I can remember one particular puzzle that the lead contractor, General Motors, and Jim and his engineers had to solve: finding just the right material for the rover's wheels. No natural or even synthetic rubber material could withstand the temperature extremes on the moon: 253°F in the daylight and –387°F at night (or in the shadows).

Moreover, no one really knew the exact consistency and depth of the top layer of lunar soil. It was thought that the topsoil might have the consistency of talcum powder—but was that surface layer four inches or four feet in depth? Jim worried that the rover wheels might quickly sink up to their hubs in the lunar soil and be of no use to the astronauts. It was just one of the hundreds of conundrums faced by the Apollo mission—none of which would find an answer until the Apollo astronauts were on the moon . . . and then it might be too late.

In the end, Jim and the NASA team of contractors and engineers brilliantly decided to build the rover's wheels out of wire mesh. But that solution only created a new set of problems—not least: what was the right tensile strength for the wire? And could it be purchased off the shelf—as there simply was not enough time to design, test, and manufacture a customized wire. The solution proved to be *piano wire*.

I can still remember listening to Jim explain all the problems that the rover development team was facing—and then all of the novel solutions that they had found—in designing mankind's very first vehicle to roll across the surface of another body in space. It was beyond thrilling; it was *transforming*.

When the mighty Saturn V engines were being tested, the ground shook in Huntsville. Knowing the planned times for the tests, which were usually reported in advance by the *Huntsville Times*, my mother would take down one special piece of her display china for fear it would fall and break.

Every time the Saturn V engines came to life, I was keenly aware, right up through the soles of my feet, that some very smart humans were building something of monumental power. The people of Huntsville were going to be part of mankind's first attempt to reach the surface of the moon. I learned right then that there is nothing more enthralling than having even the tiniest part in making history, of being even the smallest player in an epic human quest.

Chapter 4

Television Lifeline

What sort of day was it? A day like all days, filled with those events that alter and illuminate our times . . . and you were there.

—WALTER CRONKITE, *You Are There* TV SERIES

Although the technical workings of television fascinated me growing up, it was the content of those signals that truly captivated me. From the moment the signal reached my house I was glued to anything on the screen that expanded my understanding of the world.

It's not that I didn't watch many of the entertaining and amusing shows on TV—for instance, our family absolutely loved *The Andy Griffith Show*—it is just that I always found the news and the occasional history or science documentary to be irresistible.

I also loved reading. My favorite books were science fiction stories—so I found myself instantly in heaven when Rod Serling's *Twilight Zone* premiered on CBS on October 2, 1959. Even though I was just a second grader that first season, there was nothing that could get between me and a TV set when a new episode of *The Twilight Zone* was on.

To this day I fondly remember the enchantment I felt while

watching those first episodes—like "Walking Distance," in which a middle-aged executive (I was too young to know it was the great Gig Young) takes a walk back in time and visits the hometown of his youth, encountering himself as a youngster.

Walter Cronkite also played a featured role in our living room. My parents seldom missed the *CBS Evening News*, which Cronkite began anchoring in 1962. But I had known his resonant voice and presence since the fifties, as he had hosted one of my favorite series, *You Are There*, in which he treated key historical events as if they were breaking news. *You Are There* transported kids like me to historical events such as the Salem Witch Trials, the signing of the Magna Carta, the Boston Tea Party, the capture of John Wilkes Booth, the *Hindenburg* explosion, the assassination of Julius Caesar, and the fall of the Alamo.

Cronkite ended each *You Are There* episode with words I can still recite: "What sort of day was it? A day like all days, filled with those events that alter and illuminate our times . . . and you were there."

From 1957 through 1966, Walter Cronkite also narrated the great CBS documentary series *The Twentieth Century*. I tried not to miss a single one of its 222 episodes. "The Doolittle Raid," "The Times of Teddy Roosevelt," and "Paris in the Twenties" . . . it was my full immersion program in modern history. Even better were the science episodes: "Vertijets," "Reaching for the Moon," "The Satellite That Talks," and "Mach Busters."

In 1967, when I was fifteen, CBS changed the series' name to *The 21st Century*, with topics focused on the future. I was off to college in 1970 when the series ended its run. As such, it had been part of my entire childhood, its impact on my life immeasurable. It was my most important lesson in the power of television. Walter Cronkite's dedication to telling the great stories of history and technology proved to be the most important answer to my childhood curiosity—and I was thrilled to one day be able to tell him that in person.

Dark Times in a Bright Place

Television was even more than a science and history teacher in my early life—and once again, Walter Cronkite played an instrumental role. As an elementary school kid growing up in the South, television made a vital connection between me and a much bigger world outside my small neighborhood in Alabama at the dawn of the civil rights movement.

Although Huntsville, with its growing population of scientists and engineers, was much more progressive than other southern cities in advancing civil rights, there were still pockets of bigotry in many of its neighborhoods. The juxtaposition of America's intellectual leadership in rocket science alongside its persistent problem of racism was both unexpected and unsettling to witness in the years up to 1963, when the public schools of Alabama at last began to integrate. That integration began with four of the city's elementary schools. One of those schools was mine.

My family had moved from a state, West Virginia, whose governor, William Marland, had immediately taken steps in 1954 to comply with the U.S. Supreme Court's ruling against school segregation in *Brown v. Board of Education*. That had not been the case in Alabama, which had maintained its segregated public school system in defiance of federal law.

That defiance was cemented when George Wallace was sworn in as governor of Alabama in 1963. In his infamous inaugural address Wallace pledged "segregation now, segregation tomorrow, segregation forever."

Outsiders

On June 11, 1963, during the beginning of my Little League baseball season, my family watched the television coverage of the national drama playing out downstate in Tuscaloosa. There Governor Wallace stood in the doorway of Foster Auditorium at the University of Alabama and attempted to block the enrollment of African-American students Vivian Malone and James Hood. President Kennedy had authorized his brother U.S. Attorney General Robert Kennedy to dispatch Deputy Attorney General Nicholas Katzenbach (accompanied by federal marshals and troops from the National Guard) to confront Wallace and his Alabama state troopers at the registration site doorway.

Faced with the full force of the national government, Wallace stood aside and the students were allowed to register. As the civil rights movement continued to grow in Alabama, Wallace fumed: "The President wants us to surrender this state to Martin Luther King and his group of pro-Communists who have instituted these demonstrations."

My mother and father had voted for John Kennedy in 1960 and my sister, brother, and I were all enamored with the young president. In addition to the charm, wit, and intelligence that he displayed during his campaign for the presidency and at every televised news conference after he took office, we took heart in his effort to steer the nation toward equal rights under the law for all citizens.

We were "outsiders" in Alabama and had moved from a state that was formed from a group of counties in the western part of Virginia that had refused to secede from the Union at the start of the Civil War. Amazingly, this fact was brought up to me on a number of occasions by playmates who had obviously been coached by their parents on this little morsel of history. I was considered to be from a "Yankee" state.

Back when we moved to Huntsville, my family had settled into a rental home in a modest neighborhood called Terry Heights, on the west side of Huntsville, an area quite devoid of rocket engineers and scientists. The more affluent newcomers to Huntsville in the late 1950s and early 1960s—including Wernher von Braun and his team—took up residence on the east side of Huntsville on pictur-esque, 1,600-foot Monte Sano.

White Water

There had also been an incident at our neighborhood grocery store shortly after we arrived in Alabama that seriously dampened our enthusiasm over the move from West Virginia.

It was a large grocery store and I wandered away from my par-ents to the end of one shopping aisle near the back of the store. There I saw a man taking a quick drink out of a water fountain. When he stepped away, I saw a sign above it with the word WHITE. Next to that water fountain was another one, but with a sign above it that said COLORED.

Even though I was only six, my father had been playing a game each evening with me that we called "four words." I would sit on his lap while he read the newspaper, a magazine, or a book, and Dad would let me pick out four words to remember and to alert him whenever I saw the words again. After about a year of this game, I knew a lot of words, including the words *color* and *white*.

So that day, with all the mental powers that a six-year-old could muster, I quickly came to the conclusion that the sign over the "colored" fountain meant that cherry- or strawberry-flavored water—maybe orange—came out of it. I had also never seen milk come out of a fountain—but perhaps that was what that man just drank under the WHITE sign.

Without waiting for any permission, I stretched up on my tiptoes to taste the colored water. I was quickly disappointed—and a bit confused. Then a booming voice: "Boy, what are you doing?"

I ran. I scampered down the aisle back toward the front of the store. I ran around the end of the aisle and looked down the next one to see my parents at the rear of the store in a very angry exchange with a very large man. I knew I was in trouble, probably for not asking permission to take that drink. Maybe they thought I was stealing the water.

By the time my mother rushed down the aisle toward me, the tears had already welled up and were running down my face. I could feel my chest heaving in preparation for a loud sob, but I fought that. I didn't want even more adult attention to my misbehavior. And there were other kids around who I could tell were curious about what had just happened.

Then, to my amazement, my mother approached me with one of her kindest smiles. In a gentle, quiet voice, with just a touch of sadness, she said: "Don't worry, John Samuel, you didn't do anything wrong. Down here you just have to remember that you are only allowed to drink out of the water fountains with the word *white* above them."

I was so relieved to have escaped punishment that I waited until the drive back home before I cautiously asked, "Why can't I drink the colored water?" I then ventured to add a bit of very important information I had learned: "It's not colored water anyway; it's just water."

Years later, my mother, a deeply Christian woman, would say that car ride home was one of the most heartbreaking experiences of her life. She and my father were finally forced to explain to their six-year-old son that they had moved the family to a place where people were treated differently because of their skin color. On that day I learned that I was a white kid.

True Wisdom

Although my father never had the opportunity to finish high school like my mother, he remains, thanks to the ceaseless reading he pursued through his entire life, one of the most educated individuals I have ever met. To this day, my father is the only person I have ever met who actually read all fifty-two volumes of the Harvard Classics, which were part of his prized book collection.

Among the many books in his library were textbooks and guides addressing all sorts of academic subjects. When I had questions about geometry or algebra in high school, he always had a ready answer. My father even introduced me to calculus one night, a subject he had mastered from studying *A Practical Guide to Calculus*, a treasured little book that I now have in my book collection.

Home from college one weekend during my freshman year and armed with a bit of knowledge from a philosophy class, I launched into a lively debate with him over the correct use of the word *Epicurean*, which a magazine writer had used in an article about Ted Kennedy. While it was obvious from the recent coverage of the fatal Chappaquiddick incident that Ted Kennedy might be overly fond of food and drink, my father thought that the "simple life" strongly advocated by the philosopher Epicurus made this a poor word to describe the affluent Kennedy. Afterward, when I quietly consulted one of his books on philosophy, I realized my dad was probably correct.

Through my father, I learned early on that a well-rounded education of history, literature, geography, mathematics, and science often resulted, counterintuitively, in a more humble approach to life. Like generations of wise men before him, my father had realized early that, as Aristotle said, "The more you know, the more you know you don't know."

Sadly, I was living in a place and time when there were far too many adults who were comfortably certain in their ignorance and prejudices. And they were so comfortable in that misplaced certainty of their own superiority that they were willing to accept all sorts of injustice and misery in its name. And there I was, a boy growing up in Alabama in the early 1960s, bearing witness to this widespread self-delusion, cruelty, and stupidity of adults I was raised to respect.

Although George Wallace could force the agencies of the state of Alabama to implement his vow of "segregation forever," he could not control the national news broadcasts that reached into almost every home in the state. On Monday, September 2, 1963, I got home from summer football practice in time to watch Walter Cronkite deliver the evening news. With my parents, I sat down to see if there was any national coverage of the threatened action by Governor Wallace to keep the public schools in Alabama closed rather than accept federally enforced integration.

School was already supposed to be back in session that week but the actual opening date had yet to be set. At the start of the news broadcast, Cronkite announced that this would be the very first daily half-hour network news program, as CBS was now expanding its evening news program from fifteen minutes to a full thirty minutes. He then opened with the headline news that Governor Wallace had kept an Alabama school closed by a "ring of state trooper cars."

Cronkite then cut to a previously recorded interview with President Kennedy conducted on the lawn of the president's vacation home in Hyannis Port, Massachusetts. He began by asking the president for his thoughts on how the civil rights issue would affect his reelection chances in 1964. He went on to get the president's thoughts on Governor Wallace's closing of the high school in Tuskegee, Alabama, in defiance of a federal court order.

Throughout the interview, Kennedy displayed a calm confidence that school integration and equality of opportunity would indeed be accomplished across the nation, especially with continued support by local school boards. The president expressed his steadfast belief that both Democrats and Republicans would, together, support all measures needed to ensure that all Americans had equal opportunity.

The soothing and intelligent words of President Kennedy, brought to us by television, stood in stark contrast to the segregationist ravings of George Wallace and his vocal supporters, some of whom lived in our own neighborhood. As I well knew, Cronkite had throughout his career used television as a teacher of history and technology. Now, in his half-hour daily news broadcast, Cronkite began to more fully use television's ability to illuminate significant issues confronting American society.

Living History

Television had become a communications lifeline to the outside world for this eleven-year-old growing up in George Wallace's Alabama. I didn't realize it then, but television was beginning to create a shared sense of witnessing history in the making for the millions of viewers who gathered each evening around the set. Television was establishing its potential as the most powerful communications medium in history—one that, it was hoped, could be used for universal education and enlightenment.

Finally, Huntsville public schools were scheduled to open on Friday, September 6, 1963. It was a short two-block walk from my house to my sixth-grade class in Terry Heights Elementary School, which I had attended since first grade. I was actually excited to start school—my principal, Mrs. Lollie Collier, had selected me to be captain of the school's safety patrol, a group of about a dozen fifth- and sixth-grade students who showed up early and stayed late to serve as street crossing guards. We also helped direct traffic and we opened car doors for students arriving and departing in their parents' automobiles. When I had stopped by the school on Thursday to pick up my orange chest belt and captain's badge, an anxious Mrs. Collier told me to be prepared, because she didn't know what was going to happen the next morning.

When I arrived at school early Friday morning, I could not believe my eyes: Terry Heights Elementary School was already ringed by Alabama state trooper cars. I counted sixteen patrol cars with twice that many state troopers, all of them helmeted and armed with sidearms and clubs. I noticed that some troopers held cattle prods. It was an intimidating show of force for a bunch of elementary school kids.

As it happened, Terry Heights Elementary School was one of just four elementary schools in Alabama, all in Huntsville, that were each scheduled to enroll a single black student that Friday. The parents of the four children were armed with a federal court order, secured in Birmingham, and the Huntsville Board of Education had indicated its intention to comply with the order in defiance of the governor. Wallace, however, sent his troopers to close the four schools and thereby block the registration of the black students.

Having watched Governor Wallace and his Alabama state troopers back down on TV when confronted by the National

Guard and federal marshals, I actually expected that President Kennedy would send in the Army—perhaps paratroopers!—to open my school.

I could see that the state troopers were keeping parents and their kids well away from the school building. But I just kept walking toward the doorway. When a trooper tried to stop me, I told him that I was supposed to check in with my principal. Another trooper who was standing by took notice of the brass captain's badge on my safety patrol belt and said to the other: "You can let him in."

It was amazing: a student's safety patrol belt with a captain's badge got me past a barrier of more than two dozen Alabama state troopers. I was going to be right at the center of the action when the Army arrived. Maybe they would use tanks to crush the trooper cars.

The Army never arrived. But I did get to stand near the school entrance with Mrs. Collier when a dark sedan arrived. Dr. Cleveland Piggie and his little son, David, emerged from the automobile and started walking toward the school. Dressed in a dark suit, wearing sunglasses and with his chin held high, Dr. Piggie was holding his son's hand when confronted by a state trooper who told him that the school was closed by order of the governor. Dr. Piggie nodded slightly in acknowledgment and then informed the trooper that he would return with his son when the school was open for enrollment.

Little David Piggie did not have to wait long to enroll in Terry Heights Elementary School. On Friday afternoon, the Huntsville Board of Education informed the governor that it intended to open the Huntsville public schools on Monday morning, September 9. Once more, the board stated that it intended to fully comply with the federal court order to enroll the four black students who had attempted to register on the previous Friday.

My mother worked for the city of Huntsville in the Clerk Treasurer's Office. She came home Friday evening fuming at the governor's actions and told us that Mayor R. B. Searcy had "really had enough of Wallace." The *Huntsville Times* arrived on our porch that evening bearing a quote by Mayor Searcy: "This is an unfortunate situation we have been subjected to by the Governor. We did not ask for troopers to be sent in here and we did not want them."

Victory and Loss

Although Governor Wallace blocked black students from registering at all other public schools across the state the following Monday, he backed down from again confronting the city of Huntsville and its school board. This time no troopers were sent to Huntsville. The city's schools opened on time and the four black children took their seats in four separate classrooms.

It was an historic day—and the citizens of Huntsville, indeed of the United States—knew it. The banner headline atop the *Huntsville Times* that evening proclaimed: STATE BARS NEGROES ELSEWHERE, HUNTSVILLE QUIETLY INTEGRATES.

Less than three months after the integration of the schools in Huntsville, my childhood hero was shot in Dallas, Texas. That Friday, November 22, 1963, Mrs. Collier's voice came over the school speaker system right after my class returned from lunch. The president, she announced, had been shot in Texas, and she was dismissing all of us from school.

As I raced home, I focused on the word *shot*. Perhaps he had just been wounded. I cut through a yard on Barbara Drive to get home quicker. I had to get to our television set. I was home in less than five minutes. No one was there. My father and mother both worked and generally did not come home until about 5 p.m. But my adult cousin John Howell lived next door with his wife, Darlene, and their three children. Darlene kept an eye on me each afternoon after school until my parents arrived. Her boys, David and Rodney, were arriving home from school as well and she asked if I wanted to watch the news with them. I said no. For some reason, I wanted to watch it alone.

When I turned the TV set on, it was already tuned to CBS. Walter Cronkite was hurriedly sorting through real-time reports from Dallas. He recapped what facts he knew about the shooting. Then, as I watched in growing horror, rumors that the president was dead began to appear in reports from the field. Cronkite was careful to say that these reports had not been confirmed.

But then Cronkite reported that a priest had given the president the last rites. Next, correspondent Dan Rather reported from Dallas that he had a confirmed report that Kennedy was indeed dead. Cronkite acknowledged Rather's confirmation but said that it was still not official. My hopes were fading. I began to feel sick inside.

A few moments later, Walter sadly removed his glasses and announced that the president had been declared dead at 1 p.m. Central Time, some thirty-eight minutes prior to that moment. I felt as if my insides had been drained out of me.

Throughout my young life, Walter Cronkite had always connected me to the fascinating worlds of science, technology, and history. And now, on that Friday afternoon in 1963, he connected me to a national tragedy. He managed to fight back his tears. I couldn't.

Chapter 5

Visualizing Victory

Vision is the art of seeing the invisible.

—Jonathan Swift

I played a lot of sports. Baseball and, of course, football were huge in Alabama, and being part of some winning teams helped me fit in. But, more important, my time on the playing field helped prepare me for the entrepreneurial path that lay ahead.

One event still stands out after all these years. It taught me that it was okay to really believe in something that hadn't happened yet.

It was the summer of 1963. My Little League team was playing a team from Monte Sano that was one of the weaker teams on our schedule. Our coach was James Parvin, a volunteer coach who made a significant effort to mentor each of his players. I played third base, but Coach Parvin decided I had a good arm and so he put me in to pitch for the game.

It was my first time on the mound, and I was determined to do a good job. I concentrated on every single pitch. After a couple of innings, kids and their parents came over from other, finished games to watch me throw. To their amazement (and mine), I was in the process of pitching a no-hitter.

There were two outs in the ninth inning when a batter who

had earlier given me a few scares walked up to the plate. He had made contact with the ball every time he had batted. I had held my breath in the sixth inning when he popped up a fly ball into center field. Fortunately, it was caught.

But this kid was now walking up to the plate with a little more confidence. He had a chance to be a hero, too, by spoiling my no-hitter. By now, parents and kids from all over Brahan Spring Park filled the bleachers and spilled along the baselines. It seemed like everyone was screaming. As the right-handed batter kicked dirt with his left foot and took his stance in the batter's box, I tried to calm myself in the most anxiety-producing situation I had ever experienced. I took a few deep breaths and mentally pictured both the trajectory of the ball and where it was going to slap into the catcher's mitt. I had been doing this now for four innings—taking longer between pitches but throwing more strikes. "Low and to the outside, low and to the outside," I kept saying and "seeing" to myself. This kid was going to swing for the fence, but I was going to keep the ball just out of his reach.

Swing and a miss. Swing and a miss. Swing and a miss. The ballpark erupted. I fell to my knees on the mound as my teammates rushed in to knock me over and pile on. A no-hitter. Coach Parvin was beaming. He called for the ball I had last pitched. "You will remember this day," he said as he took out his ballpoint pen and autographed the ball with his signature, the date, and by my name: "no hitter."

Seeing Success

I waited the entire next day for the *Huntsville Times* to arrive. At five o'clock it finally landed, and opening it while still outside, I quickly turned to the sports section. There, under the headline

Little League Has No-Hitter, the article read: "John Hendricks walked into the ranks of no-hit pitchers. . . ." Today, that newspaper clipping and Coach Parvin's autographed baseball reside in a display cabinet behind my desk in our Maryland home. On the one hand, it's just the memento of a small childhood victory. But I cherish it, and return to it often, because it commemorates my first concerted effort at visualizing success. It wouldn't be long before I would once again put that skill to the test.

In the fall of my sixth-grade year, I was on the 120-pound football team, playing fullback. Coach Parvin was also the volunteer coach of our Terry Heights football team. Like most boys growing up in Alabama—the land of Bear Bryant and the Crimson Tide—I had played football since I was a little kid, and I knew all the plays, positions, and moves.

On the Tuesday before our first Friday game against Fifth Avenue School, one of the better teams, Coach Parvin came to me with a plan. On our very first possession of the game, he wanted the quarterback to toss the ball back to me as the entire backfield went left. I was supposed to tuck the ball for a fake run around the left end but then stop, plant myself, and throw a pass to a receiver running flat out downfield. It was a surprise play, Coach Parvin told me, and would "definitely" result in a touchdown.

I should have been honored, but instead I felt very uncomfortable. First off, Mike, our quarterback, was Coach Parvin's son and my best friend. I could see a flash of surprise cross Mike's face when his dad described the trick play. I couldn't tell if Mike wanted to make that long throw himself or if he just had his doubts about me getting the job done. As the week went on, I got butterflies in my stomach whenever I thought about the play. What if it failed? What if I threw an interception? Even though the previous summer I had gotten pretty good at visualizing where that baseball was going to go, I simply had no confidence that that mental trick would help me pull off this surprise pass play.

At practice the day before the big game, I even asked the coach if we could maybe modify the play so that I could go right and get off a more comfortable throw as a right-hander. He looked annoyed: "No." Coach Parvin then explained one more time that the awkwardness was part of the play and it would help confuse and surprise the defensive team.

Just before the game, Coach Parvin could see that I was still nervous—so he came over and told me that for the play to work, I had to believe in it. I had to see it succeeding in my mind before the ball was snapped. I had to "believe" and "own the play."

This was, to my recollection, my very first experience of someone actually coaching me about positive thinking and even visualizing my own success. As he stepped away, he smiled and said, "Don't worry, I already see your touchdown."

After our warm-ups and before the kickoff, I imagined the play over and over, with every outcome a touchdown. The coin was tossed. We were set to receive the kickoff.

Playing deep, I caught the ball and advanced it up the right side to about the thirty-yard line. Seventy yards to go for a touchdown. We lined up for the first play from scrimmage. The ball was snapped and our entire offensive line, as well as the backfield, began moving to the left as the ball was pitched back to me. It looked for all the world like I was going to make a dash around the left end. The defensive linebackers and safeties all began to track me to the left. The tall defensive end was moving into position to fend off my first blockers.

Then, as I had endlessly rehearsed in my mind, I stopped just one yard short of the line of scrimmage and threw the ball downfield as hard as I could. I can still see that football spiraling away just before two defenders smashed me to the ground.

Pulling myself up, I heard my teammates cheering and I could see a sideline full of parents jumping up and down. Our receiver, Terry Carpenter, was three steps past the nearest defender when he caught the ball. There was no way they could catch him. *Touch-down.*

Confidence

One of my very favorite quotes is by Henry Ford: "Whether you think that you can or you can't, you're right." Every kid needs a parent, a coach, a science teacher, or a piano instructor who thinks like Henry Ford and Coach Parvin. I was one of the lucky ones. Thanks to my parents and my coach, I could visualize success and was beginning to develop a confidence that I would need in the years ahead.

Just to be clear, not all of my visualizations in sports and other matters have had such happy endings. There were many times when I just blew it . . . struck out, dropped the ball in the end zone, or fumbled. But memories are merciful because they mostly allow you to remember the good times, the victories, when things worked out. And, by remembering our successes, our confidence builds.

Chapter 6

Silent Partner

The harder I work, the luckier I get.

—Samuel Goldwyn

Since I didn't come from an affluent family and needed my own cash for clothes, gas, and socializing, I took a job after school.

In the summer months, I mostly worked for my dad on his building projects. But during the school year, beginning in tenth grade, I sold clothes at a men's store in Huntsville called Budd's Men's Wear. Budd's paid me a minimum wage of $1.30 per hour and I was able to generate about $25 per week, $100 per month, from working three hours every day after school plus eight hours on Saturday.

I was a diligent worker at Budd's. When I wasn't busy with a customer, I always looked around to see if some of the displays needed straightening. I tried to look busy, especially when the owner, Barry Berman, was around. I was earnest in my efforts, but, frankly, I was not exceptional. That's because I quickly realized that, on fixed wages, extra effort did not result in extra pay. But if I did good work I would certainly keep my job and just maybe, I thought, I'd get a raise to $1.50 per hour after a year's work at Budd's.

On a Saturday afternoon during my senior year, I got a call

from Lionel Delmore, a former Budd's employee, who had left for a job at a rival men's clothing store, Bill's Men's Wear. It was one of three stores owned by local Huntsville entrepreneur Bill Fowler. Lionel had told Fowler about me and was now calling to offer me a job. But I was torn because of my loyalty to Barry Berman, the owner of Budd's. I said I couldn't come for less than $1.60 per hour. Lionel told me that I should "just go and talk with Bill." My curiosity and my hopes for a raise piqued, I agreed to go.

I was more than a little intimidated when I walked into Bill Fowler's office. His name, after all, was on the marquee of a leading retailer in northern Alabama. A large, sturdy-looking man, he glanced up from his desk, smiled, reached over to shake my hand, and said, "Lionel sure thinks a lot of you, but I am definitely not going to pay you a dollar sixty an hour. In fact, I am not going to pay you anything per hour."

I was crushed, confused, and put into my place—all at the same time. All I wanted to do at that moment was to run out of the store and hope that Barry Berman would never, ever discover my act of betrayal in meeting with his rival.

But Fowler continued. "Instead I am going to pay you straight commission, no guarantees. Just eight percent of whatever you sell. If you sell nothing, you make nothing. If you sell a lot, you make a lot."

I must have looked even more confused, because Fowler didn't wait for my reply. "You and I are going to be in business together," he continued. "Do you know what a Hickey Freeman suit sells for?" At Budd's we did not carry Hickey Freeman suits (one of the most expensive brand lines at the time), but I knew the price range. "About a hundred and seventy-five dollars," I replied.

"So, do you know what you will make every time you sell a Hickey Freeman suit?" Fowler asked.

In what was probably the fastest math calculation I had done in my life, I quickly replied, "Fourteen dollars."

"That's right," Fowler said. "Every item in my store is going to have two price tags on it—a one hundred percent price tag that the customer sees and an invisible eight percent price tag for you." He chuckled as he saw my eyes light up. He had me for sure when he winked and said: "You will be my silent partner."

Embracing Risk

I gave notice at Budd's later that day and started my new job at Bill's Men's Wear the next Saturday morning. Seldom has a customer met a more eager salesperson than when our first shopper walked through the door that morning at nine o'clock. "Go get him," Lionel said. In a stroke of luck, that first customer was the founder and president of a local engineering firm and an important NASA contractor. The gentleman had been too busy to shop for some time and he told me that he needed to "stock up" on new suits and sport coats. I think my knees buckled.

I spent nearly two hours with him, and everything he looked at had my invisible price tag on it. That first customer of mine ultimately bought four suits and three sport coat outfits, each with shirts and ties. I even sold him two pairs of Florsheim shoes, and then suggested belts and socks, which he also went for.

The total sale was an astounding $1,100—in 1969 dollars. I had no difficulty with the math for my commission: I had made $88 for two hours' work.

Suddenly, I had an entirely new attitude about work. Bill Fowler was right—he had set me up in my own little business, and that Saturday morning was my first entrepreneurial experience. It taught me forever the power of compensation tied directly to performance. Financial rewards flowed to both employer and employee alike in a compensation structure that treated workers as true business partners, as Bill Fowler's "silent partners."

Leaving the secure, but pay-limited, job at Budd's for the wide-open world of Bill Fowler's enterprise also taught me the absolute joy of embracing risk—of being in charge of my own paycheck. If I sold nothing, I made nothing. If I sold a lot, I made a lot. My fate was my own. And I loved it.

Chapter 7

A Cave of Curiosities

The mystery is what prompted men to leave caves, to come out
of the womb of nature.

—STEPHEN GARDINER

A brief diversion, both in this narrative and in my life.

It was late spring, 1969. I was seventeen and on my first long solo road trip. After cajoling my parents for several weeks, I finally got their permission to drive my car from Huntsville to Chattanooga, Tennessee, and back on a Sunday.

Chattanooga was about 120 miles and just over two hours of driving time from Huntsville. Leaving at 9 a.m., I planned to be on the road for a total of about five hours. My destination was Rock City, a roadside attraction featuring natural and man-made rock gardens, located just outside Chattanooga on Lookout Mountain. It was said that you could see seven states from the top of Lookout Mountain. Rock City was promoted on the roofs and sides of barns all along the highways approaching Chattanooga for hundreds of miles and from all directions.

The SEE ROCK CITY signs had beckoned our family on every car trip we'd ever made between Alabama and West Virginia, but we had never stopped. My folks were always hesitant to delay the beginning of our long trip north to visit relatives in West Virginia. My mother and father also never wanted to stop on the way back, when we were tired and less than three hours from Huntsville. So the magical destination of Rock City always eluded me.

In fact, I never made it to Rock City on that Sunday, either—or ever since. My curiosity, once again, got in the way. Instead I decided to stop and see Russell Cave National Monument.

I had driven nearly two hours north from Huntsville, just short of the Tennessee border, when I saw the signs for Russell Cave. They reminded me of yet another tourist destination that my family had always passed. Relishing my new freedom to explore on a whim, I turned left off Highway 72 and wound my way up the back roads to the cave site. My plan was to make a quick thirty-minute stop; instead, I stayed for three hours.

Treasure Trove

Russell Cave had been a home for prehistoric peoples for more than ten thousand years, making it one of the oldest such sites in the Western Hemisphere. The cave site was, and is, an archaeological treasure containing the most complete record of prehistoric cultures in the southeastern United States. Beginning with the first excavations in 1953, Russell Cave provided researchers with important clues about the daily life of native inhabitants dating from 6500 B.C. to A.D. 1650. In 1961, President Kennedy signed the law that permanently protected the site as a national monument.

As remarkable as the cave shelter and the surrounding fields and woodlands were, I found I could not take myself away from the intriguing displays of prehistoric tools and weapons. Fire-making bow drills, spear points, nutting stones, blowguns, and more. But it was one ingenious weapon, the atlatl, that most captured my attention. Noting my curiosity (and the lack of other visitors), a park ranger kindly gave me a detailed demonstration of the atlatl. He even let me attempt numerous throws of a replica—until I became quite proficient in consistently hitting a target some thirty yards away.

In making the very first throw, I had immediately felt the increased power resulting from the leverage in the weapon's unique design. It was clear to me that some single individual deep in our ancestral past had invented this amazing device—and in the process significantly increased the survival odds of his tribe. Refined and perfected by others, the use of the atlatl must have quickly spread throughout the ancient human populations who came in contact with it. Along with the bow and the musket, it was one of the biggest breakthroughs in the history of hunting, and thus of human survival.

Although one can imagine that atlatls were ultimately produced in considerable volume to arm entire societies, the original design was undoubtedly invented by a single human being who was powerfully driven by a curiosity to find a better way to feed and protect his family and tribe. That powerful curiosity must also have been matched by an indefatigable persistence in trial-and-error experiments, which ultimately led to the two-part throwing system that loosely interlocked a spear and a shorter throwing stick. There was no other way to do it, and it must have taken thousands of throws to get the design right. Perhaps the original inventor of the atlatl enlisted the help of a few tribal cohorts in perfecting the new weapon.

Leveraging Talent

Looking at the ancient atlatl fragments and handling the replica weapon that morning, I wondered if I could have ever invented such a clever device. I had my doubts. It certainly must have required a combination of a chance event with a special kind of observational genius—followed by a talent for tool making, a lot of patience and discipline, and some serious puzzle-solving skills. And perhaps even a well-developed sense of play.

That kind of talent doesn't come along very often, which is likely why it took thousands of years between the invention of the spear and the atlatl. But still, it had happened. The evidence was there before me. Someone had put it all together—and changed the course of human history.

The invention of the bow and arrow, the atlatl, the wheel, fire-making bow drills, iron and copper smelting, and hundreds of other advancements allowed early humans to survive. And it is possible that every one of these advancements owe their origin to a momentary, but profound, observation that sparked the curiosity of one individual—an unquenchable curiosity that drove that person to solve the problem that observation presented.

Curiosity is the fuel of human progress. That Sunday morning, at the dawn of one of the most famously inventive summers in American history, inside a cave in Alabama, that fact became clear to me. Like most seventeen-year-olds, I was a hopeless romantic—and in a strange way I felt at that moment that my own intense curiosity, suddenly ignited, had an unbroken link back through human history to the ancient inhabitants of Russell Cave. More than four decades later, despite everything that has happened in between, I still feel that link.

Chapter 8

Freedom to Create

Success is liking yourself, liking what you do, and liking how you do it.
—Maya Angelou

I first learned about the entrepreneurial spirit by observing my father.

John Gilbert Hendricks was the fourth son born to a family of builders in Matewan, West Virginia. When his father, Sam Hendricks, died, the leadership of the Hendricks Construction Company passed over to Fred, the second son. Although I never heard of anything but cordial relations between my father and his brother-boss, it became clear by the early 1950s, as he reached middle age, that Dad just had to be his own man.

He had balked at any compromise in the quality of work he wanted to achieve, especially the detailed wood craftsmanship that was the hallmark of his creations. He had worried that the rush to meet budgets and construction deadlines in large building companies had resulted in lower-quality interior finishes, particularly in cabinetry. And he believed that if he had his own contracting business, families with dreams of a new home would pay a little bit more and wait just a little longer for a house with enduring craftsmanship.

So, at the relatively ripe age of fifty-two, my father started a little contracting business of his own, reaching out to prospective new homeowners with the promise of higher-quality homes. He was finally in charge of the entire building process: the development of the blueprints with an architect, cost analysis, permits, and hiring and supervising the building crew. The process ended with the ultimate satisfaction of handing the door keys to a happy family.

It wasn't a perfect dream—few are. My father was never able to accumulate much capital in his business, and our family experienced real hardship between contracts when he was forced to work as a finish carpenter for large construction companies.

Free Enterprise

My father had been lured to Huntsville by the NASA building boom. The economy of the 1960s in Huntsville was good but my father lacked the lifelong connections enjoyed by the local builders. During my teenage years, he often worked for others during the winter. But his true joy came in the four months of almost every summer when his reputation back in West Virginia for quality building allowed him to win some of the precious few contracts to build new homes in Matewan and in the nearby town of Williamson. I spent several summers with my dad on his home projects as part of his labor crew, digging footers and carrying lumber and building supplies. In those summer days in West Virginia, I witnessed my father at his happiest—quite literally whistling while he worked.

Even though I had good grades and had been elected senior class president, my options for college were limited by my family's finances. I could dream about Harvard but I couldn't go there. I knew that it would even be a financial stretch just to pay the tuition and expenses at the University of Alabama.

When I was a senior in high school, I entered an essay contest on "The Free Enterprise System" with the hope that I could earn a little college money. It was sponsored by Insurers of Huntsville, an independent insurance agents' group. The two winners, a boy and a girl, would each get $1,000—then almost a full year's tuition at Alabama.

As I sat down to write the essay, I focused on my dad's burning desire to have his own small construction business and take charge of his destiny. When he was successful in winning contracts he could hire seven to twelve men, depending on the size of the project. But most important to me, I could see his joy in doing just what he wanted to do—despite the risks and the limitations.

And so, based on my father's up-and-down contracting fortunes, I wrote an essay about the individual's essential need for a "freedom to achieve" as the bedrock of human advancement and satisfaction.

Freedom to Build

I finished the essay at midnight and delivered it to a typist the next morning before school started. A month later, I was thrilled to learn that I was one of the two winners of the contest. The *Huntsville Times* arranged for a photographer to take our picture, and the photo and story appeared in the newspaper, much to the delight of my parents.

It's funny how the tiniest event can change the trajectory of one's life. Writing that essay was one of those moments—and I've often thought about how deeply it influenced everything that came after. Putting those few hundred words on paper forced me to really think about what motivates people to accomplish something in life, to invent or adapt new products, and to create experiences that did not exist before. My father simply wanted the freedom to build—but in doing so he created a livelihood for others, he fulfilled people's dreams, and he fed his own family. And that too made him happy.

It struck me then that humans were somehow genetically wired to be most satisfied, most pleased, when they were working freely to create something new or better for themselves and their fellow humans. And, underlying that motivation to create, there seemed to be a wellspring of curiosity within humans to identify new problems and an endless itch to solve them. And it was all there in my dad's happy whistle while he worked.

I was looking forward to college during my senior year at Butler High School in 1970. Like many eighteen-year-olds, I thought a lot about what I really wanted to do in life. When I pictured myself in the future, it was always working in a company or for a cause in a role where I was totally in charge of my own destiny. I simply could not envision going to work every day at a job where others planned my tasks. So, even then, my inner life was pointing me in the direction of entrepreneurship.

Cutting a Path

Over the years I have been struck by how many individuals have an "inner entrepreneur" even at an early age. I remember reading about T. J. Rodgers of Cypress Semiconductor, whose mother paid him three dollars in advance for mowing the lawn. He used fifty cents of his advance to buy a watermelon, which he sliced up and gave to some neighborhood kids in return for mowing his lawn. He pocketed the $2.50 profit.

But most "born" entrepreneurs, I think, discover this part of their nature about the time they enter college. Michael Dell got so absorbed setting up computers for his classmates at the University of Texas that he had to inform his parents that he was suspending his college work to set up Dell Computers. And we all know the story of Bill Gates at Harvard. It is hard to concentrate on academics or anything else when there is something new to create for the world.

Why then? I think it's because that is one's first moment of true freedom—from parents, childhood peers, the neighborhood; it's the moment you first start down that long slide to the constraints of adult life. If ever there is a moment to cut a different path into the future, it is then.

Chapter 9

Curiosity U.

College is a refuge from hasty judgment.

—ROBERT FROST

I was accepted to the University of Alabama and showed up to start classes in Tuscaloosa in the fall of 1970. My parents and my sister, Linda, drove down to help me settle into my dormitory room. The campus was beautiful and filled with excited freshmen who, like me, were looking forward to their first classes—and, more important, to sit in the football stadium to cheer on the Crimson Tide, coached by the legendary Bear Bryant.

From the very first week, I could tell that I was going to love college. My Western civilization course was taught by John S. Pancake (great name), who was a spellbinding lecturer. Even though the freshmen course was held in an immense lecture hall with about two hundred students, he somehow still made history come alive.

I had decided to major in history and so my freshman year was loaded with history classes and other courses in the humanities, including philosophy. I also had an interest in science and so I began to wonder early on if I could somehow concentrate in both the humanities and the sciences. That seemed unlikely, as most universities, Alabama included, offered those programs in two separate colleges that seemed to rarely interact. C. P. Snow's great 1963 insight into the hindrance caused by the division of intellectual life between the "two cultures" of science and the humanities was already well borne out.

Whenever the Crimson Tide played an important game—that is, whenever there was expected to be a huge crowd—the venue was Legion Field, a large stadium in Birmingham. So some of my new college friends and I packed into my Camaro to drive over to Birmingham to catch the first game of the season. It was a hot September day that turned into an unusually sweltering night, even by Alabama standards. When the Tide came onto the field, led by Coach Bryant in his iconic plaid hat, the crowd went crazy. It was my first Alabama game. Only later did I realize its historical significance.

The University of Alabama had still not entirely integrated its football team; indeed, the Crimson Tide had only one African-American player. On this hot and humid night in Birmingham, the powerful University of Southern California Trojans—who had lost only two games in three years—would be the first fully integrated team to face the Tide *in* Alabama. Although Bear Bryant had already notched three national championships as the Alabama coach, his previous 1969 season record, 6-5, was a disappointment.

The partisan crowd, which had been on fire at kickoff, slowly began to fall silent as USC's fullback Sam "Bam" Cunningham tore through the Tide defense. An African-American sophomore who hadn't even expected to play that night, he instead ran for 135 yards and scored two touchdowns. When the contest was over, USC had won, 42–21. The Trojans had gained an amazing 559 yards, almost 300 yards more than Alabama.

After the game, Bear Bryant made a point of walking over to shake Sam Cunningham's hand and congratulate him for his performance. Recently, Darren Everson, writing for the *Wall Street Journal*, put the historic 1970 game in context:

> . . . the game did have dramatic effects. Historians say Mr. Bryant—who already had a black player on Alabama's freshman team—would have added more black players sooner if it had been socially acceptable; after that game, fans recognized the need. Great black players soon started coming to Alabama. . . . The Tide rebounded to win three more national championships under Mr. Bryant, who died in 1983.

Bryant's former player and a subsequent college coach Jerry Claiborne would later say, "Sam Cunningham did more to integrate Alabama in sixty minutes than Martin Luther King did in twenty years."

Rocketing Home

It proved to be an exciting year for academics and football in Tuscaloosa. In June, I returned to Huntsville to work at Bill's Men's Wear, where Bill Fowler always held open a job for me. Although he expected me to work a full six-day week during my summer breaks, I asked him if I could have a few hours off to take a couple of courses at the local campus of the University of Alabama system. He agreed and assigned me to work for Paul Hollis, who managed his largest and most successful mall store.

I was impressed by my first courses at the University of Alabama in Huntsville (UAH). Because UAH had been developed in part to support America's space program, it had a rich schedule of courses in all the sciences as well as the expected strong program in the humanities. With important ongoing research and recent discoveries being made in its science and engineering departments, UAH was beginning to be called "the MIT of the South." Class sizes were much smaller than at the flagship campus in Tuscaloosa—just ten to fifteen students even in the sophomore-level courses I was taking. Several scientists from Wernher von Braun's old German rocket team taught some of science courses. I noted that one of von Braun's team members, Rudolf Hermann, taught astronomy—and so I quickly signed up for his class. I was also interested in diving deeper into history and so I registered to take a U.S. constitutional history course taught by Frances Roberts. Both choices would prove important.

By midsummer, I was sold on UAH, to the point that I decided to just watch the Crimson Tide on TV and stay in Huntsville for the remaining three years of my undergraduate studies. I figured that I could pay the modest UAH tuition fees out of the commissions I earned at Bill's Men's Wear. If times got tight, I knew I could always live with my parents.

Fate in a Number

Although my draft card had the 2-S educational deferment, which would last for at least thirty-six more months, until I graduated, it was an uncertain time for all of us draft-eligible young men. While I had strong misgivings about the Vietnam War, which was still raging in the rice paddies and jungles of Southeast Asia, I also knew I would have no option but to serve if called. Although some my age were fleeing to Canada to escape the draft, I could not even entertain that thought.

Earlier that year, I got word that my friend from high school Joel Hankins, an Army Ranger, had been killed in action. So, while I was enjoying my freshman year at Tuscaloosa, Joel and many of my other classmates were a world and a nightmare away facing combat.

As the draft lottery for my birth year approached, I knew that if I got a dreadfully low number—for example, below 50—I would probably be off to Vietnam in 1974 when I graduated.

The first draft lottery, held on December 1, 1969, had been excruciating to watch. It was broadcast live on CBS. Although it was not for those with my birth year (rather for those young men born between 1944 and 1950), I watched the broadcast with some older friends, one of whom groaned when his birthday was attached to the number 12.

I was at my parents' house in Huntsville on the evening of August 5, 1971, the day of the draft lottery for all of us born in 1952. It was the third draft lottery and the novelty had long since worn off. The drawing was nowhere to be found on television. Finally, we found a radio station that was reading down the list starting with number 1, which was assigned to those unlucky enough to be born on December 4, 1952. The announcer kept reading the numbers in ascending order with the birth dates attached. The local draft board had informed all of us that a number below 125 would mean almost certain induction into one of the armed services.

My father didn't make things any easier when, before the radio broadcast began, he picked that moment to tell me of the time he had made the mistake of jumping up on the bad knee of his grandfather Andrew Lewis—the knee that had been severely wounded in the Civil War and had never healed properly.

As I did my best to both nod and ignore him, my father went on to tell about how my great-grandfather Lewis was just seventeen when the Civil War broke out. Like other young Virginians, he had quickly enlisted in the Confederate Army, joining Company K of the 50th Virginia regiment. In July 1863, he found himself with the 50th on the battlefield at Gettysburg with the unfortunate task of capturing Culp's Hill.

The hill had already been heavily fortified by Union troops, who were now firing down relentlessly from the top. It was a hopeless cause and Great-grandfather Lewis soon had to take cover behind one single tree on the hill for an entire day. By nightfall, the tree had been nearly cut through by enemy fire. Under the cloak of darkness he managed to crawl back down the hill, defeated.

Although he survived Gettysburg without a scratch, at the Battle of the Wilderness a Union musket ball shattered one of his legs just above the knee. He was captured, patched up a bit by Union field surgeons, and spent the rest of the war in a Union prison in Philadelphia.

In 1910, his leg still ached. He was a sixty-seven-year-old veteran who had fought in a war for which there was little relevance to his family. They owned no slaves and they were not involved in the great political issues of their time. But like so many young men through the ages, right up to today, he served out of duty to his country—and that country for him was Virginia.

My dad was six years old when he hopped up on that bad leg and made his grandfather wince. And now, six decades later, he was sitting with his own son, waiting to learn if he too would be sent into battle.

After a while the radio announcer passed through number 125, and still my birthday, March 29, had not been called. I began to relax and a smile returned to my mother's face. Number 200 was called and still no March 29.

Finally, the announcer said "Number 343: March 29."

There are many forks in the road of life. Most often a person is in full control of those critical choices. But sometimes just dumb, inexplicable luck determines our path. Joel Hankins, like many in my generation, was dead. Four decades later, I'm still here to write this book. I have no easy answer to why this is so.

Epiphany

By the spring of 1972 I was deep into my studies at UAH. I wanted to spend more time on campus, especially in the history department, and so I applied for a work-study position with the department's chairman, John White.

I continued to work all day Saturday at Bill's Men's Wear. I had actually made a killing one Saturday before the previous Christmas when I sold more than $3,000 worth of merchandise. My take from that one day's sales was more than $240. For a college kid, it was the best job imaginable.

Professor White processed the paperwork and got me approved for a work-study position reporting directly to him. He showed me to a small office and told me that when there were no assigned work tasks, I was free to study.

My work-study assignment was to support faculty members in their course needs, particularly in ordering and reviewing textbooks and supplementary reading materials for their various courses. Also, if any faculty member wanted a 16 mm film to reinforce a topic in American, European, or Asian history, my job was to search through educational film catalogs, find an appropriate film, order it, help set up the film for projection, and then return it after the five-day rental period. White showed me the department's catalogs of book publishers as well as the distributors of educational films.

Once again my curiosity got the better of me—and soon I found myself poring through the inch-thick catalogs of educational films from *Encyclopaedia Britannica* and Time-Life, among others.

Most impressive of all were the films available from the BBC. Those catalogs contained great BBC shows and series that had never made it to America. But here, thanks to the catalog, they were available for any university—and presumably any person—to rent for five to seven days or longer.

One day Professor Alden Pearson, who taught American history, stepped into my little office to ask if I could find him a film about the Army-McCarthy hearings, which had been broadcast on television in 1954. He was teaching about the Cold War era in his modern American history class and wanted his class to discuss the U.S. Senate subcommittee's investigations into the conflicting accusations between the United States Army and Senator Joseph McCarthy.

After a brief search through the catalogs I found a good 16 mm film that contained extended footage of the hearings that, in an historic first, had been broadcast live in 1954. I ordered the film and it arrived in the mail less than a week later.

When the canister arrived, having no immediate tasks to attend to, I set up the film and projected it on an empty white wall in the corner of my office. The machine clicked loudly but the small projected image, just six feet away on the wall, was crisp and perfect.

I sat captivated by the drama of the hearings—particularly when Joseph Welch, the Army's counsel, aggressively questioned Senator McCarthy. When McCarthy had begun to counter with a reckless accusation that a young member of Welch's own law firm in Boston, Fred Fisher, had ties to the Communist Party, Welch angrily cut him off with the memorable words that had filled America's living rooms in 1954:

Senator, may we not drop this? We know he belonged to the Lawyer's Guild. . . . Let us not assassinate this lad further, Senator; you've done enough. Have you no sense of decency, sir? At long last, have you left no sense of decency?

I sat riveted by the exchanges. This was real drama about a fight for the very soul of America.

After Pearson showed the film to his class, the reel and its canister sat in my office. It was not due to be mailed back to the distributor for several more days. I knew my father and mother had not seen those hearings—they didn't own a TV set in 1954.

"Do you think Dr. White would mind if I borrowed the projector and a film for an hour this evening?" I asked the department secretary, Rene. "They just live a few miles from here and no one is showing a film this evening."

"I don't think he would mind," Rene replied. "Just have it back here in the morning."

I set up the film in my parents' living room. They were excited to see it. My dad noted that he knew a few people who had watched the hearings live on TV back in 1954 but most others in Matewan, like him, had not. It was a memorable evening.

The next day I packaged the film up and sent it back to the distributor. But something had clicked in my mind. Why, I asked myself, couldn't these great films be broadcast on television? Here I was staring at catalogs containing hundreds of documentary films, maybe thousands. And they were available only on film, as rentals.

Obsession

I've already explained how my curiosity can sometimes overwhelm me. This time I got so fired up that, unable to find any published information on the subject, I tore through the phone book and called the number for WHNT, the local CBS affiliate. I was transferred to someone who was quite amused by my idea to program Saturday or Sunday afternoons with documentaries. "We aren't interested in doing that," he said laughing. I hung up.

But I was far from done. After a while, I began to wonder if the local cable system had any channels—or maybe just part of a day or night—that might be available for documentaries. I looked up the telephone number for the local franchise of TelePrompTer, the cable company that had recently purchased the cable system serving Huntsville. I made the call.

This time a friendly, slow-talking man came on the line. In his deep southern drawl, he asked: "Now what is it that I can help you with?"

I talked fast. I wanted to get the whole idea out before he stopped me. I explained that I worked at UAH (true, but I didn't say that I was a lowly work-study student) and that I knew about a lot of documentary distributors who might be open (I had no idea about that) to providing shows that could be put on one of his channels.

Before I could go on with listing some film titles (I was really prepared), he gently cut me off. "Son, you just don't understand. The government won't let us program anything. All we can legally do is just retransmit broadcast stations. We just clean up pictures, and make them pretty and clear for folks. That's all we can do."

I was taken aback. "Really? It would be illegal for you to show a documentary—just one?" I asked. It seemed ridiculous.

"Son, we just can't do anything like that. I'm sorry," he said.

I thanked him and hung up, stunned. That was one daydream dead on arrival. I was angry with myself for not doing some basic homework on television transmission in the United States before making those two calls. How embarrassing.

The Builder

I was on a tennis court sweating in the Alabama heat. It was late morning on the last day of August 1972. I was deep into one of my almost daily tennis wars with my best friend, Mike Parvin.

Since the time we had been elementary school chums on the football and baseball fields, Mike and I had always found a way to have a friendly competition. Mike was also a history major at UAH and would go on to become a teacher before founding a small leasing company. We were midway through the match when word reached me that I needed to go to Huntsville Hospital.

As I ran into the emergency room I saw my sister, alone and in tears, walking toward me.

"We lost Daddy," was all Linda could manage to say as we embraced.

My father was sixty-eight, and just like on every other day, he had gotten up that morning to go to his construction site. He had refused to retire even following a minor stroke three years before. And though the jobs had slowed, Dad was still always able to assemble four or five good workers and find a project for their little team.

On that morning as he was standing near a doorway, he just slumped to the floor. One of the workers caught him and broke his fall. But Dad was already unconscious. Then his breathing stopped and he was gone, from a massive heart attack. He had literally died on his feet doing the work he loved.

Friends in Huntsville and relatives from West Virginia rushed to our home to provide what comfort they could. Everyone seemed to know the magnitude of our loss. My dad was a humble, gentle man whose kindness and life insights had permeated our lives. He had been my teacher since the time I was able to ask a question. Now he was gone.

For his family, friends, and his twenty-year-old son, my father's death was devastating. Then, it seemed so unfair—but now, as I write this, just a few years younger than he was, I realize that there was something beautifully painless and just about my father's departure from this life. I would give anything to have had a few more years with him—but not at the price of a worse exit than the one he was given.

I still think of him almost every day. So, in that respect, he is still with me, advising me with his wise counsel.

Skyward

For the balance of my time as a student at UAH, I focused on my studies in history, in part to fill the new void in my life. I also took elective courses in the sciences that I enjoyed, particularly astronomy. I relished my time in John White's classes on French history and Frances Roberts's classes on U.S. history.

On many nights I was out with my astronomy classmates looking through an array of telescopes set up by Professor Hermann, each one pointed toward a different celestial object. Hermann would walk around to each of our telescope stations to explain, in his thick German accent, the significance of what we were observing.

Another special treat for me was my time in Johanna Shields's American history class, especially when she offered insights on how scientific revolutions had affected society and changed the course of history. One memorable afternoon in her class, I asked her if the Newtonian revolution had any real impact on the thinking of the masses at the time. "Did it change their worldview?" I asked.

She didn't hesitate. "Newton probably made very little impact at all on the thinking of the mass of people living in the late seventeenth century. After all, how much effect is the quantum physics revolution of the 1920s having on you?"

"What's the quantum physics revolution?" a student piped up. We all laughed.

John White and the history department faculty members were organizing a UAH chapter of Phi Alpha Theta, the national honor society for undergraduate and graduate history students, as well as professors of history. My grades were good and so I was invited to be one of the first chapter members. White asked me to help him set up history forum events at which special guests would be invited to speak. One of the first speakers he had in mind was Melvin Kranzberg, a longtime history professor at Case Western Reserve University who had been recently appointed as the Callaway Professor of the History of Technology at Georgia Tech.

Kranzberg accepted the invitation to speak at UAH and White asked me to handle the logistics of the visit. I looked forward to the visit, as I had read a book that Kranzberg had edited, *Technology in Western Civilization*. There was one section of the book that had caught my attention—"Media and Education"—and in particular a chapter written by the scholar Robert C. Davis about the lack of quality educational content on television:

> When discussion swings to the positive contributions of the mass media it generally focuses on the topic of education. Critics stress the enormous gap between the potential of the media and the actual performance. They point to the fact that three quarters of the television schedule is entertainment and that cultural programs are sparse. Certainly the educational impact of television has been minor compared to its use as a "selling machine."

Davis went on to explain that recent research had found a "widespread positive and receptive attitude" toward science and other factual content that was not being addressed by mass media, and certainly not by television. From his review of available research Davis had concluded: "The 'hard core' of science enthusiasts is estimated to be about one fourth of the adult population."

Magic Number

After Kranzberg gave his lecture at UAH, he stayed to talk with a number of students. I waited until everyone else had chatted with him, then I walked up with a copy of his book and asked him to autograph it. He signed his name along with the date, October 27, 1972. I then asked him what he thought about the future of educational programming on television. I made reference to the positive findings Davis had mentioned in the book.

Kranzberg replied, "Well, about twenty-five percent of people do seem to have an interest in learning more about the world and about science. But advertisers want to reach the broadest audience, so I am not sure I can be too optimistic about more science on TV. But perhaps there will be more coverage in magazines and newspapers."

I remember nodding my head in agreement. I knew there was that interest because I considered myself among that 25 percent. But the challenge seemed enormous. It was a puzzle and Kranzberg had no solutions, either.

It was a thin reed on which to build my eventual career. And yet it proved to be remarkably accurate. Indeed, that 25 percent figure for viewers desiring science and information television still holds true even today. Somehow, almost out of sheer luck, in a soon-forgotten textbook, I had found the magic number that would one day create a multibillion-dollar industry. But for the moment it seemed only like bad news.

In the summer before my senior year, Professor Roberts lined up a special research project for me. The Tennessee Valley Authority (TVA) had contacted her for assistance in finding a researcher who could comprehensively survey and document all of the historical sites in northern Alabama. TVA had a particular interest in identifying and cataloging those Cherokee Indian sites and colonial fortifications that it had flooded when constructing the great dams on the Tennessee River in the 1930s and 1940s. TVA offered to pay a grant of $700.

I took the project and spent the summer traveling all over the state gathering historical data. I also got to make my first trip to Washington, D.C., where I was a guest researcher in the Library of Congress. My most exciting times there were when a library worker, donning white gloves, would arrive with my own gloves and a box of original documents containing correspondence from Return J. Meigs Sr., the agent for Indian affairs in the territory that would become the state of Alabama.

Torn

It was the summer of 1973, and I found myself falling in love with the excitement of Washington, D.C. The Watergate hearings were in full swing in the U.S. Senate, so history was being made around me. Professor White treated me to a fancy lunch at the Cosmos Club when he came up for a visit. Professor Roberts, also in Washington for a visit that summer, accompanied me on my first trip to Mount Vernon, where she gave me what seemed like a graduate-level tutorial on the nation's first president. She seemed to know every detail of George Washington's life.

TVA ultimately published the results of my research project. This was a somewhat unusual accomplishment for an undergraduate student—and the publication eventually caught the attention of UAH president Benjamin Graves. He invited me to his office and complimented me on my work. I was honored by his thoughtfulness.

As I approached graduation, I found myself torn over my next steps. Professor White pleaded with me to go to graduate school at Duke, his alma mater. Some of my friends wanted me to go with them to law school. Just to be prepared for the latter option, I took the Law School Admission Test (LSAT)—and scored high enough to be qualified for admission to most law schools. But I just couldn't see myself entering a profession based largely on conflict and conflict resolution, so I let the application deadlines for law school come and go. I realize now that I was anxious to get started in some business or career and that's why I was resisting graduate school. But back then, I only knew that I felt torn and indecisive.

Back to the Beltway

"Dr. Graves wants to talk to you," said Professor White. I was in my little work-study office cleaning out my things. Graduation was just a week away.

"What about?" I asked. I couldn't imagine why the president of the university wanted to talk with me.

In a disapproving tone, White replied: "I think he wants to talk with you about a job." My department chairman was still annoyed that I was not pursuing graduate school at Duke—the application deadline had come and gone.

I put on my only sport coat and tie for my meeting, and then waited in President Graves's outer office until his secretary came to get me. I walked in, shook hands bravely, and sat down in the chair in front of his desk. I decided it was best to let him speak first.

Ben Graves had been a business professor before he became a college president. Prior to taking the position at UAH, he had been the president of Millsaps College in Jackson, Mississippi. He spoke with a deep, rich southern accent.

"John," he intoned, "I need someone to go to Washington and bring us back more federal money. I need someone who can meet federal contract and grant officers and sell them on this university. I think that person is you. Frances Roberts told me you like Washington. Is that correct?"

I was a bit overwhelmed. "Yes sir, I like Washington. Would you want me to live there?"

"No, but you will need to spend a lot of time there," Graves replied. "When you are here you can help me with my community relations work. I have already decided your title. You will be our Director of Community and Government Relations."

Ben Graves was a good salesman. He had me at "hello."

Within a week of starting my new job, President Graves had arranged for me to meet Senator John Sparkman in his office on Capitol Hill. Before my departure, I went to Bill's Men's Wear— this time as a customer. I bought three new suits with ties, shirts, and a new pair of shoes. I made the young salesman's day. He made $64, by my calculation.

I remembered to breathe while I waited in Senator Sparkman's outer office. I was twenty-two years old and was about to have an important meeting, my first as a professional, with the man who had been the Democratic Party's candidate for vice president in the year I was born.

My mission was simple: I needed to convince Sparkman to help me make contacts in Washington. I also wanted him to provide letters of support when UAH grant proposals were in competition with universities located in other states. Even though funding for university projects came through federal agencies, it never hurt to have a proposal endorsed by a powerful congressman.

Senator Sparkman, who was quite elderly by this time, welcomed me into his office with a warm smile. I lingered just a bit while walking by a framed photo on the wall of him at the inauguration of my hero, President Kennedy. In the photo, he was sitting just behind the new president and between Harry Truman and Richard Nixon. It was more than a little daunting.

The meeting proved to be a success, probably because Senator Sparkman took a liking to me. Over the next few months, he helped me learn the ropes in Washington and was always available to take my call. On one occasion, when I was convinced that I had submitted the best proposal for the funding of a campus educational opportunity center, he wrote a personal letter of support to Caspar Weinberger, then secretary of health, education, and welfare. I'll never know the true impact of that letter, but we did win the $1 million competition.

After eight months on the job, my work was paying off for UAH. I was earning my keep and I was making new D.C. contacts every week—and I was getting noticed. Unknown to me, there was a college consultant making inquiries about me for a position at the University of Maryland. He had noted that million-dollar federal grant—and especially that I had won it in spite of competition from much larger universities.

It wasn't long before I was contacted about a newly created position within the Office of the President at the University of Maryland. I interviewed for the position and received a job offer. After some reflection, I knew that it was time for me to leave Alabama and take up residence in Washington full-time. That's where my future seemed to lie. I accepted the job.

Part Two

Discovery

Chapter 10

From the Sidelines

*Nearly every man who develops an idea works it up to a point where
it looks impossible, and then he gets discouraged. That's not the place to
become discouraged.*

—THOMAS EDISON

The process of becoming an entrepreneur, of taking the field in
the great game of free enterprise, is mercurial. Because the path
of each entrepreneur is different, there is no simple and universal
road map.

However, over the years I've observed that there are some
shared experiences in the creation of any successful entrepreneurial enterprise. I passed through all of these stations while creating
Discovery and I believe they are common to most entrepreneurs:

1. Curious observation
2. Preparation
3. Ignition of passion
4. Idea
5. Plan
6. People
7. Brand

We'll visit each of these in turn. For now, we'll look at the first: *Curious observation.*

I decided to leave Alabama in February 1975, a month short of my twenty-third birthday. I took with me not only my furniture and car, my work experience at UAH and Bill's Menswear, and my growing rolodex of D.C. contacts, but also that "curious observation" I had made in college about the lack of documentary entertainment on television—and the statistic that 25 percent of the public would eagerly consume this kind of content.

The Central Administration of the University of Maryland was located on the campus of the institution's flagship campus at College Park, less than ten miles from the nation's capital. President Wilson Elkins presided over a five-campus system, with a chancellor to administer each campus (the titles have since reversed). I was offered the position of Director of Corporate and Foundation Relations in the Office of the President. My job was to assist faculty members and college deans throughout the university system in their quest for funding to support their research projects and other activities.

One of my first assignments was to help a noted physicist, Joseph Weber, find grant support for his breakthrough research in gravitational wave detection. I was fascinated by Weber and his attempt to build detectors out of two large aluminum cylinders, each chilled to within a few degrees of absolute zero (0-459.67°F). The detectors were positioned thousands of miles apart so that any local vibrations and movements of the earth could be identified and eliminated.

Einstein had predicted that when extremely massive objects in the universe were disturbed they would radiate waves or ripples that would actually deform the space-time fabric of the universe. We were able to get aluminum giant Alcoa interested in supporting the project. Although in the end Weber, like so many others since, failed to make a confirmed detection of the elusive gravity waves, it was exciting for me to observe the hunt.

The Challenge

One day in 1975, an article appeared in the *Washington Post* that caught my attention. Time Inc., the story announced, had decided to establish a new television service called Home Box Office (HBO), which was scheduled to launch on satellite for cable television distribution across the United States. Although federal rules were already in place to keep cable operators from offering content that might siphon viewers away from free over-the-air broadcasting ("anti-siphoning rules"), the Federal Communications Commission (FCC) had just recently, according to the article, created even newer and stronger rules that would block HBO's plans. Time Inc., the story continued, was now taking the FCC to court claiming that its new rules infringed on HBO's First Amendment right to free speech.

Finally, I said to myself, someone was challenging the ridiculous set of laws and regulations that prevented cable from offering its own content. That curious observation I had made back in college about the potential for documentaries to air on cable now seemed more relevant—especially if HBO's claims were successful in court. And if there was going to be a movie channel, why not a documentary channel?

But for the moment, these were just musings. For the rest of that year I was fully engaged in my new job at the University of Maryland. I gave absolutely no thought to actually trying to create a documentary channel. I just hoped, as a potential viewer, that someone else would. However, I did make a mental note to follow that promising HBO court case.

Nexus

Looking back, I can now see that, even as I focused on my new job, larger forces were at work in my life—and that they now were beginning to flow together. For example, I had unconsciously tucked away that factoid about informational TV watching—almost as if I knew that one day I'd find a use for it. By the same token, that *Washington Post* article had leaped out at me not by chance, but because, for years now—even when I wasn't thinking about it—I had been looking for the right opening in the marketplace. And now, as I began to track the HBO story on a daily basis, I was also unconsciously forming a strategy—one that I would consciously elucidate once the FCC, or the courts, reached a final decision.

At the time, none of this was obvious to me. Rather, it all just seemed to engage my curiosity in a different and exciting way. In the meantime, I went on with my life. I was still waiting, though I didn't know it, for the spark.

Difference

I have come to believe that successful entrepreneurs think differently from everyone else in some important way. Some of that difference may be baked in early as genetic or learned character traits. But even then, those traits will lie dormant unless they encounter the right *opportunity*. And almost always, that opportunity cannot be identified without some prior knowledge about new technologies or ideas or possibilities to which others haven't been exposed.

Famously, Bill Gates was introduced to computers in high school, when personal computers were in their infancy. Computers fully engaged his curiosity and, by age twenty, he had spent thousands of hours as a programmer. That gave him a knowledge and comfort level that was unique, and the result was Microsoft. By the same token, Steve Jobs early on needed the presence of a true computer genius, Steve Wozniak, to open his eyes to the possibilities of personal computing.

Ben Cohen and Jerry Greenfield, founders of Ben & Jerry's Ice Cream, both had ice-cream jobs as young men—Ben as an ice-cream truck driver and Jerry scooping ice cream in his college cafeteria.

Fred Smith, the founder of FedEx, started the company after a stint in Vietnam, where he and his friends did a lot of short-hop flying. After Vietnam, he wrote a college paper at Yale in which he outlined how to organize an overnight mail delivery system. Although Fred got a C on that paper, he was confident in his new delivery system that used a central sorting site as the hub. Doing all that logistics work as a young man in Vietnam got him thinking hard about how to move supplies around by air—and so, when the opportunity arrived, he was ready to make his move.

You now know my story. My curiosity, my early fascination with television as a teaching medium, my college work-study job exposing me to the producers and distributors of documentary films—no doubt other people had similar experiences during that same era, and yet, for some reason, in my mind they compounded upon each other, building a strategy beneath the surface of my consciousness that could be switched on and executed when the right factors were at last in place.

Did I tell myself that one day, when the moment was right, I was going to found a new television network dedicated to documentaries and educational content? No. Not even that day when I read about the HBO lawsuit. Rather, I was thinking about my new job, about adapting to my new life in Washington, D.C., and a thousand other things. And yet I do remember the odd sensation, as I read that article, that I was checking off another box on some mental checklist that I barely knew I was keeping.

Making Your Move

As I grow older, I'm convinced more and more that anyone looking back on his or her life will see comparable streams of experience converging, establishing a possible destiny. But I'm also convinced that only a fraction of the population has this inner checklist that tracks these events, both internal and in the outside world—and that then drives their choices and tells them when the moment is right to act.

What fraction of the population is born with this internal monitor? It would be ironic, but not unlikely, if it was the same 25 percent drawn to documentary and educational television. Why? Because both are driven by the same kind of curiosity to understand the world around them, to piece together how things work, and to recombine these pieces into new forms that create something new and valuable.

And everyone else? Are there no entrepreneurs in the remaining three-quarters of mankind? Of course there are, and they exist, I believe, *because curiosity not only is born; it also can be taught.* And it can be taught to anyone, at any age, anywhere in the world.

It has become the challenge of the second half of my career to find out how this can be done—and then to make it happen for the world's emerging billions of newly "wired" citizens. We'll revisit this quest later in the book.

Curious observation will remain just that if it isn't supported by *Preparation*.

Before players are ready to join the "show" of Major League Baseball, they typically need to spend a few seasons on a minor-league team, perfecting their skills. The same is true for most would-be entrepreneurs. Michael Dell labored hard to assemble just the right components to suit the unique computing needs of each of his college friends. After college, Jeff Bezos worked as a computer scientist on Wall Street. At a company known as Fitel, Jeff helped to build a network for international trade. And while it may seem that Mark Zuckerberg was impossibly young when Facebook had its celebrated initial public offering, the fact is that he spent years at Harvard perfecting and growing that service.

In other words, Dell, Bezos, and Zuckerberg spent time in the minors perfecting their skills and honing their instincts. All three were getting prepared to make their debut into the major league of free enterprise.

And it is easy to forget that it was *eight* years between Wozniak's prototype of the Apple 1 and Jobs's introduction of the Macintosh computer.

A Time of Change

In 1976—coincidentally the year of that first Apple computer—I unexpectedly found myself anxious to strike out on my own. It wasn't that my work at the University of Maryland was boring; it was just that it suddenly seemed important to me to be in control of my own destiny. I needed to be on my own. I desperately wanted to be able to explore and develop ideas without any constraints. It sounds a little crazy now—and it seemed that way even then—but that's the best way I can describe the emotions I felt.

It was also a year that once again reminded me of the preciousness of life and of those we hold dear. At age thirty-seven, my beloved sister, Linda, whose vibrant personality had been the dynamo of our family, died tragically, the victim of medical care gone awry.

Three years before, she had noticed a small lump in her breast. After a biopsy indicated that the tiny lump contained cancer cells, she had a mastectomy. Since the disease had been caught extremely early there was no need for further treatment, although precautionary radiation treatments were recommended—which she chose to do.

All seemed well and there was no reoccurrence of the cancer. Then, horribly, she began to exhibit symptoms of a radiation overdose. An investigation found that the radiation equipment used in her treatment had not been properly calibrated. The tissue of my sister's esophagus began to dissolve—until it was of no use. A feeding tube was inserted. My sister's situation grew desperate.

There was only one surgeon in the world who had successfully reconstructed an esophagus using a portion of a patient's own stomach. That surgeon was Dr. Henry Heimlich, already famous for the Heimlich maneuver for choking victims. Dr. Heimlich immediately took over Linda's case and successfully reconstructed her esophagus, performing the surgery where he practiced, at Cincinnati Jewish Hospital. Sadly, the effects of the overdose continued. Her spinal cord was also damaged and her heart was weakened. She died in her sleep of a failed heart.

Linda's death took a devastating toll on me. It was months before I could get my head back into work or anything else. Feeling helpless, I spent a lot of time with Linda's two boys, Martin and Alan, then fourteen and thirteen. We have remained extremely close ever since, as I have with their father, Jim Sisson.

Martin went on to become one of the most successful architects in Alabama, specializing in hospital design. Alan became a Harrier pilot for the U.S. Marine Corps. Before retiring after combat tours in Bosnia and Iraq, he rose to the rank of lieutenant colonel and commanded Marine Attack Squadron 542. My sister would have been very proud of her two boys and the men they have become.

Freelance

One day, after I came back from a visit to my family in Huntsville, I saw an opportunity that began to rejuvenate my flattened spirits. I read in the University of Maryland newspaper about a new university policy that allowed professors to consult for organizations, companies, and government agencies for one day a week without losing any pay. During my time at Maryland a number of organizations had asked if I could help them with fund-raising. I had always declined due to the potential conflict with my job at the University of Maryland.

Now I called the general counsel of the university to see if the new policy applied to those of us who worked in the administration. He said it did and that I was free to consult as often as one day per week without any reduction in pay, so long as my consulting work was in the same field. The rationale for this consulting policy was that, for example, engineering professors who actually got into the field and helped design a new bridge or new industrial plant would bring those enhanced skills and experiences back to their university teaching and research work. I asked about my avoidance of conflicts of interest and the general counsel said he saw none unless I consulted with another university that was in direct competition for funding against Maryland.

I was off and running. I quickly landed a contract with Huntsville Hospital in Alabama. They had called to see if I could help them get federal funding for a new wing. Pretty soon, I was too successful for my own good: I had more work lined up than I could possibly accomplish in one day per week. And the sum of all my pending consulting contracts was almost triple my university salary. I walked into the office of my boss, Bob Smith, and explained that I needed to resign so that I could pursue my consulting business. Bob was encouraging but he didn't want to lose me entirely.

He asked if the University of Maryland could be one of my new clients. Win-win. I cheerfully agreed.

Chance Encounter

I resigned from the University of Maryland but, on the same day, executed a contract for consulting with the university for about four days each month. Before long, I had also executed a new and expanded consulting agreement with Huntsville Hospital and I was under contract with other organizations such as the Police Boys and Girls Club of Washington, the Montgomery County Hospice Society, the Children's Defense Fund, and the Black Student Fund of Washington.

At a University of Maryland event, I met Richard Ford, an affluent, philanthropic individual from Indiana who was involved in supporting a number of nonprofit organizations in the Washington, D.C., area. Over the next few years he introduced me to a number of prospective consulting clients.

On one memorable occasion, Ford arranged for me to meet the headmistress of Madeira School in McLean, Virginia, one of the most exclusive schools for young women on the east coast. I was very impressed by the well-dressed headmistress. She was both charming and engaging as she described her school and its upcoming capital campaign. I left the school encouraged, but it was not meant to be: within two weeks of our meeting, headmistress Jean Harris shot and killed her lover, Dr. Herman Tarnower (the "Scarsdale Diet doctor"), in one of the most famous crimes of the era.

Maureen

I incorporated my consulting business in Maryland as American Association of University Consultants (AAUC) in late 1976. Just twenty-four, I was now an entrepreneur and what I wanted most to be: my own boss. I soon began to hire some of the staff at the University of Maryland to work with me under that same one-day-per-week consultancy rule. I loved the simple equation of it all: the harder I worked, the more consulting fees came my way. I then used those increased finances to expand my business opportunities.

In 1978, while still in the midst of building my consulting business, I met Maureen Donohue at the Apple Tree, one of Washington's most popular nightspots for young professionals. At the Apple Tree, young staffers from Capitol Hill, lobbying epicenter K Street, federal agencies, and local universities would dine, mingle, and dance the night away. I often went there to escape the pressures of the week.

Maureen, twenty-four, was pretty and fit with, as the saying goes, "the map of Ireland on her face." I was instantly attracted to her, even more so when I discovered who she was: Maureen worked for a U.S. Navy contractor that supported the Naval Underwater Sound Lab, a unit that developed acoustic wave propagation loss models for submarine navigation and tracking. In particular, Maureen translated complex mathematical models into Fortran programming code. Her resulting computer programs were used in the Navy's effort to track Soviet subs with detection technologies that factored in the depth, salinity, and temperature of the ocean water.

Maureen also had a top security clearance, and so she could only say so much about her work—which added to her mystery. She had obtained her degree in mathematics from the University of Rhode Island and would soon complete her master's degree in numerical science at Johns Hopkins University.

How could I resist? We immediately started dating—and were married three years later, on January 10, 1981. Mike Parvin, my best friend since childhood, came up from Alabama to serve as my best man.

New Venture

Shortly after we returned from our honeymoon, I uncovered a major new business opportunity for my little company. Thanks to my experiences at UAH and Maryland, I knew that most colleges couldn't afford an office in Washington to hunt for federal funding. Indeed, fewer than twenty major universities actually maintained grants offices there. That left almost 1,500 small colleges across the country needing better information about funding possibilities—and better access to Washington.

It struck me that a comprehensive newsletter for these other colleges, published quarterly, targeted at each academic discipline, might be a winning proposition.

So, I set my little band of consultants to creating a test newsletter, this one to be aimed at college chemistry departments and titled (somewhat drearily) the "Chemistry Funding Information System." My consultant/researcher Margarete "Peg" Hall worked tirelessly on the first issue. We managed to send out about 1,500 personalized packages targeted at chemistry department heads at every U.S. college and university. Each contained a signed letter from me, a sample first newsletter issue, and an order form. Annual subscriptions were set at $1,000—big money, but worth it to subscribers *if* we could consistently deliver useful content.

That was my next lesson in entrepreneurship: offer your customers what they need, set a price based on perceived value, then work your butt off to match, then exceed, what you are offering. Too many start-ups die because they fail at one or more of these three variables: they either don't understand their customers' needs, they price too low to grow and thrive, or, worst of all, take the money from the customers and then don't do *whatever it takes* to deliver on their promise.

I tried to calculate how long it would take before a department chairman would receive the package, read it, and respond. I figured the first responses would arrive within a week to ten days. It was a long week.

Confirmation

The next Monday morning, I opened my mailbox at the College Park post office and was heartbroken to see that there were still no responses, just a few bills and a yellow slip of paper. I was almost out of the post office when I noticed that the yellow slip was a notice that I had a package to pick up at the counter.

The counter clerk, a middle-aged woman, returned with a plastic bin. "These are for you. We just started putting these in a bin this morning after we saw that there would be no room in your box. Sir, you need to get a bigger box."

Every struggling entrepreneur needs an exciting, confirming moment that all the risks and sacrifices they've made are worth it. This was mine. I counted twenty-seven packages, each containing a $1,000 order. And this was just the first day.

I rented a bigger box.

I thought I was a pretty big deal at that moment—but I was still in the minor leagues, learning my craft, taking some swings, getting on base. But I had just hit a home run. And now, for the first time, I knew I could play at the highest level of the game.

Passionate Viewing

Although I had always been fond of watching documentaries, especially shows on science and history, two series that aired during the 1970s utterly changed my perspective on my life and, ultimately, my life's work. These series resulted in my entering the *Ignition of passion* stage of my entrepreneurial life.

The first was *The Ascent of Man*, an epic thirteen-part series that was produced by the BBC and Time-Life Films. The series was written and hosted by Jacob Bronowski, a legendary mathematician, biologist, and historian of science. Adrian Malone was the executive producer. It aired in the United States on PBS in the mid-1970s; I was spellbound by every episode as Bronowski walked me through the history of science and civilization.

I babbled so much about *The Ascent of Man* at work that one of my colleagues at the University of Maryland went out and bought me the companion book to the series. To my great satisfaction, Bronowski's foreword to the book described the unique strengths of television as a teaching tool:

> Television is an admirable medium for exposition in several ways: powerful and immediate to the eye, able to take the spectator bodily into the places and processes that are described, and conversational enough to make him conscious that what he witnesses are not events but the actions of people.

Yes! I said to myself as I read his words.

And then, in the eleventh episode, "Knowledge or Certainty," Bronowski showed just what the medium could do. In one of the most powerful and spine-chilling moments in television history, Bronowski stepped into the ash-strewn pond at Auschwitz and said:

> Into this pond were flushed the ashes of some four million people. And that was not done by gas. It was done by arrogance. It was done by dogma. It was done by ignorance. When

people believe that they have absolute knowledge, with no test in reality, this is how they behave. This is what men do when they aspire to the knowledge of gods.

Then he reached down and grabbed up a handful of the muddy black ash, symbolically and literally touching those lives, including those of his own Jewish relatives, lost in the Holocaust. No one who saw that scene has ever forgotten it.

Billions and Billions

A few years later, Maureen and I sat down to watch a new thirteen-part documentary series on space, *Cosmos*, presented and written by Carl Sagan (along with Ann Druyan and Steven Soter). It too was executive-produced by Adrian Malone.

Cosmos was brilliantly innovative in explaining the wonders of the universe. Carl Sagan used the device of a "spaceship of the imagination" to whisk viewers around the galaxy and beyond. The series was a national sensation and, at the time, the most widely watched series in PBS history. Sagan himself became a celebrity—and a regular guest on Johnny Carson's *The Tonight Show*.

These were incredibly promising developments for television and, as a viewer, I wanted more—even if I had to do it myself.

Realization

There is a vast gap between the *dream*, which is the vision that arises at the confluence of all of those curiosity-driven streams of experience, and the *idea*, which is the road map for the practical implementation of that dream.

As I've already said, I think most people I meet, at least from what they tell me, have such dreams. I also think that a sizable percentage of folks even turn their dreams into ideas. But only a small fraction of those "idea" people ultimately become entrepreneurs and execute on their ideas. Thus, if we are to develop more successful entrepreneurs in our society not only will we have to cultivate curiosity at the front end; we will also need to teach the skills needed on the back end to turn ideas into practical implementation.

I had now reached that point—and my practical education was about to begin. And I was lucky to have a mentor to guide me through.

Knowing my interest in education and educational television, Richard Ford introduced me to Edward Bauman, a professor of theology at Wesley Theological Seminary at American University. Ed Bauman was also a well-known television personality in the Washington area—WJLA, the local ABC broadcast station, produced a weekend show in which Ed presented programs about faith that incorporated both music and art.

Market Research

Bauman was convinced that one of the series he created at WJLA deserved regional, even national, television distribution. After watching it, I agreed. It was called *The Children of Abraham*, and it described how Christianity, Judaism, and Islam all traced their origins back to the Patriarch Abraham.

Ed asked me if I could help distribute the theological series as well as generate funds to support his work. I took up the challenge.

There was no Internet (as we know it today) in 1981 and so I began spending my afternoons in McKeldin Library at the University of Maryland College Park campus. There I combed through their periodical collections and read *Broadcasting Magazine*, *Variety*, *Multichannel News*, *Television/Radio Age*, *Channels*, and *Satellite Week*. These trade magazines provided a wealth of information on new cable channels being planned, such as Music Television (MTV), which launched in August that year.

I also confirmed that the law was now well settled: HBO had won its court case and cable television was now free to offer its own content. Broadcast television had lost its regulatory protection from competition. I searched for cable channels that might potentially air *The Children of Abraham*—but there didn't appear to be any. There were some fundamentalist Christian networks that were attempting to get cable carriage—but these outlets would not accept Bauman's "interfaith" approach. Meanwhile, there simply were no educational or documentary networks in operation and, as far as I could tell, there were none being planned.

Choosing Sides

In 1981, only a few of the major cable networks we know today were in operation. HBO had been on satellite since 1975. Ted Turner was next to create a national cable channel when, in 1976, he uplinked his local Atlanta broadcast station WTCG-TV (later renamed "superstation" WTBS) to satellite for broader distribution. USA Network and ESPN had been launched in the late 1970s. And, just a year before I began my research, Ted Turner had gotten CNN on the air.

Although some channels were now making "themed" content promises to consumers—CNN for news, HBO for movies, ESPN for sports—no one, it seemed, had yet thought of science, nature, or education as a content theme for a cable channel. There was a cable "news" network and a cable "sports" network—and even plans for the imminent cable "music" network (MTV)—but there was still no cable "educational" network.

On the Clock

For the first time since I had formulated my vision for cable educational programming, I began to sense—and worry—about an impending deadline to make it real. Like many other entrepreneurs in the same situation, I began to fret that there might be others out there not only with the same idea—but also further along in making that idea real. What if they beat me to market? What if their strategies were better than mine?

Most of all, *what if they lived out my dream and left me behind with a lifetime of regrets*?

I think most entrepreneurs will agree with me that they too went through a similar point of inflection sometime in their career. Before that moment, their dream, their idea, was more an idle fantasy that might be realized someday. After that point, it becomes an obsession; the clock is ticking, and every new day may be too late. And what sparks that moment is the sudden realization that you may not be alone in your quest, that there could be other competitors in the race.

In my case, what spurred me to action—and terrified me—was not only that there might be others inching toward my dream, but that they might be some of the smartest and most dynamic players in American industry. Surely someone like Ted Turner, or even a broadcast network executive, would soon recognize what I already saw—if they hadn't already. If I was going to make my move—and I would never forgive myself if I didn't—I would have to do it *now*.

Questions and More Questions

The University of Maryland had a strong radio, television, and film department, and its media library collections were rich and comprehensive. So that would be my base for industry data. My research intensified. Who made the satellites, how did they work, and how much did it cost to lease a transponder? Who were the major cable operators, how did their systems operate, and who were the people who ran them? What commercial television advertisers also sponsored quality content on PBS, what kind of shows did they sponsor, what were the ratings, and how much did they spend? What individuals and companies were making documentaries, where were they being made, how much did they cost, and how were their television rights managed? How do you run a television operation, what are the key staff positions, and how much do people make in the business? What was the viewership on any outlet, broadcast or cable, for nonfiction content? Was the interest among the public for more science and educational content still standing at about 25 percent, as I had learned in college?

As you can see, the questions I was asking had changed. In the dream mode it had been enough to surf atop the surface of academic theory and market tastes in order to confirm the overall concept. At the idea stage, I was looking at structures, players, market sizes, consumer trends, and timing.

Now, as I prepared to execute, I became much more specific and empirical: Exactly how big were those target markets, and what were the cost structures involved in delivering content? Who would be my suppliers, strategic partners, and distributors—and what cut of my profits would they demand? It was not only a much more precise set of questions, but also a longer list—frankly, it seemed as if I could come up with an infinite list of questions I wanted answered. And the fact that I couldn't possibly come up with all of those answers only added to my fear that I was missing some vital piece of the puzzle, and that that would ultimately lead to my ruin.

How much nicer it would have been to have stuck with my pretty dream—the one in which I couldn't possibly fail. I could still spend the rest of my life, as others lived out my dream, claiming (though few would believe me) that I had thought of the idea first. But my personality wouldn't let me take that easy way out.

Quest

I soon gave up on distributing Ed Bauman's film series. That seemed hopeless anyway. I let him know and he understood.

I was now a man on a mission. Was there an existing opportunity I could seize? Did I know something that no one else had realized?

I was increasingly haunted by that one question: Why had the network news divisions at CBS, ABC, and NBC not thought to start a news network or a documentary network? Was I still missing something? Was somebody, somewhere already on to the idea and working behind the scenes to lock up contracts with the BBC and TVOntario and all the other quality documentary producers?

And that was just the beginning. Right behind that "why" question was the "how" question: if I was not already working inside a major television network organization, how could I find the financing to launch a new channel?

I worked all through the end of 1981, struggling to find answers not just to those questions, but to the scores of new ones that seemed to erupt in my mind each time I came up with an answer. It wasn't until early February 1982 that the answers finally began to outpace the questions. My idea, now fully investigated, was finally becoming fully formed. The time had come to make it real—but would I be willing to take that step?

I was now convinced that the United States, and quite possibly the world, wanted—even if they didn't know it yet—a dependable high-quality cable channel devoted solely to engaging and informative programs about science, technology, nature, history, travel, and human adventure. I was further convinced that this massive latent demand would, within the next two years, power the creation of just such a channel. All that remained was who would build it—and who would fund it.

The time had come. I had been sitting on the idea for months, but I couldn't keep it in anymore. I desperately needed to market-test my idea—and thus risk publicly exposing it for the first time—to make sure I wasn't completely crazy. The audience would be my wife, Maureen. And that brings us full circle to that Sunday morning in February 1982 with which I began this book: "What would you think about a new cable channel that just showed great documentary series like *Cosmos*, *The Ascent of Man*, and Walter Cronkite's *Universe* series? You know, informative but entertaining shows about science, nature, history, and medicine?"

Almost immediately Maureen blurted out: "That would be awesome!" But then, after a brief moment of reflection, she asked: "But if this is such a good idea, why didn't Ted Turner do it?"

Starting Line

Why indeed? Maureen's response had pierced right to the heart of my idea. Her enthusiasm for my idea matched my own, and her question about Ted Turner tapped into my own self-doubt and paranoia. I took away from that conversation the comfort that I was perhaps on the right track—but that I needed to dig much deeper into my idea.

So, I continued my research throughout the spring and summer of 1982. By the end of August, I had found enough answers to give me the confidence that I was not only on the right track, but, more important, also still ahead (briefly) of the competition. It was now or never.

I swallowed my fear and jumped. In early September I began hiring people and writing checks. I knew from the start that I would need to form a legal entity, a company, through which I could both receive financing and sell shares to investors. And for that I needed experienced legal advice.

I knew a lawyer, Kenneth King, who had worked for Ed Bauman's organization, and I asked him to prepare the incorporation papers. I had not yet determined the actual brand name for the new channel. Knowing it would take a while to decide, I instructed Ken to file under the name "Cable Educational Network, Inc." On September 8, 1982, the articles of incorporation were filed in the state of Maryland. My new company was born.

The forty-page business plan for the new network took me nearly a year to write—a pace that would never work in today's fast-moving digital world. The plan called for $25 million in start-up costs, which I figured was enough to pay for transponder time to relay the signal, programming rights for a full schedule of documentaries, marketing costs, and employee salaries.

That, of course, was too much money to try to raise in the initial phase. No investor would take such a risk on an unproven concept led by an unproven entrepreneur. Instead I figured that I would first need to raise an initial $5 million in a first round of financing just to get on the air and operate for five to six months. By then, after (hopefully) being picked up by cable operators and proving the value of our channel, we would likely have an easier time getting the other $20 million. With full financing, my plan was to reach "break even" and enter into profitability within about three years of launch.

While researching the business plan, I learned that twenty-four of the twenty-five top-rated shows aired by PBS were documentaries (rather than dramas or the ballets and symphonies) and that when NBC put on one of its *White Paper* documentaries, it inevitably enjoyed good ratings as well. That information was welcome, but it only reinforced what I already believed: that not only was there a television audience out there for something beyond mindless entertainment, but we could also make a good business out of delivering it.

I like to solve puzzles, but the deeper I dug the more pieces it seemed I needed to fit together. For instance, my plan was to feature a lot of documentaries from the BBC, but I got a big surprise when the BBC staff informed me that they didn't even know if they owned the rights to their content.

As it turned out, the "Beeb" had never licensed its work to a cable provider before and had a serious question about what undefined rights its "talent" and associated production partners and contractors might claim. In today's digital, multiplatform, multimedia world that would be unimaginable. But even as late as 1983, it was a question that the BBC still hadn't taken the time to answer.

We eventually resolved the matter, but it quickly became obvious that we were operating in new territory on this and many other issues. For example, there was the technical question of how to reconfigure older 16 mm footage into a video form that we could send out, bounce off a satellite, and land in people's homes via cable. But slowly, we made our way through, solving each problem in turn—and putting together our puzzle in the process.

Jettison

During my months of cable network business planning Maureen and I had largely lived off income available from my consulting and from my college newsletter business in addition to Maureen's salary. But I could already see that the day was coming when I would have to go all in. I had already quit my Maryland job and the subsequent consulting contract. It was also soon clear that I had to cease all consulting activity for AAUC clients.

It wasn't so much that I didn't have the time or physical energy to continue with this existing work. Rather, it was that I could no longer share my attention or my mental energy on that work. My new venture had fully captured my imagination and I had no doubt that it was going to demand all of my attention and then some.

That moment when you jettison your career and go all in on a new venture has been called the scariest part of being an entrepreneur. It sure was for me. Had I been single, it would have been a lot easier to make the leap—though perhaps more difficult to get to that point, because marriage had given me more focus and purpose. I couldn't help thinking about the implications of failure. Would we lose our house? Our savings? Would a black mark on my résumé make me unhireable? Was I about to put my loving and supporting wife through the hell of bankruptcy and poverty?

And then, just to make the risk even more tangible and daunting, a new responsibility came into the world.

Our precious daughter, Elizabeth, was born on March 1, 1983. We now had a new baby and the financial obligations of a young family. Did I really dare to risk my little family on my dream, my obsession?

If the decision had been left to me, I'm not sure I would have taken the leap. But, thankfully, Maureen had the same level of confidence as I did in the business plan and, even more, she believed in me. So when I floated the idea of taking a second mortgage loan on our home to fund the new business idea, she readily agreed.

We raised $100,000 for the start-up operations that way. Then I also threw in all of my remaining savings from the consulting work. Altogether, that gave us $130,000—everything we owned—to start our new cable network. It was an insanely high-risk venture. And now by default, because we had just spent her college education funds, even baby Elizabeth was going along for the risky ride.

Teammates

In launching the new cable network I knew from the start that I had to put together a team of *People*—the next step—with the experience and aptitude to tackle each of the business challenges we faced from day one. Things were going to move too fast, and the decisions that needed to be made were too important for on-the-job training.

I also knew that as founder, chairman, and CEO, I had the job of meeting with prospective investors and finding that $25 million. Whatever skills I had developed raising money for other causes and organizations I now had to put to work for my own project. I quickly discovered that fund-raising for yourself is a whole lot more serious business.

I also wanted all of our marketing materials to look exceptional. Too many new companies don't take this part of the business seriously and hire friends or family to do the work. That's a big mistake. There should be nothing amateur or homemade in a company that plans to play in the big leagues—and that included our "look," the first thing about us that our clients and customers would see.

So I recruited Edward Peabody, a talented public relations and graphic design professional who had worked with me before. I knew that he understood what I was looking for—and he delivered, designing and producing all of our initial marketing materials, including a program guide magazine. He brought our first logo to life. Working in Canada with TVOntario, Eddie also supervised the production of our first promo tape. Eddie made us look big-time before we really were. In an odd twist, we were driven to live up to those first promotional images we projected of our network ambition.

I was also fortunate that the chairman of the Department of Radio, Television, and Film at the University of Maryland was hugely enthusiastic about my plans for the new channel. Robert McCleary even left his post at the university to provide the in-depth television experience that I needed—a very brave move given our humble start. In addition to his years in academia, Bob had also worked at broadcast stations and he was experienced in all aspects of television operations. That's why I placed Bob in charge of all production operations and program scheduling.

Bob McCleary quickly realized that he needed help scheduling the network, so he recruited a talented and experienced program-ming professional with the aristocratic name of Michael du Mon-ceau. Michael, who had been on the faculty with McCleary, had a natural instinct for content—so he was put in charge of construct-ing the daily program schedule for the network.

I took a gamble that really paid off when I hired Suzanne Hayes to head up programming for the network. Although she had no television experience other than her communications studies at the University of Virginia, she did possess all the sales skills and busi-ness savvy needed to conduct business with the entrenched film suppliers like the BBC, TVOntario, Granada TV, and all of our early sources of content.

Suzanne's natural advantage was that she was smart, persistent, and fearless. She knew how to get people to say "yes"—a far more important skill than any particular expertise in the field. In fact, I first met Suzanne when she sold us word processing equipment for our AAUC consulting business. She was so good at selling me that I figured she should be doing that to our content supply partners who needed a lot of convincing about our viability as a network.

There is a tendency in start-up companies to identify the senior management slots you need to fill—and then to rush out and fill them as quickly as possible. It's not a bad strategy, because it enables you to get under way fast and then fix any mistakes as you proceed. But I chose the opposite—and I think even better—strategy of filling those slots with the best people you can find, no matter how long it takes.

The weakness of the latter course is that you can waste a lot of time recruiting before you ever get started. But the advantage is that you don't have to suffer the internal confusion and dislocation that comes from shuffling staff while you are still building the company. It also makes it less likely that the company will make a mistake so devastating that you won't recover from it.

I even went so far in my recruiting that I actually hired people whom the company didn't really need yet. For example, although there would be no network for cable affiliates to carry and no advertising to sell until we were transmitting on satellite, I still wanted us to begin making pitches to cable operators and potential advertisers. No one was going to beat us to the market, even if it didn't yet exist. So I hired a seasoned ad executive, Joe Maddox, to head up ad sales. Steve Eldridge, an engaging young man with a passion for cable television, was hired to begin meeting with cable operators.

While learning about communication satellites, I was fortunate to meet Lew Meyer, who had recently retired as chief financial officer for Comsat General Corporation. Lew offered to serve as my head of finance. Lew gave us instant credibility in the area of financial stewardship. Nothing makes investors more comfortable than a veteran finance guy.

Finally, I want to be sure to mention our very first employee, Michael Donohue, Maureen's brother. He had come to Washington in 1982 looking for work after graduating with a finance degree from the University of Connecticut. After serving as the chief assistant in my consulting work, Michael became the very first person on the cable network payroll. Though officially engaged with bookkeeping, Mike was in fact that most vital early employee in a start-up: the guy willing to do any job to make the company succeed.

We rented office space in Landover, Maryland, near Amtrak's New Carrollton station. It was cheap, and I figured that easy commuter train access might help with recruiting. I put all my new employees on the payroll—which meant that I was now starting to spend the funds borrowed through the second mortgage on our home.

In other words, I needed to start raising money—fast. But first, I needed to finally decide on a company name.

The Brand

It was spring 1984 and I was on one of my very first fund-raising trips. My target was Storer Communications, parent company of the local cable system that served Prince George's County, Maryland, where our office was located.

The general manager of Storer's local cable system was Winfield "Win" Kelley. Win Kelley liked my channel idea—to the point of offering to set up a meeting for me with senior management at Storer's headquarters in Miami.

At the Miami meeting, Ken Bagwell, Storer's president, quickly made it clear to me that Storer was in no position to invest in my company. He explained that his current bank covenants prohibited any new investments outside their cable distribution business.

However, when the discussion turned to carriage of my network, the Storer executives in the conference room were optimistic.

One of the marketing executives then spoke up and said that we really needed to finalize a name for the channel. Cable Educational Network, our corporate name, was, he said, "way too boring." I told him that I fully agreed and was working on the final brand name. The meeting ended on that note and I headed for the airport.

On the flight home, I revisited each of my final candidates for the channel name: Horizon, Vista, Discovery, Explorer, and Wonder. I got out a pad of paper and played with each name and added the word "network" and, alternatively, "channel" to each one. Here was my reasoning:

> "Horizon" brought up images of the future, perhaps of the hiding place of the unknown just "over the horizon"—but it lacked a sense of drama and personal involvement by the viewer.

> "Vista" had similar strengths and weaknesses.

> "Wonder" was the front-runner for a while, because that's the emotion, the response, I wanted to inspire. We would be presenting the wonders of the world to our viewers. However, maybe it wasn't quite serious enough.

> "Explorer" also was close to my goal because it implied a "reaching out" for information—the quest to answer questions raised by our curiosity. Yet it also had the feel of a *National Geographic* kind of program where you go along for an exploration of the Amazon. I wanted that, but I also wanted more.

By the end of the flight I had circled the word "Discovery." To my mind the name implies an active search to find something important and rewarding at the end. People like the process of discovery, the feeling of reaching the successful end of some kind of quest or effort. I also thought that viewers could "discover" the future through our science and technology programs, and they could likewise "discover" the past through our history documentaries.

In 1983, I had read the now-famous book by Daniel Boorstin about humanity's enduring quest to discover *The Discoverers*. Boorstin's book had captured the amazing human spirit that was the heart of my network's planned content. Discovery Channel would be a good name. I felt both relieved and excited as the plane touched down at National Airport.

That was Friday afternoon. On the following Monday morning, I asked that all of our letterhead and marketing materials be changed to reflect our new brand.

Chapter 11

Connections

A chain is no stronger than its weakest link, and life is after all a chain.

—William James

The clock was ticking on that little $130,000 war chest that Maureen and I had managed to scrape together. Only $25 million to go . . .

I knew that raising that kind of money was going to require my every single waking moment. Running AAUC's operations had now become a distraction, so with regrets I shut the company down. Now, having burned all of my other economic bridges, my family, my employees, and I were even more out on a lonely tightrope.

Even creating that tiny war chest had been a struggle. A local branch manager at Suburban Bank (now part of Bank of America) worked hard to get us the loan. However, the difference between what Maureen and I owed on the first mortgage and the appraised value of our home was about $70,000. He had to go to his supervisors to get approval.

They approved our requested $100,000 second mortgage loan conditioned on Maureen and me signing personal guarantees. If we defaulted on the loan, and the sale of our house under foreclosure did not produce enough proceeds to pay off both the first and second mortgages, the bank wanted to be in a position to collect any other assets (car, home furnishings, etc.) we owned.

That was it: we had now put everything on the line. We would stake our future—and our company—on $130,000 and a handful of credit cards. If we failed, we would be raising Elizabeth in a generous relative's house or in the cheapest rental apartment available.

By March 1, 1984, our daughter Elizabeth's first birthday, that cash balance was down to $106,000. I was spending about $12,000 per month to cover office lease expenses, marketing material design and printing, legal fees, and staff salaries. Meanwhile, travel costs were beginning to escalate as Suzanne was starting her trips to London to meet with the BBC.

I calculated that we could survive for another eight months at this monthly burn rate. I just had to find funding. We were running out of time.

Deep Pockets

I had to start networking. I had to get introduced to individuals who could write $50,000 investment checks and to companies that could invest $1 million or more. I simply had to get linked up to people with money, or people who knew people with money. But all my previous funding experience had been with federal grant officers and foundation staff members, not in soliciting major gifts from wealthy individuals.

But I did know Richard Ford and knew he had some good connections. Ford introduced me to a group of businesspeople who had come together to support the drama department at Catholic University. They called their fund-raising effort "Father's Purse." Father Gilbert Hartke was the charismatic founder and head of the department, and in the past he had mentored actors such as Jon Voight and Susan Sarandon. He was in constant need of scholarship support for his students.

One evening, at a gathering of the Father's Purse group in Mel Krupin's restaurant in downtown D.C., I mentioned to member Tom Newman that I was starting a new cable channel. After describing the concept to him, and my need for $25 million in start-up funding, Tom looked up from his drink and said, "You need an investment banker, probably one in New York."

"Do you know any?" I asked, hoping he would have connections at Goldman Sachs, E. F. Hutton, or one of the other leading investment banks.

"Well, no," he replied, "but I do know a securities lawyer in Georgetown, John McCarthy. He worked with that guy Harry Hagerty, who started Digital Switch."

I had heard about Digital Switch Corporation. It was a local success story, the first company to develop digital switches for telephone companies. All telephone companies were now converting their antiquated mechanical switching to these new devices.

Tom agreed to make the introduction—and within a week I was sitting with McCarthy over lunch in a Georgetown restaurant. McCarthy immediately took a liking to my idea and wanted his client Harry E. Hagerty Jr. to hear about the concept as well. It was March 1984, and I had yet to decide on the Discovery Channel brand name. So I simply described the company as the nation's first "cable educational network," a channel devoted exclusively to documentary entertainment in science, nature, history, travel, and human adventure.

Hagerty, an engaging guy, had a great sense of humor and a ready smile. I liked him the instant John and I sat down with him in his Georgetown office. After I described my plans for the channel, Harry leaned back in his chair.

"Well, I'd watch it," he chuckled. "Hell, I don't know if I'd ever watch *anything else* if you got this on cable." He turned to McCarthy and said, "Dick Crooks at Allen and Company should see this."

We spent the rest of the meeting talking about what we liked on television and complaining about what little there was on TV worth watching. After mentioning that I grew up watching Walter Cronkite's series, such as *You Are There* and *Twentieth Century*, Harry remarked: "Yeah, I did, too, but why did CBS cancel his *Universe* series? I hope there are people other than us that like to watch this stuff. You know, Allen and Company is going to want to see a lot of research on this."

"I know and I'm working on it," I said.

I left the meeting excited that John and Harry were going to try to set up the meeting with a New York investment firm—and knowing that my team and I would have to rush to get some better presentation materials together, especially on our potential audience. My excitement was also tempered by a gnawing worry regarding Harry's remark about CBS canceling Cronkite's *Universe*. I had heard this before while describing the channel concept. I even wondered about it myself. Had science television already been proven a failure? I needed an answer—fast—because I knew that the smart analysts at Allen & Company would be all over this.

Chapter 12

The Most Trusted Man
in America

I want to say that probably 24 hours after I told CBS that I was stepping down at my 65th birthday, I was already regretting it. And I regretted it every day since.

—Walter Cronkite

Of all the topics covered in my business plan, I knew my audience research was the weakest.

My plan was comprehensive and complete on almost every other subject. I had a complete analysis of programming costs, as well as transponder and uplink expenses. I had a detailed marketing and sales plan to get carriage on cable systems. And Suzanne Hayes had made enough progress in her content search that I had a long list of programs and series that could make up a credible program schedule.

But the question I hadn't fully answered was the big one: *would anybody watch?*

Detailed ratings information was hard to come by. In fact, I only had access to the audience ratings for a few PBS series, such as *Cosmos, Civilization,* and *The Ascent of Man.* R. H. Bruskin Associates had conducted a survey of viewer interests in March 1982—and I had a summary report of that study. It offered the best evidence I could find; its results indicated that 62.5 percent of adult Americans wanted to see more programs about science.

However, I also knew that was just what people said in a phone survey, maybe to prove how intelligent they were to the pollster. But would they really watch? Only real ratings data could actually prove or disprove my case. I knew there had to be someone out there who had that critical information I needed.

It was now late March 1984 and the all-important first meeting with Allen & Company was less than three weeks away.

I stared at my phone. Would it actually be possible to get in touch with Walter Cronkite himself? He would know his own ratings. But would the most trusted man in America even take my call?

I hesitated. Who did I think I was even thinking about calling the great newsman, the one person I most admired in the world of television, the man who had provided the voice track of my life? If I was going to embarrass myself, I certainly didn't want to do it with Walter Cronkite.

And That's the Way It Was

It was one of those moments when you either go big or go home. I steeled myself, threw caution to the wind, and dialed the CBS News office in Manhattan.

"This is John Hendricks. Can you connect me to Walter Cronkite?" I said with the most confident voice I could muster. I expected the receptionist to say, "And just who the heck is John Hendricks?" Instead, she put me on hold.

Finally, she came back on the line. "He's working over at his Time and Life Building office today. I have the number."

In somewhat excited disbelief over such quick cooperation, I wrote down the number and dialed. A woman answered the phone and I asked to speak to "Mr. Cronkite"—which I immediately realized indicated I was not an acquaintance.

"He's out at the moment. Can I take a message?" she politely replied.

I knew this message was vitally important and so I decided to tell the woman all about why I was calling. I explained my plans for a new documentary channel for cable and why I thought Walter Cronkite would be interested. She didn't interrupt so I kept talking.

In other words, I probably sounded hopelessly obsessed. Finally, mercifully, after one of my pauses, the woman spoke up. "How about this? Why don't you put all this in a letter to Mr. Cronkite? Keep it short, no more than two pages, and I'll make sure it gets in front of him. Be sure to include your phone number so that we can reach you."

How many times had she given this same advice to other hapless callers?

She gave me the office mailing address and I thanked her. I then asked her name. "Blanche Lafitte," she replied. I loved both her name and her willingness to help. Afterward, I made sure to cover my letter to Walter with a letter addressed to her.

Then I waited—likely for the nicest rejection letter or phone message one could imagine. What the heck, I told myself, it was worth a try.

Summons

I was just about to leave the house one morning about a week later when the phone rang. I figured it was for Maureen but answered anyway.

"Is this Mr. Hendricks?"

"Yes," I replied. It was . . . the voice.

"Mr. Hendricks, this is Walter Cronkite, and boy, I think you are really on to something. I've just read your letter, twice in fact. Could you come to New York to meet with me?"

"Absolutely," I replied, beginning to tremble. "I can be on a train anytime."

He then told me he would have Blanche call to set up a time, as he was still at home. Blanche had given my letter to Walter as he walked out the office door the day before; she figured he might read it that evening. I loved that Blanche.

Soon I found myself in New York with Walter Cronkite— *Walter Cronkite!*—for not one, but two meetings within a two-week period in April 1984. He also made plans to come down to Washington on May 10 to meet with my staff and support network. He wanted to be of any help he could.

When I told Walter that I would probably need his help with introductions to financial people in New York, he replied, "I would be glad to. I know a few people."

Yeah . . . he knew a few people. Behind him on the wall as he spoke were two framed photos, one of him walking on the Normandy beach with Dwight Eisenhower and the other of him in front of the Great Pyramid with Egyptian president Anwar Sadat.

A Fair Share

During my meetings with Walter that April, he had explained that the ratings for *Universe* had been good but hadn't always met the expectations of CBS management.

The three broadcasting networks at that time were still dividing up an astounding 90 percent share of the total television viewing audience. So, a third of that amount, or a 30 percent share, was expected for CBS prime-time shows.

Universe, a science and technology series, typically garnered a 25 percent share—a number that, once again, was consistent with the early research I had first encountered back in college. It seemed that it really was a world that was 25 percent full of curious people. Unfortunately, CBS had viewed that glass of human curiosity as being 75 percent empty while I was seeing it 25 percent full.

Walter went on to say that CBS canceled his *Universe* series largely for "audience flow" reasons.

"John," he explained, "the audience that shows up for an informative show like *Universe* will just not stay on for the sitcom that follows. We had a nice audience for *Universe,* but they just abandoned the network when our show was over at eight-thirty. They probably turned the TV off to read a good book.

"However," Walter added, "if you can get a cable channel up and running with back-to-back shows on science and other educational topics, these viewers will finally have a TV channel that they can stay with all day." He smiled like a co-conspirator and said, "This really is an idea whose time has come."

I asked Walter if he would put what he had just said in a letter to me—especially that part about "an idea whose time has come." He readily agreed, asking Blanche to come in and work with me so that I could take the letter with me when I left. "I'll make phone calls, too," he promised.

Before I left with his endorsement letter, I talked to Walter about ways that we could work together. He told me that he was very disappointed about how things had worked out at CBS: he had planned to work on *Universe* for years—only to see it canceled and buried.

I told him that I would need a lot of help programming my network, and I wanted him to be a producer and host once I secured my financing. "It's a deal," he said.

It was April 11, 1984, and the most trusted man in America was on my side. I could not believe my good fortune. The man who had most inspired my passion for quality television was going to be my production partner.

I floated out of the lobby of the Time & Life Building at Fiftieth Street and glanced across busy Sixth Avenue toward the neon lights of Radio City Music Hall. As I hailed a taxi for the train station and looked up at the skyscrapers of Manhattan, I knew I had come a long way from Hatfield Bottom.

Chapter 13

Not All Angels Are in Heaven

All money is a matter of belief.

—ADAM SMITH

In late April 1984, Harry Hagerty and John McCarthy accompanied me on my first trip to Allen & Company.

Armed with a solid business plan and an endorsement letter from Walter Cronkite, I was feeling especially confident. "I can win them over," I told myself as the three of us entered the building at the corner of Fifth Avenue and Fifty-Fifth Street.

Allen & Company was a "boutique" investment bank known for its savvy deal making, especially in identifying promising new start-up ventures. It was also known for pulling off large and complicated transactions with a remarkably small staff.

Even then, Allen & Company was regarded as the premier investment house in the media and entertainment sector. In 1973, Allen & Company had acquired a significant interest in Columbia Pictures—then, in 1982, had sold that stake to Coca-Cola at a substantial profit.

Allen & Company now occupied several floors of a building bearing the Coca-Cola logo. As we entered, we walked past large framed posters of upcoming movies from Columbia Pictures. This was the big time, a world I couldn't have imagined a decade before.

On the ninth floor we were greeted warmly by Thalia Crooks. John McCarthy explained to me that Thalia was the wife of Dick Crooks's late brother. She was originally from Crete and spoke with a very slight accent. Dick relied on her for a lot of the due diligence required on projects under consideration by the investment bank. I knew that, polite as she was, Thalia was about to run me through the wringer.

We walked into a wood-paneled conference room. I was astounded to see original Norman Rockwell paintings on the walls—paintings I had seen only in magazine and book reproductions. Now here were the originals hanging on the walls of the room where I was to make my presentation. My confidence started to ebb; did I really deserve to run with this crowd?

Yes, I told myself. After all, Walter Cronkite believes in me. Just hang on to that.

Dick Crooks walked in, smiled, shook my hand, and settled back into one of the chairs. He had a relaxed manner and immediately put me at ease. He, Harry, and John McCarthy chatted for a bit. I could tell they all had a history together.

Before I could start, Dick asked Thalia to go get Manuel Roxas. While Thalia stepped out of the room, Dick explained that Manuel Roxas was a smart young staffer who would be important in the evaluation of my plan. He said that Manuel was the grandson of a past president of the Philippines. He had recently graduated from the Wharton School and was now working as an analyst at Allen & Company.

Walk Through

With the group finally assembled, I began to walk through each component of my plan. As expected, Thalia had a lot of questions. Manuel was also relentless in his probing and chased after every detail. I will list here some of the things Manuel and Thalia wanted to know, to give the reader a glimpse of what one of these interrogations is like:

1. How many cable channels are still available and on which systems?
2. Do you have any written evidence that cable operators are committed to carrying your channel?
3. What advertisers have you actually talked to, and could we have their names and phone numbers?
4. Where is your contract for the satellite transponder? *I didn't have one.*
5. Why not?
6. What is the term length of contracts that could be executed on programs, and from which suppliers?
7. Where are the actual rating reports from Nielsen?
8. What will you do if CBS or another network just decides to start a competitive channel tomorrow?

Dick posed the occasional question, but, in that first meeting, he mostly listened to Thalia and Manuel pepper me with questions. I could tell that at times he was amused. By the nature of some of his questions, it struck me that he was probably going to go with his gut. I hoped that he would simply visualize himself personally watching the channel, just like Harry had done.

I left the meeting exhausted. And as I walked out, I wasn't even sure if it had been a success or failure. Dick Crooks had been noncommittal but he offered to continue to meet with me. "You've still got a lot of work to do," he told me. "Come back when you have more answers."

And so began the twelve most torturous months of my life.

Obstacle Course

On the way back to Maryland, provoked by the meeting, I struggled in my mind with one overwhelming obstacle after another.

How could I possibly execute a multimillion-dollar satellite contract without first getting the financing in place? How could I get a carriage commitment from any cable operator without first getting a signal up to satellite so they could watch it? Would any program supplier, like the BBC, tie up its libraries for years without a huge up-front payment?

Knowing that a network had to reach 15 million homes before Nielsen could begin to measure audience size, how would it be possible to get advertisers interested enough to make a sponsorship commitment now before we had even uplinked a signal?

Most important, how could I manage to keep the lights on until I solved these puzzles? Cash was now down to $85,000—and burning fast. And now I had to spend it at an even faster rate.

After thinking pretty hard about the situation, it seemed the only way to pull things off was to somehow be real—or at least *appear* real—enough to the cable industry to convince cable operators across the United States to make carriage commitments to us. Our little outfit was going to have to sufficiently puff itself up to look like a major, established enterprise. And that wasn't going to be easy—even with a letter from Walter Cronkite.

The next major cable event, the Western Show, wasn't scheduled until early December in Anaheim, California—and my existing cash funding would certainly run out before then. In any event, we would have to produce a promo tape of the quality that the industry was accustomed to seeing from giant networks like HBO or CNN. The price tag for producing such a high-quality, ten-minute promo tape could be as much as $100,000. Allen & Company understandably wanted to reduce the risks for any investment clients they might bring to the table, but operating at this high level with so little cash seemed impossible. Still, I went to work determined to make it happen—and hoped for a miracle.

Putting Up Wins

Our little team fanned out to tackle all of these challenges in parallel. And we started to enjoy some victories.

After endless meetings in Stamford, Connecticut, we convinced Group W Satellite Communications to prepare and execute a detailed services agreement proposal, requiring no immediate deposit. This confirmed all the pricing elements for uplink and master control. As a division of satellite builder Westinghouse, Group W also identified a transponder on the company's Westar V satellite and reserved it for our use. When we commenced operations, the uplink and master control services plus the satellite transponder would cost us $336,000 each month—a stunning amount for an entity that, when we received the signed pricing commitment on August 1, 1984, had just $60,000 left in cash.

Meanwhile, I managed to talk Harlan Rosenzweig, the Group W Satellite Communications president, out of demanding a deposit or payment before we received financing. Harlan was confident in the ultimate success of the Discovery Channel. I asked him if he would share his enthusiasm with Allen & Company and he promptly sent a letter. In Group W, we now had our first strong corporate ally.

By July 31, Suzanne Hayes had negotiated an agreement with TVOntario for the provision of 100 hours of content at a license fee of just $1,000 per hour. The bad news was that TVOntario also wanted a first payment of $50,000 by September 30, and the balance of $50,000 by the end of the year. I just couldn't sign the agreement, which TVOntario had already executed, as there was no way I could meet the payment terms. It would have left us broke.

Suzanne labored on until September 25 to renegotiate the terms. Remarkably, her renegotiated terms required us to pay only $4,000 per month, beginning October 4. *That* deal I could sign. I knew it might mean having to reduce everyone's already meager salaries, but now at least we would have a promo tape—and ultimately, even a revenue source. I simply had to have TVOntario's rights-cleared content.

Ultimately, when we did make that initial $4,000 payment to TVOntario, Discovery Channel was down to a cash balance of less than $25,000.

Ironically, now that we finally had the content to create the demo tape, we didn't have the money to produce it. TVOntario had also given us a price to produce the promo tape using excerpts from the shows they were licensing to us: $65,000, payment up front, with none of that flexibility they'd shown on the content deal.

Increasingly desperate, one day I walked into Lew Meyer's office and straight-out asked him if he thought his old employer Comsat General would sponsor the production of the first Discovery Channel promo tape. I told him that we would be showing it to the cable industry—and, as a satellite company, perhaps Comsat General would see a value. After I told Lew the cost of the TVOntario production, he said, "Let's give it a try."

We soon met with Robert Kinzie, president of Comsat General, to pitch the sponsorship idea. As Comsat General had few dealings with the cable industry, the rationale for such a sponsorship was a stretch. Luckily, I had the inspiration to mention that the demo would also be shown to our prospective advertisers, including companies such as GM and Boeing.

That seemed to turn the tide. He agreed to the sponsorship, and Lew secured the check for $65,000 within a week. It was now early November. We finally had money for the promo tape, but the cable industry's Western Show convention in California was less than a month away. I asked Eddie Peabody to race up to Canada and supervise the production.

Making Noise

Now, assuming that we did manage to get the demo tape completed in time, there was still the matter of getting noticed. There had to be a better way than just showing the video at one of a hundred booths at a noisy, busy cable TV convention.

I had a better idea: Thanks to the deal, we now had access to 100 hours of TVOntario's documentary content, and we soon would have a high-quality video logo that could easily be adapted for interstitial use between programs.

So, what if we convinced Harlan Rosenzweig at Group W to donate a week's worth of satellite time to us in mid-December? Cable operators all across the country would then have a preview of our upcoming network, even if they weren't at the convention. If operators were interested in carrying the Discovery Channel, they could return a reply package, not to us, but instead to an independent accounting firm that could certify the results.

Even if cable operators serving just 1 million homes replied positively, it would be confirming evidence that we had a channel idea that could gain carriage. And that, in turn, would help get us over the top in securing financing—and Harlan in turn would get a new revenue stream of $336,000 a month from a new network customer.

That was a lot of ifs. However, though Harlan needed some convincing, he soon recognized that it was a win-win proposition. Group W agreed to provide the satellite time without fee.

New Arrival

Just a few days before, on October 29, 1984, Maureen and I had raced to the hospital when she went into labor with our second child. Elizabeth's delivery had taken thirty-six hours, so I brought along plenty of reading material.

As Maureen was getting settled on the maternity floor, I strolled downstairs to fill out the paperwork. Ten minutes later, the phone rang at the registration desk. The receptionist urged me to go immediately upstairs as my wife was now delivering the baby. I thought it was a mistake. It wasn't.

Andrew John Hendricks had his own rushed deadline. He was born within minutes after I ran into the delivery room. We cherished the arrival of Andrew just as we did when Elizabeth entered our lives twenty months earlier. Today, when I look at my wonderful full-grown children, I'm reminded that Elizabeth is as old as my decision to start Discovery, and Andrew is as old as the channel itself.

From the Heart

In mid-November 1984, two weeks after Andrew's birth, the $65,000 check from Comsat General was transferred north of the border to TVOntario, whose producers were hard at work on the promo tape. Lew Meyer walked into my office. I knew he had come to talk about our dire financial situation.

We were now down to just $511. I had maxed out my MasterCard over the previous three months. We then started using Maureen's Visa card, but that was soon maxed out as well. Maureen then discovered that her American Express card had no credit limit as long as we paid the entire outstanding balance each month. So that became our next monetary lifeline. But we had recently used that American Express card to pay for all staff travel and for other expenses.

Now the American Express balance was up to $75,000, and there was no way we could pay that off. We couldn't even make a partial payment. Maureen started to get calls at home every three days from American Express demanding payment on the overdue account. She had held them off and the card was not yet canceled.

When Lew walked in, I told him the encouraging news that Maureen's American Express card was somehow still active and that we might be able to buy an airline ticket and book a hotel room in Anaheim with it. Combined with the $511 left in the bank, it might just be enough for at least me to get to Anaheim, show the promo tape, and meet with cable operators.

Lew was a pro. He had managed the finances of businesses for four decades before reaching retirement age the year before. He had seen a lot, but I guessed he was never involved in a business with national ambitions but just $511 left in the bank.

Before I could tell him about Maureen's American Express card not being canceled, Lew put a hand up to stop me.

"John," he said, "I talked to my wife last night. I believe in what you are doing and she believes in what you are doing, too. We want to help bridge you to the financing. I think we can make it through the winter with this."

Lew then reached into his inside coat pocket and handed me a personal check for $50,000. "It can just be a loan to the company that you can convert into stock for me when we close the first round."

I sat for a long time staring at the check. Of all the things that could have happened that day, this was the most unexpected. For the first time in a professional setting with a work colleague, I felt tears begin to well up. I was the most grateful entrepreneur in America at that moment.

Too often, when we talk about business and entrepreneurship it's about numbers: stock option prices, revenues, per-share earnings, and on and on. But if it were only about the money, or the products, the world of business—and especially entrepreneurship—wouldn't satisfy the way it does. What we don't celebrate often enough is the human side of this world. It is those stunning moments of nobility, decency, courage, and trust that make it all worthwhile.

This unbelievable act of loyalty and sacrifice by Lew Meyer and his wife was one of those moments. It not only saved the company, and my dream, but also brought a new, personal dimension to the company that I hope it never loses. As for myself, I will never forget that moment—and I will always be grateful.

After I thanked Lew profusely, he noticed that I had laid his check on my desk. "John," he said softly, "you've got to give the check back to me. I've got to go deposit it and get a partial payment off to American Express."

I laughed and handed the check back to him. I never knew what percent of Lew's retirement savings that $50,000 represented, but I suspected that it was significant. And I'm writing this with that same swell of emotion I felt twenty-eight years ago.

The Pitch

Armed with Lew's funds, we quickly went to work preparing packages to send out to the top two thousand cable systems in the country. It was quite an effort. We included a handsome brochure about the Discovery Channel and instructions about how operators could take a look at the service on satellite. And we announced that we would be transmitting twenty-four hours daily for a preview week beginning December 17, 1984. Finally, if a package recipient was interested in carrying the service, I requested in my cover letter that he or she return the enclosed reply package to Arthur Andersen, the accounting firm we hired to certify results.

We assembled a six-hour selection of documentary content that we delivered to Group W. They would just repeat the six-hour programming block four times each day during the seven-day preview week. Also with Lew's loan, I was able to bring my entire little team to the Western Show in Anaheim—where they helped staff a pitifully small booth that was more like a desk with a logo mounted behind it.

There were five of us at the convention. We rented a suite at the nearby Hyatt hotel, where we set up a large TV set and showed our promo tape to cable operators we had invited over. And on the convention floor we tirelessly told everybody we encountered about the preview week that would be starting on satellite less than ten days away.

After the holidays, Arthur Andersen reported that responses from cable operators were starting to come in. They planned to give me a report on February 1, 1985.

We waited on pins and needles. Would we get responses from operators serving at least 1 million homes? Once again, I found myself waiting for the mail to arrive, just like that day in the College Park post office years before.

On February 1, I opened the envelope from Arthur Andersen. I saw first that they had sent a copy to Allen & Company, as I had requested. Then I quickly scanned down the report to the numbers. Arthur Andersen certified that 911 cable systems had responded indicating they wanted to carry the Discovery Channel. In total, they served more than 4 million homes.

I remember whispering "Yessss!" as I read the report. It was an amazing response. And it had an amazing impact: within two months, after completing the necessary paperwork, Allen & Company completed our initial round of financing.

Over the previous nine months, I had met with more than two hundred prospective investors to plead my case, urging them to take a risk on the Discovery Channel. A few of them "believed" and they were now poised to invest in the first round of financing. Our goal for the initial round was $5 million, an amount we considered sufficient to get us on the air for about five to six months.

During this initial operating period we would then seek the balance of the estimated $20 million that would cover our losses until break-even operations. I calculated that we would reach operational break-even within three years of launch.

Our expenses, once we launched on satellite, would total about $1 million per month. That was a lot of money—and a few years before, I would have found it overwhelming even to contemplate. But if there is one thing I've learned in business over the years, it is that with practice you can become accustomed to financials, whatever their magnitude. What was astonishing in the thousands can become everyday news in the millions—and even a common unit of exchange in the billions.

Betting on the Bankers

For now, though, those days were still in the future. Right now, a million dollars per month was a very large sum of money. And I needed to line up investors to provide those millions.

One of the most important investors that I had recruited, after a chain of referrals, was New York Life Insurance Company. New York Life had recently created a $50 million venture investment fund, and its manager, David Glickstein, and his supervisor, Irv Culpepper, pledged to invest $1 million in the first round. I sensed that they would also participate in subsequent rounds of financing. They were believers.

I also had met with a number of prominent individuals in the Washington, D.C., area, and they were waiting to receive the final investment documents. Two banks, American Security and Suburban Bank (since acquired by Sovran Bank and then ultimately Bank of America), were surprisingly eager to invest. Venture America, a new venture group in northern Virginia headed up by Dan Moore and Jim Ball, wanted in as well.

At Allen & Company, Dick Crooks had agreed to personally make a substantial investment and, in March 1985, he was rounding up investment commitments from his colleagues in the firm. Thalia invested and so did Jack Schneider. Those were particularly satisfying investments since they came from the savvy analyst and trading ranks at Allen & Company.

Only after Dick Crooks had committed to invest would Herbert Allen, the firm's principal, consider risking his own money or that of the firm. It was smart policy—assuring Herbert Allen that any proposed investment project had been fully vetted by one of the firm's partners.

That moment had now arrived. Dick asked me to come to New York to meet with Herbert Allen as a final step before closing the first-round investment. The paperwork was all but complete. Dick had even collected some investment checks from his associates that we could hold in escrow until the final closing date of the transaction.

I had a good meeting with Herbert; then Dick went off to chat with him. He came back with a handwritten personal check from Herbert for $250,000. He said that Herbert believed in the project and was going to make a few calls to his friends, associates, and clients that afternoon.

In those calls, made over just a few hours, Herbert Allen raised more than $2 million in investment funds for Discovery. When I looked down the list of my new shareholders, I saw names like Ray Stark, the Hollywood producer, and Robert Strauss, the former chairman of the Democratic National Committee.

Meanwhile, as you might imagine, it was a good plane ride back to Washington. Herbert's check for $250,000 was the largest check I had ever seen. I pulled it out several times on the way back just to hold it, and to look at it. Some very important and smart people believed in me.

Countdown

During April 1985, all of the checks for the initial $5 million round of financing had been collected, along with stock purchase agreements signed by each investor. The investment round, managed by Allen & Company, then closed. The funds were released from escrow and transferred to the Discovery Channel company account. Suzanne Hayes contacted all of the program suppliers and sent off the initial payments required under their contracts. I called Harlan Rosenzweig and told him to get ready to light up the transponder on the Westar V satellite. The launch date for the Discovery Channel was set for June 17, 1985—just two months away.

Chapter 14

Bon Voyage

The real voyage of discovery consists not in seeking new landscapes but in having new eyes.

—Marcel Proust

Monday, June 17, 1985.

At noon, we gathered in the conference room on the single floor we had leased in the office building in Landover, Maryland. Almost all nineteen employees of the Discovery Channel, except for a few stationed at our uplink site, managed to squeeze into the room where a television set had been connected to our rooftop dish.

We were anxiously waiting for 3 p.m. EST. That's when Group W would beam the first Discovery Channel signal up from Stamford, Connecticut, to the Westar V satellite positioned 22,236 miles above the earth's surface at the equator. At that altitude, the $250 million satellite was in geostationary orbit and its orbital speed exactly matched the earth's rotation. Since the satellite appeared to be "fixed" in the sky, cable television operators across the country could receive the retransmitted television signals from the satellite through their own fixed dishes, just like the one mounted on our roof.

A Space Odyssey

In an article published in *Wireless World* in 1945, Arthur C. Clarke had first suggested that if just three satellites could be placed in a geostationary orbit, then the entire planet would be fully blanketed with retransmitted signals from space—and would usher in a world of instantaneous global communications.

However, in 1945 no rocket existed that could lift a satellite even into low earth orbit. In America, that feat would have to wait until January 31, 1958, when the powerful Jupiter C rocket built by Wernher von Braun and his team in Huntsville, Alabama, lifted the nation's first satellite, Explorer I, into orbit. Intelsat I, launched on April 6, 1965, became the first geostationary satellite for tele-communications over the Atlantic Ocean. In 1975, Satcom I had launched and was soon retransmitting the television feed of Home Box Office, an event that marked the birth of cable satellite pro-gramming. Now, just a decade later, we were taking our place in the sky aboard Westar V.

At precisely 3 p.m. the crisp television signal with the animated Discovery Channel logo burst onto our television screen and the room erupted into cheers. At long last, we were real.

Then a curious thing happened: no one could leave the room. We were transfixed by the television feed that we had worked so hard to assemble.

It had been a team effort, and now the team wanted to stay together in that room and share our success. Hundreds of hours of programming—from the BBC, from TVOntario, and from a score of other suppliers around the world—had been acquired by Suzanne Hayes. It was enough to fill our schedule for months, if not years to come. Bob McCleary and Mike du Monceau and their teams had skillfully assembled the content into a schedule containing commercial breaks, promotional spots, and other interstitial elements. Joe Maddox had somehow managed to land mighty General Motors as one of our very first sponsors and so we waited for that spot to run. The high-quality marketing and promotional materials that Eddie Peabody produced had been used by Steve Eldridge to convince cable operators to launch us on day one.

But Steve had not been able to confirm if any operators were actually launching our service simultaneously with the very first satellite transmission—so there was the small possibility that we, in that small conference room in Landover, Maryland, were actually the only people in America watching our new channel. But we put that out of our minds. We told ourselves that soon millions would be watching.

Our pressing work on hold, we all settled down like a big family to watch the very first Discovery Channel show, *Iceberg Alley*. It was a TVOntario documentary about the frigid waters of the North Atlantic.

Viewer Number One

Within minutes after the first transmission began, the phone in the tiny lobby began to ring . . . and ring. We looked around at each other. It turned out that our office receptionist was standing in the room with us watching *Iceberg Alley*. Her eyes met mine and she quickly dashed out of the room to answer the phone. I assumed it was either Harlan Rosenzweig or Dick Crooks calling to congratulate us on the launch.

The receptionist returned. "Who is it?" I asked. "It's some teacher in Kansas," she replied. "She wants to know if she can tape *Iceberg Alley* on her VCR and show it to her class."

A grin formed on every face in the room. We really *did* have viewers.

I turned to Suzanne and asked, "Do we even own the educational rights?" "No," she grinned. "But I'll see if we can get them."

We learned later that cable systems serving about 156,000 subscribers had simultaneously started carriage of the Discovery Channel when we beamed up to the satellite at 3 p.m. EST on June 17, 1985. One of those systems, in Kansas, had told its customers about the planned launch of the channel and a teacher had been standing by her TV set. Within a few moments, she had called the cable system office to find out our phone number. In doing so, she had made our day.

Characterizing Cable

We never forgot about that teacher from Kansas.

We managed to accomplish a lot of things in the first year after the launch, but one of our highest-priority items was to secure educational rights to many of our shows. That would enable teachers to legally tape these "rights-cleared" shows for use in the classroom without further compensation to the program producers.

In order for this content to be easily identified by teachers, we created a one-hour program block that aired at the start of each weekday called *Assignment Discovery*, in which rights-cleared content in science, history, and other subjects was free for teachers to tape and show in their classrooms.

Soon the Discovery Channel was appearing in homes all across America. We would end 1985 with almost 5 million homes able to watch our programming.

I think it's important at this point to explain the different business models of cable television.

From the beginning Discovery was a "basic" cable service—that is, it was included in the lowest-priced service package sold by cable operators to their customers. If you got basic cable service from these operators, you typically received the Discovery Channel along with CNN, ESPN, MTV, WTBS, and a host of other advertising–supported networks.

Other cable networks, like HBO, were "premium" services and therefore carried no advertising to support their programming. These "premium" networks (sometimes called "pay" services) had to rely solely on subscription revenue generated by an extra purchase decision, beyond basic-level cable service, made deliberately by cable customers.

The advertising subsidy worked powerfully to minimize the subscription cost of basic service to cable customers in the same way that it had made broadcast television "free." However, no television content is truly free. Advertisers recover the cost of the billions of dollars that they spend in advertising by setting higher retail prices paid by consumers for their products and services. Thus "free" television is a great illusion.

Basic cable television networks that have a specialized theme, such as Discovery, CNN, and ESPN, enjoy the same dual stream of revenue (from advertising and from subscription fees) that also supports, in the print world, such specialized magazines as *Scientific American*, *Time*, and *Sports Illustrated*. Magazines and newspapers, which all carry advertising, generally cost much less than publications, including books, that carry no advertising.

An advertising supported newspaper, like the *Washington Post*, also consists of a bundle of different types of content—sports, opinions, local news, movie theater listings, etc.—that, because of advertising revenues, is priced very affordably for the consumer. Some readers may never read the sports section or the movie listings but they are still, of course, paying for this unread content.

Now, imagine if these unhappy readers complained about the

content they never read but still paid for, and the government then forced the *Washington Post* to break apart its editorial bundle and sell the individual sections separately, creating, for example, a separate *Post* sports newspaper, a *Post* opinion newspaper, and a *Post* entertainment newspaper. The interest in each of these new narrowly targeted newspapers would be less, readership for each would be diminished, and advertising would plummet since none of the new independent special-interest newspapers would attract the entire readership of the original *Washington Post*.

Different Interests, Different Channels

In the same way, basic cable contains a variety of different content, each appealing to different consumer interests. Because it penetrates into all cable homes, basic cable generates substantial advertising revenue and makes the whole bundle affordable to the consumer. If you break apart that bundle, the economic model also breaks down—and consumers will find themselves having to pay more for a few "à la carte" channel choices than they previously paid for the entire basic 50–100 channel package.

It is important to understand this characteristic of cable because, in 1985, we were setting out at Discovery to distribute television through cable systems—and we had two choices, "basic" and "premium."

Now, let's say a network owner—like we were—decided to launch its channel as a basic cable service and it was available in all 100 million U.S. households. And imagine that this network needed revenues totaling $1 billion annually to pay for its programming and operations.

Then that network would only have to charge a wholesale subscription fee of just $.42 per subscriber per month to generate half of its break-even revenue, $500 million per year, from those 100 million subscribers. Due to the universal reach of its programming, the basic network could easily generate the other half of its revenue, $500 million, from advertisers.

This also means that a cable operator could carry 100 of these channels and pay wholesale subscription fees of just $42 on behalf of each of its subscribers. Now, obviously, the cable operator would have other costs than just for programming, and so the basic retail fee might be realistically set at $60 to $80 for each customer.

That would be attractive and a low cost to the customer: 100 or more channels, each transmitting twenty-four hours a day. Remember: a price for just one movie or documentary on a DVD costs about $14.99. So, for the price of just four or five DVDs, a cable subscriber can enjoy an entire month of programming from 100 or more channels. That is the power and attraction of the basic cable bundle.

Now, by comparison, let's look at the "premium" or "pay" model. The most successful premium service in history is HBO. Yet, after more than four decades of marketing, it has penetrated just 28 percent of cable and satellite homes. HBO in 2012 had 28 million subscribers. Thus, when a cable network is not provided as part of the basic package—even if it is HBO, with its compelling schedule of entertainment—that network can only attract about one in four cable customers as subscribers.

Needless to say, most specialized cable services attract far lower consumer interest than does HBO—typically just 10 percent of homes.

Now, suppose that a network has to recover its annual expense budget of $1 billion from just 10 million homes. Because it doesn't even qualify for ratings measurement by Nielsen (which requires a minimum distribution of 15 million homes to qualify for measurement), the network will attract little or no advertising revenue. Consequently, this premium network would have to charge each of its 10 million subscribers $8.33 per month to recover its $1 billion annual expense budget.

So, if a cable consumer were to subscribe to just fifteen of these "à la carte" premium channels, then his or her monthly bill would be a whopping $124.95. That's a dramatic step backward in programming value per dollar spent.

Charting a Path

That's why, in 1983, even as I was developing my business plan for Discovery, I knew I wanted to go the route of a "basic" service. I did not want the Discovery Channel's future distribution limited to perhaps only 10 million homes, serving only those people who could afford an expensive "premium" service. However, in those days "basic cable" was still a delicate business model, and the powerful force of government had been tinkering with it through regulations.

For example, cable operators were subject to the FCC's "must carry" rules, which protected local broadcasters from competition for a channel slot by cable programmers. Those rules required that a cable operator had to first carry all local broadcast stations before providing any leftover channels to cable networks. That meant that a cable operator, for example, had to provide carriage to a seldom-watched, poorly programmed local independent TV station carrying reruns of *Gilligan's Island* before it could carry CNN.

In other words, cable networks were second-class citizens in the eyes of the law. Cable programmers had to settle for the scraps of channel capacity left over after broadcast station carriage. As you can imagine, this severely stunted cable network growth.

In 1984, Ted Turner filed a lawsuit against the FCC over these must-carry rules. Turner prevailed when the courts agreed that the FCC rules were an unconstitutional violation of free speech. That ruling gave all of us a little breathing room, that is, until 1994, when the courts reversed their earlier decision and must-carry rules were reinstated.

Start-up cable networks, including Discovery, did not initially enjoy universal distribution, as did the broadcasters. Consequently we had difficulty attracting advertisers. We desperately depended upon the monthly subscription fees paid by cable operators, who in turn collected those fees from their subscribers.

Washington Intervenes

Once again the government, prodded by broadcaster lobbyists, stepped in, this time to thwart the development of our revenue stream just as it had done to distribution efforts. The feds heavily regulated the retail rates that cable operators could charge their subscribers. So, if a cable operator wanted to pay Discovery Channel even just a nickel per month for each subscriber, government price controls would prevent the operator from adding that increased wholesale cost to the retail rate charged to its customers.

Finally, Congress decided to stand for fairness and competition, and began to take steps to deregulate cable pricing through the Cable Communications Policy Act of 1984. A transition period was established for the implementation of the act, which began on December 29, 1984, and ended exactly two years later at the end of 1986. It was during this two-year period that we were seeking critical early carriage agreements for the Discovery Channel. However, during this transition period, state and local jurisdictions could still regulate the pricing of basic cable services. Cable operators would therefore be largely prevented from increasing their consumer rates during 1985 and 1986 to pay for new services like the Discovery Channel. Retail rate increases to pay for new services would have to wait until the first monthly cable bills were sent out to customers in January 1987 when deregulation came into effect.

This was a big problem for a struggling new start-up like Discovery. It was difficult to convince cable operators to pay any kind of subscription fee for a new channel that launched during this period. We had unfortunately launched Discovery at a time when networks had to provide their service free of charge to get carriage. What this meant was that we would have only meager advertising revenue with which to fund our operations in addition to my precious investment capital.

That prospect made our chances of survival even more dismal. The entire investment community suddenly seemed to recognize the difficulties faced by any new start-up cable channel.

Dog Days

By August 1985, Allen & Company was having difficulty finding investors for our second round of financing—money we needed in place by November, when the $5 million proceeds from our first round would be exhausted.

Our operating expenses were now running $800,000 per month, the biggest portion of which was the monthly payment of $336,000 to Group W for the Westar V transponder lease and uplink and master control services. We had already abandoned hope of raising the entire $20 million that we needed to carry us through to break-even in 1988. Now we set our sights lower to just $6 million in a second round. This would buy us seven more months, until May 1986, to find the rest of the financing.

So now, just when I thought that we were finally in the clear and on our way, Discovery Channel slid into its darkest days—and desperation reentered my life with a roar.

Chapter 15

A Near-Death Experience

There is a time to take counsel of your fears, and there is a time to never listen to any fear.

—George S. Patton

Throughout the fall of 1985, I traveled to New York, Los Angeles, and anywhere else there was a potential investor. In meeting after meeting, people were polite but just not interested.

I soon understood why. Even though the Discovery Channel was a terrific service, getting great reviews, and climbing above 4 million homes in distribution, it seemed that word had spread that basic networks were a poor investment. Even though some relief in the deregulation of cable rates was expected to begin in January 1987, the long-term success of cable networks still looked like a challenge.

Advertisers certainly weren't flocking to pay for the meager audiences of many of the new cable networks. And it didn't help that buying cable was a lot of work for advertising agencies. An agency could make three calls, place a $10 million order on ABC, CBS, and NBC, and earn its 15 percent agency commission of

$1.5 million. Conversely, the agency could spend a lot of time and effort meeting with fifteen or twenty cable networks to place that same order amount for that same commission, with no guarantee of equivalent ratings. Which one would you pick?

Aiming Low

Although I initially hoped we'd have to sell only 20 percent of our company to secure the $6 million second-round investment, Allen & Company felt that it was a stretch to argue that Discovery in its entirety was worth more than $15 million. Allen was right, and in August 1985 we lowered our sights—and decided to sell 40 percent of Discovery for a measly $6 million. (For some context, that 40 percent equity stake is today worth about $9 billion.)

Even at this depressed (and depressing) company valuation, there were *no* takers. I had an amazing story to tell and people listened, but then they declined to participate. Most said that cable programming was just not one of their investment priorities. Allen & Company did their job in getting meetings with blue-chip prospects but, one by one, they said no. By late September 1985, I had been turned down by Coca-Cola Entertainment Group, Universal, Disney, and others. And their refusals quickly filtered down to individual investors, who followed their lead.

By October, the balance of funds remaining from the first round of financing was getting dangerously low—just $600,000 remained. When the Group W monthly invoice arrived I knew that I couldn't send off more than half of my remaining funds to them. I needed the funds much more urgently than Group W did. They were, after all, a subsidiary of mighty Westinghouse.

They can wait until we close the next round, I told myself, whenever that is. I wondered how long it would be before they noticed.

California Calling

Then, in late November, about the time our cash was down to the last $100,000, the unexpected happened once again.

Dick Crooks called. "You're not going to believe this," he laughed. "E. F. Hutton just called and said they have a client who wants to fund the entire six-million-dollar round."

It almost sounded like a joke. "Who?"

"I don't know, they won't say until we have a meeting," Dick replied. "Can you come up tomorrow?"

Oh yeah, I could make the time.

The next day, the two young investment bankers from E. F. Hutton explained that they represented the venerable Chronicle Publishing Company, based in San Francisco. I knew that the Chronicle owned Western Communications, which was a cable operating company with systems in a few western states and Hawaii. It also owned the *San Francisco Chronicle* newspaper and KRON-TV, the longtime NBC affiliate in the same market.

The E. F. Hutton bankers explained that they had come for a "get-acquainted" meeting. Following the meeting, they said they would put us together with the Chronicle's chief finance and planning officer, Leo Hindery. They told me that Hindery thought highly of the Discovery Channel and had convinced his colleagues at Chronicle management to pursue a substantial ownership stake.

We tried our best to hide it during the meeting, but we were ready to shout, do high-fives, and turn cartwheels. Not only had we been rescued, but it had been by media people who truly believed in what we were doing.

The celebration was brief. We were now completely out of cash and, even with the Chron's promise in hand, we still had to work fast to close the transaction, no later than the end of the year. Otherwise the creditors would be chasing us—and if we went dark it might be impossible to start up again.

E. F. Hutton's lawyers pored over all of our agreements with cable affiliates, advertisers, and program suppliers in their due diligence work. At Discovery, we called all of our vendors, many of whom we had not paid in several months, and asked them to be patient for just a few more weeks. We promised we would get a check out to everyone by December 31.

I was particularly worried about the long-overdue $500,000 payment we owed to the BBC. Suzanne Hayes and I got on the phone with them, as well as other major producers, to explain the situation. The BBC and the others agreed to be patient until the end of the year.

Buying Time

Things started getting dicey when the due diligence dragged on into the new year. By mid-January, the patience of our vendors was exhausted. Many threatened legal action. We were just days away from programs being pulled from our schedule due to payment default.

That was bad enough. But then Group W threatened to pull us off its satellite. Obviously, they had noticed. We had not paid the previous three months of transponder lease payments and the bills for other services, and we owed them more than $1 million.

Worst of all, we now had to suspend paying our hardworking, loyal staff. That was a tough message to deliver, especially since everyone knew the next round of money was on its way.

We were now approaching the end of January, and the closing date for the financing had still not yet been set. Finally, E. F. Hutton informed us that the Chronicle would be ready to close the investment and wire funds to us on Tuesday, February 18, 1986.

We were ecstatic and crestfallen at the same time. The end was in sight, but how were we ever going to survive until then? After our endless promises, would Group W, the BBC, and all our other suppliers now believe us when we said the money was on its way?

Luckily, Harlan at Group W agreed to give us one more chance. Wisely (and this is a lesson to all budding entrepreneurs) we had kept him closely informed of our negotiations with the Chronicle, and so he agreed to one more payment delay.

It was a time for unexpected turns of events. For example, about the time I was telling our employees that their pay would be suspended, we began to notice an odd increase in the number of subscriptions to our monthly *Discovery Channel Magazine*, a publication containing articles about our shows and a complete guide to our schedule. We had promoted the magazine on the air and suddenly orders for the $11 annual subscription jumped. Now they were pouring in at a rate of nearly 1,000 each week. That unanticipated $11,000 per month in revenues enabled us to reinstate our employee payroll. Thus viewers were now directly paying our staff salaries.

The Message

Somehow, we survived. And on the morning of February 18, 1986, Dick Crooks came down from New York to be with us for the closing of the Chronicle investment.

It was scheduled to take place in John McCarthy's Georgetown law office at 11 a.m. Understandably anxious, we arrived early and waited for Leo Hindery and the E. F. Hutton bankers to arrive. They seemed to be running a bit late, so Dick Crooks, John McCarthy, and I walked over to the Four Seasons Hotel for coffee and waited for a message calling us back to the office.

Beginning life in the hills of West Virginia, circa 1955. *From left:* my father, John Gilbert Hendricks; my brother, Kenneth; my sister, Linda; my mother, Pauline Daugherty Hendricks; and me, age three.

Already working the phone at age two.

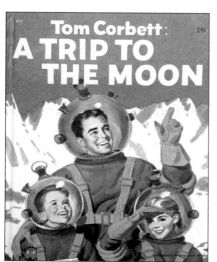

The power of the written word. This little Wonder Book in 1957 inspired my interest in the universe.

Ready for the 1967 football season in Huntsville, Alabama. I learned through sports to visualize victory before it happens.

Our newborn daughter, Elizabeth, arrived on March 1, 1983, just as my wife and I secured a second mortgage loan to finance the Discovery start-up.

Taking a break at the Allen and Company Sun Valley Media Conference to go white-water rafting with my children, Andrew and Elizabeth, in 1995.

On location in Kenya in 1989 with my wife, Maureen. The beginning of a great co-production relationship with the BBC.

Although Ted Turner failed in his 1988 attempt to merge CNN and Discovery, we remained friends. Here we are at a 1990 Discovery event held at L.A.'s Griffith Observatory with Yue-Sai Kan and Buzz Aldrin.

The two men who came to my financial rescue in 1986. With my great partners, Bob Miron and John Malone, at Discovery's Twenty-Fifth Anniversary Gala in New York in June 2010.

By 1992 Discovery was exploring global issues with world leaders such as former president Jimmy Carter, who led a Discovery-televised forum on the Middle East.

Walter Cronkite inspired me as a kid growing up in Alabama. It was a dream come true when he became an executive producer for Discovery. Here I am with Walter in 1992 on the set of *Address to the Nation.*

The late, great Steve Irwin surprised our family with a visit on the occasion of Discovery's twentieth anniversary in June 2005. Steve was later tragically killed by a stingray barb while filming underwater off the coast of Australia on September 4, 2006.

Taking a thrilling ride with the Blue Angels out of Colorado's Grand Junction Airport in 2001.

Winning the championship of the world's first women's professional soccer league, with the Washington Freedom. Mia Hamm *(in front)* was team captain.

Expanding internationally—with our team at the Great Wall of China in 2004.

With well-known stars of Discovery, *from left:* Mike Rowe, Paul Teutul Sr., Johnathan Hillstrand, Andy Hillstrand, me, Buddy Valastro, Paul Teutul Jr., and Dave Salmoni.

At the *Frozen Planet* premiere in New York in 2012 with Discovery Group President Eileen O'Neill, Executive Producer Alastair Fothergill, Senior Producer Vanessa Berlowitz, me, David Zaslav, and two penguins.

With all global offices of Discovery hooked up via satellite television, David Leavy, David Zaslav, and I celebrate twenty-five years on the air.

Our headquarters building in Silver Spring, Maryland, has a visitor each year during *Shark Week*.

With Oprah Winfrey, our partner in OWN, at a 2012 dinner in New York.

With former presidents George W. Bush and Bill Clinton, Laura Bush, and my wife, Maureen, at a 2012 event in Washington to support the Flight 93 Memorial. Aboard the tragic flight was a cherished Discovery employee, Elizabeth Wainio.

In 2005 I created Gateway Canyons Resort in Colorado as a place to explore the wonders of the world within one of the planet's most spectacular landscapes.

As you might imagine, our spirits were high. We had managed to stay on the satellite, and the Discovery Channel signal was still lighting up TVs across the country. Back at the office in Maryland, our finance staff was gathering up all of the bank wiring instructions for the funds that we would promptly transfer to grateful vendors at 9 a.m. the next day.

Eventually a hotel staffer walked through the lounge holding a sign with "Mr. Crooks" written on it, and announcing, "Phone call for Mr. Crooks!"

"I guess they're here," I said to McCarthy as Dick jumped up and left to take the call on the house phone.

We were gathering up our briefcases and preparing to head back across the street when Dick returned. His face was ashen.

He could barely speak. "E. F. Hutton said the Chronicle board didn't approve the investment. The closing is off." Dick slumped into his seat and said, "No one is coming."

Blindsided

We were dumbfounded and nearly speechless. I felt as if I were dying. Frankly, dying might have been less painful.

Neither Dick nor John McCarthy had ever witnessed the cancellation of a closing on the very day of an investment. It just didn't happen. Approvals for a transaction are secured well before a closing date is even set. When he could speak, Dick said that E. F. Hutton was as stunned as we were, and they were worried this catastrophic turn of events would damage their future relationship with Allen & Company.

We sat for a while longer. There was no place to go. We were at the end of the line.

"John," Dick said to me as he finally stood up to leave, "you've got to start getting your head around the company's shutdown and bankruptcy."

I desperately wanted to get home to Annapolis, Maryland, to talk with Maureen. Nonetheless, feeling it was my duty, I first stopped by the Landover office to break the bad news. I told the staff that the closing had been canceled, not postponed. I didn't have to say anything more—they knew what this meant. They were well aware that a major financing like this one takes months to pull together. There was just no time left to put together another such deal.

"How did it go?" Maureen cheerfully asked as I slumped through the door.

"We need to talk," I said.

Postmortem

We spent the rest of the evening analyzing how this could have happened. From the brief conversation he'd had with E. F. Hutton, Dick Crooks surmised that Leo Hindery had also been taken aback by the Chronicle board's surprising action. Leo was new in his job at the Chronicle, and Maureen and I speculated that he had misjudged company management.

We talked all evening, but we knew the cause of the calamity didn't matter. All that counted was that the Chronicle investment was dead—and stupidly, I now realized, I had failed to use the intervening months to solicit any other investor prospects. After signing the confidentiality agreement with the Chronicle back in November, I had assumed the deal was done. We had shaken hands.

What I couldn't bring myself to talk about with Maureen that evening was the improbability of continuing payments on our outstanding second mortgage loan. This would likely result in foreclosure on our house.

"You've put so much into this," Maureen kept saying over and over. Yes, I had—and now I had failed.

It was the darkest day we had ever experienced. Maureen has referred to it ever since as "Black Tuesday."

Resurrection

When morning came I stopped despairing and began searching for a solution. There had to be someone out there who would help. I could not let this be the end of Discovery.

On the drive in from Annapolis to work I realized that I had to get Dick's head back into the game. He had actually used the word *bankruptcy* the previous day. I just couldn't let that awful word linger in anybody's mind.

As I drove, I remembered a brief interview that I had read in a cable trade magazine. A reporter had asked John Malone, the leading force in the cable industry, for his thoughts concerning January 1987. That was the date, still more than a year away, when cable operators would finally be able to adjust their rates upward, reflecting what the market would bear.

"How will the industry spend its new revenues?" the reporter wanted to know. Malone replied that the industry would be wise to invest some of its increased revenue in content because "people don't buy cable service for the coaxial cable, they buy it for the programming."

I had filed Malone's little comment away in my mind, but now, as I approached the Beltway and our office building came into view, it took center stage. I had to get to John Malone.

I had never met the man. But, like everyone else connected in any way to the cable business, I knew all about him. He led industry giant Tele-Communications Inc. (TCI), based in Denver, Colorado. In 1986 TCI served more homes (more than 4 million) than any other cable distributor. I also knew that a programmer soliciting channel space rarely got an audience with "the Doctor." Rather, John Sie, his senior vice president, dealt with programmers.

I knew that John Malone had earned degrees in both electrical engineering and economics at Yale, and earned his Ph.D. in operations research at Johns Hopkins. From all accounts, he had an intimidating intelligence—in fact, the word *brilliant* seemed to appear in every feature story about him.

I was certain that John Malone had to be one of the world's most curious individuals. Surely he would value the Discovery Channel. He was my last hope.

The Doctor

Dick Crooks needed no bucking up from me. By the time I phoned him at his office, he had already spoken to Harlan Rosenzweig and explained to him that Group W wouldn't be getting a wire transfer that morning. Dick had even somehow managed to talk Harlan into keeping us on the air despite our million dollars in unpaid fees.

"Harlan is furious at the Chronicle," Dick told me—and Dick had skillfully helped redirect Harlan's anger into helping us find a solution. "I am turning Group W into an investor," Dick said.

When he finished his report I asked, "Does anyone at Allen know John Malone?"

"I'm pretty sure Paul Gould has had some dealings with Malone," he replied.

I told Dick about the cable magazine interview. Maybe Malone might be interested in helping us.

"Let me talk to Paul. I'll call you back," Dick said and hung up.

Paul Gould was one of the most senior managing directors at Allen & Company. He had joined the firm in 1972 and had quickly risen through the ranks to become one of the company's top deal makers. I expected that I wouldn't hear back from Dick until the afternoon, maybe the next morning. Yet the phone rang barely a half hour later.

"Yeah, Paul knows John Malone," Dick said, "and he just got off the phone with him." I held my breath. "Malone told Paul: 'We can't let Discovery go dark.'" Dick then explained that Malone was putting John Sie on a plane to Washington to meet with me.

"Black Tuesday" had come and gone. This was Wednesday morning, and a beacon of light was now shining from John Malone's Denver office.

Chapter 16

The Napkin

All great change in America begins at the dinner table.

—RONALD REAGAN

What happened at Allen & Company on that cold February morning in 1986 is the best illustration I know of the valuable role an investment bank can play in the life of an unconnected entrepreneur.

Entrepreneurs typically emerge out of left field, from backgrounds and circumstances far removed from affluence and from connections that can get an idea funded. If they even have an extended personal network of friends, it is likely the wrong one for building a company. You can try to call the rich and powerful—but a "cold call" usually rates only a cold shoulder. Top executives at giant companies are well versed in the art of setting up barriers and filters to access.

However, a trusted colleague, friend, or associate can easily vault those barriers—as Paul Gould did that morning with John Malone. Additionally, if an investment banker is truly engaged, or has "skin in the game," as did Dick Crooks, he or she will move heaven and earth to not let a private deal turn into a public failure.

Within the week, John Sie, TCI's senior vice president, arrived in Washington from Denver. I met him in the suite of his hotel downtown, where we talked for several hours about the Discovery Channel. He evinced an almost superhuman curiosity about every little detail of our operations.

This time I wasn't surprised. I had done my homework on Sie, and I knew what a remarkable man he was.

A native of China, John Sie had come to America in 1950 when he was fourteen years old. After staying at a Catholic orphanage until he finished high school, Sie went on to earn a bachelor's degree in electrical engineering from Manhattan College and a master's degree in the same field from Polytechnic Institute in Brooklyn. Before joining TCI, Sie had worked at Jerrold Electronics Corporation and at Showtime, the movie service. He had a quick and probing mind—and a kind of genius for getting to the heart of any business challenge. The sheer power of his intellect was intimidating.

I had come to the meeting alone but soon wished I had brought along Suzanne Hayes. Sie quickly overwhelmed me with detailed questions about our programming rights, the terms, territories covered, and exclusivity provisions. I answered the best I knew but told him he'd need to have a follow-up meeting with Suzanne Hayes. He agreed. And I worried whether he thought I knew enough about my own business.

Turning next to a possible investment by TCI, I told Sie that I couldn't survive a long due diligence process. I needed to send checks out that week, even if they were just partial payments, to a list of suppliers. I showed him the list. I then explained that Dick Crooks was handling Group W, which had agreed to wait for the outcome of our negotiations with TCI.

I told him that even partial payments of $25,000 each would be enough to buy some more time, perhaps even a few weeks, from most suppliers. Finally, I told him I needed $500,000 that very week. It just couldn't wait. Sie said he would talk to Malone and see if he would approve a wire transfer before the week was out.

Betting It All

We all tend to rise to occasions, often to our surprise. Looking back at this meeting, in which I was on the brink of business failure, in which I was admitting to having led my company down the path to that failure, and in which I was asking for—almost demanding—a gigantic sum of money with the claim I could fix that failure, I am astonished at my fearlessness at that moment.

A large part of it, I think, was that it wasn't me, the individual, talking to John Sie; instead, it was me, the CEO of Discovery Channel, who held the career fates of a couple dozen Discovery staff in my hands.

Sie and I then discussed the amount of the next round of financing. I professed my hope that, with TCI's help, we could raise $20 million in a single round so that we could focus on programming and growing the business, not fund-raising.

Sie said that he and John Malone had talked briefly about the possibility of forming some sort of partnership with other operators to help with the financing. I told him I thought that was a good idea. Privately, I had worried about the prospect of having only one dominant shareholder who could control the company with an equity stake of 51 percent or more. Raising $20 million all at once from one investor certainly presented that risk.

When I asked Sie whom he had in mind as co-partners, Sie replied that there were a number of candidates. In particular, Malone had told him that Bob Miron of Newhouse had to be the first potential investor we talked to. Malone knew that Bob Miron was a well-respected industry statesman and his involvement would provide a valuable endorsement. Malone told him that "Bob Miron could attract others to the table."

Before I left his hotel suite, John Sie suggested that we next meet in Dallas at the National Cable Television Association (NCTA) annual convention. It was just a few weeks away.

"Bring Suzanne Hayes along, and I'll set up a meeting with Bob Miron," Sie said. Then with a grin, he added: "We'll have Chinese food."

The Cable Statesman

It was a good plan, but only if Discovery could financially survive for three more weeks. We desperately needed that $500,000. Thank God we didn't have to wait long: within forty-eight hours, TCI had wired $500,000 into our company account. They actually wired the funds before I signed the unsecured loan agreement letter. The $500,000 in funding was structured as an unsecured loan to Discovery, a loan that TCI could convert to equity at the closing of a future investment round.

The $500,000 loan was a lifesaver, but even as we started paying off our bills, or at least sending partial payments, I was already starting to worry about the Texas meeting. It was insanely important. What if Bob Miron didn't want Newhouse to invest in Discovery? What kind of message would that be to TCI and the rest of the industry? I told Suzanne, "We just have to make this sale." "I know," she replied. We were both a little terrified.

Robert Miron was a member of the legendary Newhouse family, which had created an enormous American media empire that, by 1986, included numerous newspapers across the United States. Through its Advance Publications, Newhouse also owned many well-known magazines, including *Condé Nast Traveler*, *Architectural Digest*, *Vanity Fair*, *Vogue*, and *Parade Magazine*. By 1986, Bob Miron's cousins Donald Newhouse and S. I. Newhouse Jr. had also expanded the empire into broadcasting and cable properties.

Miron himself had worked at various Newhouse-owned newspapers in high school and college. After attending Syracuse University, Bob set out in 1958 to work in several Newhouse broadcast stations—including the NBC-affiliated station in Birmingham, Alabama, whose signal had reached my Huntsville home via cable. Newhouse also owned the *Huntsville Times*.

Bob had moved over to NewChannels, the cable side of the business, in 1966, becoming president and CEO eight years later. By 1986, Bob had achieved leadership status within the industry and was a key spokesperson on regulatory issues. He had a reputation as a "peacemaker," even in complicated negotiations such as the industry's licensing of music rights. He was known to be thoughtful and friendly, but very direct.

Off the Menu

I navigated my rental car through the streets of Dallas trying to find the Chinese restaurant where John Sie had made a reservation. We were running late. Finally, we realized that the restaurant was located in a shopping center. I parked the car and we scampered inside.

John Sie and Bob Miron were already seated. Luckily, they were both smiling.

Sie proceeded to dazzle us with his orders of Chinese food items, almost all of them off-menu. The staff dashed around attending to his bidding. It was an impressive start to an important dinner.

We soon got to work talking business. Like Sie, Miron went right to the details. A veteran broadcaster, he was familiar with every aspect of putting a program schedule together. He and Sie grilled Suzanne on program supplier relationships and on how each contract might be improved. I could tell that both men were searching for competitive advantages that we could secure through program exclusivity and long-term "output deals."

To my relief, both wanted to explore how we might strike output deals quickly, even in the next few weeks. Perhaps, they suggested, we could freeze supplier pricing at favorable levels for five years or more. They knew that an investment by TCI and Newhouse would change our financial fortunes in the eyes of our content suppliers.

"If these producers knew that TCI and Newhouse were going to invest in Discovery, your programming costs would skyrocket," Sie gestured upward. Miron agreed. We would have to act quickly to solidify long-term pricing.

As we began to talk about cable carriage, I noticed that Bob Miron looked to his left and grabbed a paper napkin off an empty table next to ours. He pulled a pen from his inside coat pocket and began to scribble on the napkin.

Soon we were deep into an analysis of all U.S. cable systems. It was so exciting to be working with industry insiders at this level that I almost forgot my troubles. We looked at the various owners of the cable systems and the chances of us convincing each one to give increased carriage to Discovery. I explained that we needed to get to 15 million subscribers before Nielsen would provide ratings data—and how that was crucial because many ad agencies simply refused to buy unmeasured media. Discovery was growing, but we would still finish the month just shy of 8 million homes.

Miron kept writing on the napkin. Finally, he announced, "Let's go through your expenses one more time. Item by item."

Knowing our cost items by heart, I ticked off the transponder lease payment, uplink and master control costs, editing costs, personnel costs, marketing, and programming costs. We had just increased the programming costs to account for new incentives, which we hoped would convince suppliers to sign up. Bob Miron then looked up from his napkin at Suzanne and me and said: "That's $975,000 a month, about a million dollars a month, in costs."

We then talked about the dismal revenue situation. Both of them knew, of course, that cable operators were not yet free from regulation and so subscription fees, derived from rate increases to consumers, were nonexistent. Like other start-up networks in this period, Discovery Channel had offered free carriage to the industry. Our hope was to survive until government deregulation, then renegotiate our cable distribution agreements and secure a modest subscription fee. Apart from just a few companies and agencies who wanted to associate with our content, we had precious little income from advertisers—less than $75,000 per month. Bob Miron winced.

The other three of us could tell that Bob Miron was vigorously working on that napkin. The conversation paused until Bob looked up.

"You need twenty million homes and a nickel per sub," Bob announced with finality. "Is that possible? That's the question on the table."

Heart of the Matter

I knew in an instant that he was right. If we could get 20 million subscribers, and get paid just $.05 each month from cable operators for each of those subscribers, it would create for us an income stream of $1 million a month. "Anything you get extra from advertisers would then be profit," Miron added.

This was the first time I'd ever been excited working with a master number cruncher.

"Look," I offered, "if we get to twenty million homes—that is, beyond the Nielsen threshold—we should be selling $250,000 of advertising per month."

Back to the napkin Bob went. He started to list cable companies starting with TCI and NewChannels. By each company name, he listed a number. Sometimes he would glance over at Sie and ask a question like, "How many subs do you think we can get from Cox?"

I could tell that Bob was heading for some kind of decision point. As he looked up from the napkin, he said: "People will want Discovery in their homes. Even if they don't watch it, they will say they watch it. Discovery has a 'wholesome' quality about it." He then told us that his wife, Diane, was a teacher and that she would love the service. Suzanne and I smiled and told him about that teacher who had called us from Kansas just moments after we had gone on air.

Bob glanced back down at the numbers on the napkin, as if to confirm his calculations one last time, then back up to meet my eyes. "I believe we can get that twenty million homes and that nickel," he said. "I'm in."

Years later, standing in the Discovery boardroom, after we had passed 100 million U.S. homes in distribution, 400 million international homes in distribution, and $4 billion in annual revenues, Bob Miron winked at me and said, "We should have saved that napkin."

Chapter 17

Restart

Every new beginning comes from some other beginning's end.

—Seneca

We quickly moved to close a $20 million investment round with a group of four cable investors, each contributing $5 million in capital to Discovery.

John Malone and John Sie made a call to Gene Schneider, the head of United Cable, also based in Denver. I flew out to meet with Gene and his top executives, and United Cable decided to join in the funding.

Bob Miron contacted Amos Hostetter at Continental Cablevision and Brian Roberts at Comcast, but both declined to invest. Bob then contacted executives at Cox Cable Communications in Atlanta. After I spoke at length on the phone with Ajit Dalvi, a senior vice president, a meeting was set up with Jim Robbins, president of Cox Cable, and with Robbins's boss, Bill Schwartz, president and CEO of Cox Enterprises.

The two were on the way to Europe, so I flew up to JFK Airport in New York to rendezvous with them in the Scandinavian Airlines lounge. Schwartz was brusque and difficult but I could tell that Jim Robbins was intrigued. Still, I could not get a commitment. However, as I left, Jim pulled me aside and, glancing at Schwartz, said, "Let me work on him."

I wasn't confident that Cox was in, so I turned to a potential backup investor. A former president of Cox Cable, Bob Wright, had just taken over at NBC and I thought there was a chance the network might consider coming in as an equal investor with the three cable operators.

Priorities

Since I was already in New York, I stopped by to discuss the idea at Allen & Company. I talked to Jack Schneider, one of the managing directors at Allen, and a Discovery shareholder. Jack knew Wright and said, "Let's go over and see him." With that, he placed a call and we were on our way.

It was obvious that Wright was still settling into his office in Rockefeller Center. He had arrived at NBC just weeks earlier. I gave Bob a briefing on Discovery, then Jack and I together outlined the investment offer. Bob listened politely and asked a few questions. Then he explained how a Discovery investment was just not a fit for NBC. Bob simply said, "We're in the broadcasting business, not the cable business."

Even as I walked out of his office, I knew that Bob Wright's business definition for NBC was wrong. NBC's real business was "the television business," or "the content business"—and instead, he was, perhaps unconsciously, making the perilous choice to tie NBC to a particular delivery technology in an abbreviated, shorthand definition of the business. It was an understandable abbreviation in 1986, one that Wright later corrected through his aggressive development of cable networks like CNBC and MSNBC.

It was a powerful lesson for me: from that day in 1986 forward,

I have always tried to think of Discovery as being in "the business of satisfying curiosity." Our charter mission is to satisfy curiosity through all forms of media distribution technologies as they evolve through time.

A week later, I got a phone call from Ajit Dalvi confirming that Cox wanted to join the investment group. We had our fourth $5 million investment partner.

Meanwhile, since the previous October, in 1985, Dick Crooks had been working to convince Harlan Rosenzweig at Group W to take ever-larger stakes in our venture. Would Group W accept Discovery stock and warrants instead of cash for satellite, uplink, and master control services?

Harlan had to ask his superiors in Pittsburgh for approval. Luckily, there Harlan and Discovery found an ally. Bill Baker, the president of Group W Broadcasting, was impressed by our efforts and gave Harlan his blessing. By accepting stock in lieu of cash for an extended period, Group W secured an equity position comparable to the stake held by each of the four incoming cable investors.

A New Lineup

By mid-1986, I had $20 million in new cash funding secured. This proved to be more than adequate to finance Discovery for the two years until we reached profitability. At last, after nearly a year of begging, I could now focus solely on building the business.

I already knew I needed to strengthen my management team to successfully navigate the next phase of our growth.

In program acquisition, I could already count on a strong duo. Suzanne Hayes, of course, was invaluable—and she was even more effective with Clark Bunting, whom she'd hired just a month after our July 1985 launch. Together, Suzanne and Clark made it their mission to find every great documentary made anywhere on the planet. Clark ultimately retired as president and general manager of the Discovery Channel in 2011. One of his great finds was Eileen O'Neill, then a graduate student, whom he made a programming intern. Today the company's preeminent programmer, Eileen is president of the Discovery Channel and TLC Networks Group.

Bob McCleary and Mike du Monceau continued to create our compelling programming schedule. Their brilliant innovation was to take the many hours of individual documentaries and package them into themed "anthologies" to cultivate extended viewer interest. Our viewers also quickly became enchanted with series such as *Disappearing World* and shows such as *Young Einstein*, *A Duck's Tale*, and *Otto, the Zoo Gorilla*.

In August 1986, recognizing that Discovery needed an experienced industry veteran at its helm, I recruited Ruth Otte, a senior marketing executive at MTV, to serve as our president and chief operating officer. Cable operators liked Ruth. A former teacher, she was intelligent and had a ferocious work ethic.

Ruth soon recruited several individuals to our organization who would make impacts for decades to come, including:

> JUDITH McHALE, also from MTV, as general counsel. In 2004, Judith became Discovery's president and CEO. She left us in 2006 and shortly thereafter became U.S. undersecretary of state for public diplomacy and public affairs.

> MARK HOLLINGER joined the legal team—and eventually became general counsel and senior executive vice president. Mark is currently president and CEO of Discovery Networks International.

BILL GOODWYN joined the affiliate sales team in 1987 and ultimately became the industry's leading expert in distribution. Today he is president of global distribution and CEO of Discovery Education.

Back on Offense

The investment by the four cable operators in 1986 gave Discovery a new start. It was a new start for me as well: I could finally direct all my energies into programming and building the network. As we entered 1987, I had assembled a team of dedicated and passionate people, some of whom are still with me today. We were still a small operation, reaching just 14 million homes. Most people in America had not yet heard of us. It was now our job to change that.

Chapter 18

Russia: Live from the Inside

Americans wanted to settle all our difficulties with Russia and then go to the movies and drink Coke.

—W. Averell Harriman

"There's a very persistent man on the line who wants to talk to you about Russian programming," my assistant announced from my office doorway. It was the first week of February 1987.

"I'll take it," I replied, thinking it was a distributor who might have films on Russian history.

"You don't know me," said the voice on the line, "but would you consider preempting everything you have next week to air live Soviet television?" Oh great, I thought, I'm on the line with a prank caller. But before I could cut him off, the man kept talking at breakneck speed. He had his chance and he was taking it.

"My name is Ken Shaffer and I'm an electronics inventor. I invented the wireless microphone system for rock groups and I found a way to take down television signals from Soviet satellites. I've gotten the signal to Columbia University and the faculty and students are studying them—"

Now I did interrupt—because I knew that Soviet satellites were not in geostationary orbits. Since the bulk of the landmass of the Soviet Union was so far north, fixed satellite dish receivers didn't work because they would have to uselessly point at the ground well below the southern horizon if they were directed at geostationary satellites positioned in orbit over the equator.

As a result, the unfortunate Soviets had to launch four communication satellites—the "Molniya" system—that moved in highly elliptical polar orbits (traveling north-south rather than east-west), reaching their highest altitude over the Northern Hemisphere. The Molniya system guaranteed that at least one of the moving satellites would always be visible to Soviet soil. Interestingly (especially to our intelligence people) these orbits also meant those same signals hit American soil.

"How in the world did you manage to receive Molniya signals?" I asked.

Kenny Shaffer calmed down a bit. He no longer had to worry about me cutting him off. He then explained that, using his computer, a special decoder he'd invented, and a motorized dish mounted on the roof of his New York apartment building, Kenny was able to capture the signal off the moving Soviet satellites. He had since improved the signal reception quality and it was now being used by Professor Jonathan Sanders in teaching Soviet studies at Columbia University.

I recognized Jonathan Sanders's name. Kenny reminded me that Sanders often appeared on the *CBS Evening News* as Dan Rather's expert on Soviet issues and developments.

Coincidentally, at that moment the most anticipated program on television was the ABC miniseries *Amerika*, a controversial television project that portrayed America ten years after its conquest by the Soviet Union. It was set to premiere on Sunday, February 15, 1987.

When ABC announced its plans, many commentators noted that the series was grossly ill-timed given that glasnost was in full swing under Mikhail Gorbachev. Many thought (myself included) that ABC's *Amerika* was an exploitive piece of Cold War hysteria that could damage the thawing relations between the United States and the Soviet Union. Now, what Kenny Shaffer was offering was the chance to counterprogram ABC's *Amerika* with actual live Soviet television. Americans could now eavesdrop on what their Russian counterparts were watching.

It was a fascinating idea—a perfect programming counterpunch to ABC. My only hesitation, beyond the obvious technical challenge, was making sure that there would be no political messaging at all. But how could we control the content in a *live* Soviet feed?

Kenny had already visited communications officials in Moscow—and told me that the Soviets would not change or alter their television feed in any way. There would be no "messages to the American people" inserted by the Soviet leadership, he assured me.

I was still not completely sold on the idea. So I put Shaffer on hold and walked next door to Ruth Otte's office.

"We're going to New York tomorrow to talk to this guy on the phone," I told her. "He has the craziest idea you've ever heard."

The next day, in front of a TV screen at Columbia University, Ruth and I sat transfixed by the live Soviet feed. We first watched a game show and tried to decipher what was going on. Soon we were surrounded in the viewing room by faculty and students who spoke Russian. They helped us understand what we were seeing.

We then asked to see tape-recorded samples of other shows. Soon we were laughing at children's shows and engrossed by the Russian soap operas, so much like ours but so different in dress and settings.

Then a news program caught our attention. The news anchor sat in front of an animated map of the world that changed to close-ups of each region with Russian text script overlaying the country maps. When a map of the United States appeared, I asked what they were talking about. After listening a bit, one faculty member spoke up. "They're reporting about Bill Casey's resignation." William J. Casey, the director of the CIA, had just resigned and the Soviets were reporting this news.

I wanted it.

After we watched the feeds at Columbia and discussed the technical obstacles, Ruth and I stepped into a hallway by ourselves. Ruth was confident that she could rally the staff to make it happen. And I could tell that she was excited by the challenge. "Okay," I said, "let's go for it." Within hours, she was assembling staff at our uplink site at Group W in Stamford, Connecticut.

I called the board members to let them know our plan. They were somewhat hesitant. However, after we talked through all the details, they each concurred. It would be an historic event in American television, and we wanted the credit to go to Discovery.

Overnight Sensation

Within days, we announced to the world that the Discovery Channel would premiere *Russia: Live from the Inside* on Sunday, February 15, 1987. For the first time in history, Americans could watch live Soviet television. We further announced that Discovery would air sixty-six fully translated hours over the course of the week.

Already keyed up by ABC's *Amerika*, the press jumped on the story. Soon newspapers and TV stations were calling for interviews. By week's end, we had a national sensation on our hands—indeed, with almost every newspaper in the country carrying stories, it was getting more publicity than *Amerika*. Then local television stations started running stories using promo footage that we delivered to them by satellite. We had a tiger—or maybe a Russian bear—by the tail.

On Friday morning, February 13, 1987, just two days before the historic premiere of *Russia: Live from the Inside*, my assistant once again appeared in my doorway with an odd look on her face. "Someone from the State Department just hand-delivered this letter for you," she said, then handed me a sealed envelope.

It was a letter addressed to me from the U.S. secretary of state, George Shultz. It advised me that Discovery's planned reception of Soviet satellite signals for retransmission to the American public was in violation of the INTELSAT Treaty to which the United States was a signatory party.

What the letter was referencing, I soon discovered, was that the INTELSAT Treaty prohibited any broadcaster or any other entity from direct reception of another nation's communications signal for retransmission to the public. To be in compliance with the IN-TELSAT Treaty, all transmission feeds of foreign television had to pass through the INTELSAT satellite communications system.

Short, clear, and to the point, the letter informed me that the U.S. government was stepping in to stop Discovery's *Russia: Live from the Inside*.

Cloak and Dagger

The letter hit me like a sledgehammer. How could my government do this to me? The cancellation would cause humiliating damage to our brand. It would be an embarrassing setback for Discovery, just when it was showing real promise.

I dreaded calling my board members but I had to let them know quickly. But first I had to talk to our lawyers. Surely they would find some loophole under the First Amendment rights, or something.

It wasn't long before our legal staff was deep in consultation with outside counsel preparing a response to the State Department. It was a novel legal situation—and the lawyers could find little prior law or precedent. One thing working in our favor was that the courts had recently held that cable networks and their owners enjoyed protection under the Constitution as "First Amendment speakers."

Our argument, developed in just a few hours by the legal team, was that the constitutional rights of U.S. citizens to free speech would "trump" any provision of an international treaty that violated those rights.

Early Friday afternoon we sent a message back to the State Department stating that we intended to proceed with our plans to air the live Soviet feed, adding that if the federal government took any action to interrupt the exercise of our "free speech" we would file for immediate injunctive relief in the courts.

As we waited for the reply, we took comfort in the fact that, as a cable network, we were not required to hold a broadcast license from the FCC. So, what could they do to us? When no response came by 4 p.m., we began getting hopeful.

Little did we know . . .

State Pulls the Plug

Late Friday night, Group W Satellite Communications, the company that uplinked the Discovery Channel television feed to the Westar V satellite, received a call from the corporate headquarters of parent company Westinghouse in Pittsburgh. The FCC had given Westinghouse a terse warning. If Westinghouse's satellite communications division in Stamford even touched the "illegal" Soviet transmission feed, the FCC would immediately suspend the broadcast licenses of all Group W stations across the country. The FCC would make Westinghouse broadcasting go black.

Harlan Rosenzweig from Group W called me with the news.

"Sorry, John. We love you, but we can't even consider putting our broadcast stations at risk."

All seemed lost. Then Ruth Otte called me with Kenny Shaffer on the line: "Kenny thinks he can talk the Soviets into hitting an INTELSAT bird over the Atlantic. If they do that, then we can legally downlink the signal at the COMSAT site in West Virginia. Then the signal is legal.

"We can then re-uplink the signal to another satellite. Group W can downlink that feed and we can insert our interstitials. Group W could then resend the live stream up to Westar V."

I couldn't help but laugh. "How many satellite hops is that?" I asked.

Kenny broke in: "Actually four hops, counting the one that the Russians have to use to hit the Atlantic bird."

It was a brilliant solution—in theory. But even if the Soviets agreed to the plan, it would be very expensive. I was also concerned that the Soviets would now be directly involved. I just wanted our American audience to eavesdrop on their programs. Kenny again assured me that the Soviets would not do anything to embarrass us. He was confident that the Soviets wanted the event to happen without any controversy.

After listening to his arguments, I authorized the unexpected transmission expenditures and Kenny got off the line to call the Soviets. Group W was alerted to the plan and its staff readied to receive the "legal" signal from COMSAT.

Kenny reached the Soviets on Saturday. His Soviet contact said they would favorably "consider" the request. We hoped for written confirmation and even test broadcasts well before the announced Sunday evening airtime—but none came. It was maddening. Would we get a signal or not?

Kenny urged us to keep the faith, but we were rapidly running out of it. No confirmation or test feeds were sent on Sunday, the day of telecast.

Moments before the scheduled airtime, there was still no Soviet feed. Then, precisely at the appointed 8:00 p.m. airtime, the monitors in the control room blazed to life with a strong color television feed. It was live from the Soviet Union. The Soviets had redirected an uplink dish and were sending television directly into American households. We cheered, then slumped with relief.

America had never seen anything like it. Discovery Channel's week-long Soviet television event became "must watch" TV in the lucky 14 million households that had our service. Beginning on Monday night, Johnny Carson started joking about *Russia Live* in his monologues.

CARSON: Now you want to see some interesting television coming? How many of you get a channel called the Discovery Channel, on satellite?

[Audience clapping.]

Soon they're going to show—start showing—sixty-two hours of programming—Russian programs. Actually as they were produced in Russia.

So I guess we don't get it on regular network but on the Discovery Channel.

You, are you ready for a game show like *Name That Tractor*?

[Audience laughing.]

And they're going to have a Russian version of *The Price Is Right*; behind curtain number one is a fur coat, behind curtain number two is a KGB agent.

As a bonus, I have three of these . . .

[Johnny Carson laughing.]

You know the old comedy rule, "as a bonus" . . . a show featuring a little old lady who gives sex advice to the Politburo, called *Ask Dr. Ruthless*.

[Clapping and laughing.]

Viewers across America began calling their cable companies. They wanted the Discovery Channel. The Soviet programming helped propel us to become the fastest-growing cable network in history.

A year later, in recognition of our historic *Russia Live* event, the industry honored us with a Golden Ace Award, its highest accolade. Actress Shelley Duvall presented it to me on the HBO telecast of the awards ceremony.

And it was all due to the crazy idea of an inventor who decided to make a cold call during the waning days of the Cold War.

Chapter 19

Captain Outrageous

If I only had a little humility, I would be perfect.

—TED TURNER

I had not forgotten my wife's question when I had first described my idea for a documentary channel. "But if this is such a good idea, why didn't Ted Turner do it?"

Well, in the aftermath of *Russia: Live from the Inside*, I learned that Ted Turner had started asking the same thing.

And when he didn't have an answer, Turner telephoned me one morning in 1988.

"You know," he said, "the thing I regret the most is that I didn't start the Discovery Channel."

That was how he began the conversation.

"You know I love documentaries, and I've tried to do as many as I can on WTBS," he continued. "And now I'm watching way too much of the Discovery Channel!"

We both chuckled.

"I should have been the one to start the Discovery Channel, not you!"

I laughed harder.

The marvelous thing about Ted Turner was that he would absolutely say anything that crossed his mind. There was a reason why he was called "Captain Outrageous."

The Man Without Limits

Everyone knows who Ted Turner is. But few, I think, know his full story.

Robert Edward "Ted" Turner III was born in 1938. In 1963, at age twenty-four, Ted inherited his family's billboard business following his father's suicide. The business, called Turner Outdoor Advertising, was worth about $1 million when Ted took it over.

Ted entered the television business in 1970 when he purchased an Atlanta UHF station, WTCG Channel 17. Watching HBO go on satellite in 1975, Ted realized the opportunity to expose his television station audience to millions more viewers through cable. So, a year later, Ted uplinked the signal from his WTCG to satellite.

Also that year, Ted purchased the Atlanta Braves baseball team, put it on his new satellite-delivered channel, and gave the team a national audience. In 1978, the cable channel was rechristened WTBS, the Superstation. In 1980, Ted Turner created and launched CNN, bringing twenty-four-hour international news coverage to cable. In 1986, Ted attempted to acquire CBS, but failed. That same year he purchased the MGM/UA film studio and library from Kirk Kerkorian for $1.5 billion.

Deeply in debt after the transaction with Kerkorian, Ted had to sell off parts of his newest asset but still managed to retain valuable portions of the MGM library, including such film classics as *Gone with the Wind*. By 1988, Ted was planning the launch of a new broadcast network, TNT.

Now Ted Turner was calling me to discuss a potential merger between Discovery and CNN. "They just belong together," he told me.

He had a point. News and documentary productions did live side by side in most network news organizations, from CNN to CBS. However, Discovery's programming was more than just extended versions of news programs. We offered multipart series in history, anthropology, paleontology, and other subjects that no news organization would ever tackle.

There were also even bigger differences that made any discussions of a merger a fruitless exercise.

For example, our distribution was now soaring toward full penetration of the cable universe; we were now crossing the 30 million mark of households in distribution. It was also clear to all of us on the board of directors that Discovery Channel would one day be worth $500 million, $1 billion, or even more. So why sell out now when the value might be only $150 million? The third reason was that no one on our board wanted to combine our interests with Turner Broadcasting, which still had significant debt.

Last, we knew that Turner's more mature assets would certainly be valued much higher than the Discovery Channel, a network that was just commencing to blossom financially. Thus, the result of any merger would be that our shareholder group, myself included, would become minority shareholders in a company controlled by Ted Turner and his existing shareholders.

Not surprisingly, no one on my side of the table even wanted to talk about a merger. We were willing to discuss joint productions between CNN and Discovery, but any merger talks would be unproductive. Turner and I did share a common shareholder in TCI—but I doubted that John Malone would be interested in a merger, either.

I explained all of this but Ted was persistent. "What's the harm of a meeting?" he asked. "I talked to Malone and he said there's no harm in talking."

Okay, that was annoying. Ted had already talked to John Malone before talking to me. However, by that time, I knew Malone well enough that I suspected he was just leaving Turner to me to handle.

"Come down to my office in Atlanta," Ted cajoled me. "We'll have a great time. Have you ever been here? We'll just talk. I'll show you around CNN. You'll love it."

"Okay," I finally agreed, "I'll come down to see your place. I've heard it's great. I'll just need to call my board to let them know about the visit."

"Absolutely," said Ted enthusiastically. "You are going to love CNN Center."

In the Lion's Den

I had been with Ted Turner on a number of occasions since I had become part of the cable industry. The CEOs of all the cable networks sat on the Programmers Committee of the National Cable Television Association (NCTA). This NCTA committee met about two or three times each year and that was when I would see Ted. But it was always in a group setting. This would be the first one-on-one meeting between us.

After CNN's launch in 1980, the news network soon outgrew its first home, a former country club on the outskirts of Atlanta. In 1985, Turner purchased the Omni International hotel, located in downtown Atlanta, and moved CNN to its new home in one of the towers. The complex was rechristened CNN Center; it was a showcase for that network's studios. I had once stayed in the Omni hotel before Ted purchased the complex, but I had never seen CNN Center. Despite myself, I was excited about the visit.

"Look, I have a bedroom here," Ted said as he walked me to the end of his expansive office. He opened a door that led to a bedroom, complete with closets and a shower. "Sometimes, I just don't go home," he admitted.

Ted could not have been more charming as he showed me around the executive offices. We talked only briefly about a potential partnership. He was no longer pressing the issue. He had promised to give me a tour and he delivered.

"Come on, let's go down to see CNN," he said as excitedly as any proud parent. "You're not going to believe it."

We got in the elevator to go down to the lobby level, from where we would walk over to the CNN studio and office tower. Another man joined us on the elevator. Then, about halfway down, the door opened and a striking young blond woman in professional attire stepped into the elevator.

I'm sure all of us had the same thought, but only Ted blurted out: "Wow, you are so good-looking!" It didn't stop there. "Do you work for me? No? I sure wish you did."

If there was any doubt before, I now was certain I was with the real Ted Turner.

After our tour of the spectacular facilities, Ted announced, "C'mon, I have to show you where my Braves play." Off we went to the parking garage, where I climbed into the passenger seat of Ted's modest compact car. Ted announced, "We're running out of oil, John. We just have to drive smaller cars."

On the way to the stadium we talked about Ted's nonprofit organization, which he called the "Better World Society." Ted was the most idealistic individual I had ever met. It was hard not to admire him.

As we approached the stadium, Ted said, "You like baseball, John? If we get together, you'll have a piece of the Braves." He grinned at me. He couldn't help himself. Ted was still selling me.

At the end of the visit, I thanked Ted for his hospitality but I explained again that a combination of Discovery with his company was just not in the cards.

One Last Pitch

About a week after I returned from Atlanta to Maryland, Dick Crooks called. "Ted Turner wants to meet with the Discovery board," Dick said. "He's going to drive all of us crazy until we meet."

"I guess he is going to have to hear it from everybody," I told him. "Let's see how many we can get to the meeting."

Five members of our nine-member board could make the meeting. It was held at Allen & Company in the conference room with all the original Norman Rockwell paintings.

Ted began as animated as ever. But he soon looked rather crestfallen as it became clear that the diverse interests represented on my board—venture capitalists such as Venture America and the venture fund of New York Life; Allen & Company, an investment bank focused on a future IPO; Group W, which wanted to maintain Discovery's satellite uplink center out of Connecticut; four cable operators who were all becoming quite proud of their Discovery investment; and an entrepreneur who greatly valued his independence— were just not interested in such a premature acquisition.

"I really want to thank all of you for your time," Ted said as we all rose to leave the room. Even though he had not been successful in his run at Discovery, Ted remained a southern gentleman to the end.

Last Word

I had to admit that I was flattered Ted Turner thought so highly of Discovery. Ted always had a passion for quality, meaningful content. And he showed good instincts in pursuing us. He was just too late.

Five years later, Ted Turner's fascination with the Civil War led to the movie *Gettysburg*. The world premiere was to be held at the National Theater in Washington, and he was kind enough to send Maureen and me an invitation. It was a star-studded event with actors Tom Berenger, Martin Sheen, Jeff Daniels, and other cast members mingling in the lobby prior to the show.

Ted was one of the last to take his seat down front. Before he sat down he turned to gaze up at the full theater. He saw me about fifteen rows back. When our eyes met, he just couldn't help himself. "Hey, John Hendricks!" he grinned and yelled. "Movies are more fun than documentaries!"

The crowd roared with laughter. We all love Ted Turner.

Chapter 20

A Board Divided

In a crisis, don't hide behind anything or anybody. They're going to find you anyway.

—Bear Bryant

"John, we just have to bring Discovery to Europe," the accented voice pleaded on the other end of the line.

It was Hungarian-born Nimrod Kovacs, one of my board members, calling from London. It was 1988 and cable was getting traction in Europe and especially in the United Kingdom. Nimrod, working for United Cable, was spearheading that American company's move into Europe. He realized that the new cable systems would need differentiated programming to drive business—just as it had in the United States. European cable systems needed a movie channel, a sports channel, a news channel, and a documentary channel, among other specialized services. We had already proved in the States that viewers wanted a documentary channel. And we knew that if Discovery didn't expand into Europe to fill that slot, then someone else would. Then we'd have a competitor running loose in the world.

I already knew we needed to compete in Europe and I had been looking into the costs. It was going to be expensive: a whole new

185

satellite delivery infrastructure involving multiple transponder leases, European content rights, and a heavy investment in language translation. And I knew that after we set up in Europe, we'd need to move to Asia, as cable distribution was incubating there as well.

It was becoming abundantly clear that multichannel television would soon sweep the planet. But the enormous cost of setting up satellite delivery to international markets, with their few subscribers, was just too daunting an investment proposition. Most U.S. cable networks decided to just stay home, where distribution and revenue growth were soaring.

The Discovery Channel was riding the crest of that growth—and even promoting it. Consumer research had uncovered the fact that Discovery, along with American Movie Classics (AMC), was driving cable penetration into the homes of "cable holdouts." Cable had passed by these homes for years, but their residents had refused to subscribe. Typically they were light TV viewers and were simply not interested in any more television—until Discovery and AMC came along.

Distribution of cable networks also accelerated once cable operators were liberated in January 1987 from the constraints of rate regulation. They were now free to adjust their retail rates upward to cover the wholesale costs of new networks like Discovery and AMC. We now were being quickly added to the channel lineups of America's cable systems.

Buoyed by these two trends, Discovery was adding new subscribers at the rate of 1 million per month.

A less appreciated reason for our industry-leading subscriber growth was an ingenious distribution incentive developed by our board member John Sie.

Until 1986, when Sie joined the board, we were offering our

service free in order to gain carriage while the industry was still regulated. We figured that if we could get more subscribers, we could at least sell more advertising. And we hoped that once we proved our value, we could one day renegotiate our cable operator agreements to secure a monthly subscriber fee.

Sie had a better idea: "Let's give cable operators a piece of the advertising action," he proposed. "If operators tear up their old free-carriage deals and sign a new affiliation agreement that gives us a nickel per month—and if they commit to an aggressive rollout of Discovery to all their subscribers—then we'll sell more advertising. We can set aside twenty percent of our advertising revenue into a 'rebate pool' that we can give back to our new 'rebate affiliates' as an incentive to do the new deal."

It was a brilliant, revolutionary plan, and it worked. Cable operators began to tear up their old deals, paid us a sub fee, and launched us everywhere they could. The more Discovery subs an operator added, the greater their share of the advertising rebate pool.

Thanks to this distribution innovation, by mid-1988 Discovery was profitable. Needless to say, our investors were thrilled, and we celebrated. It had been a long, tough haul. But for the Discovery team it also meant something even more exciting: we were now able to begin original productions.

Original Thinking

We hired Tim Cowling, an award-winning producer at National Geographic Television, to head up our new production effort. He quickly began work on our first original production, *Ivory Wars*, which chronicled the plight of African elephants due to poaching.

Armed at last with production funds, I was finally able to sit down with Walter Cronkite. Over a series of meetings we out-lined future series—*Understanding, Great Books, Cronkite Reports,* and *Cronkite Remembers*—that he would either host or serve as ex-ecutive producer for. Walter in turn formed the Cronkite Ward Company with his longtime *CBS Evening News* producer Jonathan Ward to produce these series and more.

During the presidential campaign of 1992, Walter also pro-duced and hosted *Address to the Nation*, a Discovery Channel pro-gramming event in which each of the presidential candidates was invited to give a twenty-minute televised address. Walter moder-ated a follow-up discussion by a panel of experts.

I pursued another of my old heroes as well: Adrian Malone, the executive producer of *The Ascent of Man* and *Cosmos*. Adrian had been producing *Smithsonian World* for WETA, a major public television station based in Washington, D.C., and the series had enjoyed nationwide distribution on PBS. He came on board as well—and among other projects for Discovery, Adrian produced "Uncertainty," an episode of Cronkite's *Universe* series on the topic of quantum physics, which was clearly the series' most challenging undertaking.

My long-term goal had been for Discovery to be a world leader in original documentary entertainment. In pursuit of that, we had attracted some of the best minds in documentary production to help. Now we needed to invest in high-quality productions to match this talent.

I expected this new initiative to be expensive. What I didn't expect it to do was brew trouble in my boardroom.

Divisions

In 1988, I served as chairman of Discovery's board of directors, a position I continue to hold. Today, we have an eleven-member board, but in 1988 our board was composed of nine members. As the company's business began its growth explosion, and as we launched our in-house production initiative, it also became evident to me that the board was dividing into two equal camps—and that I was the swing vote between them.

On one side were the four cable operators: Bob Miron, representing Newhouse Cable; John Sie, representing TCI; Nimrod Kovacs, representing United Cable; and Ajit Dalvi, representing Cox Cable. On the other side were the four venture capitalists: Dick Crooks, representing Allen & Company; David Glickstein, representing New York Life Insurance Company; Dan Moore, representing Venture America; and Harlan Rosenzweig, representing Group W, a supplier that had converted receivables to venture equity.

In terms of equity holdings in Discovery, the venture capital group held 53 percent, the cable operator group 40 percent. After the full $25 million of financing had been raised, I had still managed to hang on to 7 percent. While at that point there had been no formal valuation of the company, we all generally believed that Discovery was worth between $200 million and $250 million. But we were also growing fast—and if our earnings kept pace with our revenues, then we would surely be worth $300 million or more in an initial public offering (IPO) of our shares.

An IPO—"going public"—had of course been a key objective of my early venture investors. They had purchased their Discovery shares for as little as $.40 per share in 1985, and, with those same shares worth ten times that, were now looking forward to a spectacular return on their investments. And, if earnings kept growing, those stakes would grow even higher.

Needless to say, the venture capital camp on my board began to closely watch our bottom line. That was one thing, but then they began to resist major new expense projects that might temporarily depress earnings and derail us from our track toward a successful IPO. Meanwhile, the board's cable camp, whose own companies would also benefit from new Discovery programming, was gung ho for moving ahead.

I first began to notice this rift when, in early 1988, Ruth and I proposed significant spending increases in programming and marketing, especially for those ambitious new productions.

The members of the cable operator camp were enthusiastic over our content spending plan—not just because it would bring new subscribers to the cable industry, but also because they believed that Discovery's proposed new spending would be easily recovered with bigger audiences and future rate increases.

By comparison, the venture capitalists on the board were horrified about the damage to the bottom line that significant new programming and marketing expenses would cause. They could not understand why we would voluntarily depress earnings and spoil our great record of bottom-line performance, one that would surely impress investors. They wanted us to suspend any such plans for a couple of years, until after an IPO.

Needless to say, it was a difficult meeting. And the next one promised to be even worse.

And it was. Nimrod and I walked in with a proposal to spend tens of millions of dollars to expand into Europe. The other cable guys, Bob Miron, John Sie, and Ajit Dalvi, were already on board with international expansion. They all had experience in cable distribution and knew the perils of not seizing channel space the moment it was available. Cable was proving to be a "first player" industry: if you were first in movies, like HBO; first in sports, like ESPN; or first in documentaries, like Discovery, then you enjoyed a perpetual carriage lead over the number-two and number-three competitors in your category. For that reason, we had no intention of being number two or number three in our category anywhere in the world.

To put it mildly, the board discussion did not go well. The members of the venture capital group—no doubt having reached an understanding among themselves beforehand—voiced their strong opposition to the international expansion. They would not vote for it.

I chose not to exacerbate the situation by forcing a divisive vote. However, as we all left the meeting, we knew that we had a board in deadlock. If the issue of international expansion was pressed to a formal vote at the next meeting, I was going to be the swing vote in a 5–4 decision. And that was the kind of board decision that would cause as many problems as it solved.

Taking Sides

Dick Crooks was the first to call me. He made a compelling argument about how Discovery, after a successful public offering, would have all the resources it needed to expand. We could get to a public offering in less than two years if we just kept establishing a profitable growth record. If I just hung tough with the initial investors who had brought me to the dance, he told me, we could make it to a successful IPO.

Next to call was John Sie, who reported that the four cable companies had huddled after the meeting. He said it was absolutely clear to them that Discovery could not afford to miss the expansion opportunity in Europe. That opportunity would only come once, he reminded me, because the new cable systems in Europe, particularly in the United Kingdom, would be determining their channel lineups over the next six months. That meant we had to quickly announce a Discovery Europe service to get in the game. Any delay could cost us our global future.

Two men who represented the best in their respective professions, and both of whom I respected immensely—and they were trying to pull me in opposite directions.

I called Dick Crooks back, but he was not budging. He made it clear that New York Life, Group W, and the other initial venture investors were with him.

John Sie called again, this time with even more urgency: "John, the four of us MSOs [multiple system operators—the big cable companies] have set up a meeting in Chicago to discuss the future of Discovery. We are at a real crossroads, and you need to be there."

I hesitated, uncertain if my fiduciary duties to all my shareholders even allowed me to meet formally with a subset of board members. Sie assured me that his counsel Jerry Kern was comfortable with the meeting. "We just want to talk," he told me. "We just want to try to find a way out of this mess, and Jerry Kern is exploring possible solutions."

I agreed to come to the Chicago meeting.

Then I gave Dick Crooks a courtesy call to tell him I would be meeting with the operators. He was concerned, but I told him that I would share whatever came out of the meeting.

Divided Loyalties

As I traveled to Chicago I was a man torn by conflicting loyalties, and alarmed over the fate of my company.

On the one hand, there never would have been a Discovery Channel had not my initial investors, led by Allen & Company, taken a huge gamble to fund my idea.

But the cable operator investors had tossed me a lifeline after the disastrous Chronicle deal exploded. They had saved me from bankruptcy. My cable operator investors had dramatically accelerated our distribution in the United States. Now, like me, they recognized an enormous, and impending, global opportunity.

Just as important, the cable operators were long-term players. And I, as company founder, was the longest-term player. I had created Discovery to realize a dream, not as some get-rich-quick scheme. No matter the valuation of an IPO, we could not take a chance on missing global expansion and the opportunity to create a world force for quality nonfiction television.

I had made my decision even before landing in Chicago: I would side with the cable operators.

Clean Slate

At the Chicago meeting we agreed that the only fair way to resolve the crisis was to approach the venture investors with a buyout offer that matched their expected value of a public stock offering.

The four cable operators understood, and I reminded them that the venture investors had played a critical role in the creation of Discovery. Consequently, there would be no attempt to "lowball" an offer at, say, $2 per share. Instead, the offer price, to be funded entirely and equally by the four cable companies, would be above $4. The initial investors would get their tenfold return.

It was a fair deal—and after brief negotiations, the venture capital team accepted it. In the end, the cable operators purchased all of the outstanding shares in Discovery except mine. The valuation of Discovery at the time of the buyout transaction was approximately $300 million.

As we finalized the buyout, our plans to launch Discovery Europe were publicly announced and our rapid global expansion began. The five of us remaining on the Discovery board committed to keeping the company private as long as possible. That way we could invest all of Discovery's revenues, in excess of expenses, back into growing the company domestically, internationally, and with new, original content.

Discovery emerged from the board crisis a company transformed. What appeared at the time to be a financial dispute proved to be a debate about the soul of the company. In the end, we had chosen long-term growth over a short-term payout—and that decision put us on the path to become a global media giant.

When you are building a company, you don't think much about how many shares you own. After all, if the enterprise fails they won't matter anyway. Instead those shares become a kind of barometer of *control*—how much control of the company you give away to investors and employees, and how much you retain for yourself.

Control Matters

My role in Discovery's board crisis taught me that my shares, and my ability to retain them, would largely define my role in the company in the future. Had the board's venture capital team forced a shareholder battle, the cable team directors and I might have lost—and I might well have been driven from my own company. I needed to be more vigilant in the future.

Like so many entrepreneurs, I had made decisions and choices throughout the start-up period that ultimately affected my level of ownership in the company I'd founded. Using debt instead of equity sales to finance my start-up would have preserved more of my ownership, but it was simply not available. Even if it had been, I would have probably missed the opportunity to form a strategic investment alliance with four of America's largest cable operators—support that now meant Discovery was destined to be a multibillion-dollar company.

I made the choice to own a fraction of a future global media giant rather than all of a modest, also-ran company. But that decision required a concurrent commitment to find major investors whose board representatives shared a common growth vision with me. I had barely escaped the consequences of a company with a board that was deeply divided on growth strategy.

We reconstituted the board in 1989, and then enlarged it when we finally went public, some two decades later, in 2008. Happily, we have not had another split vote by the Discovery board during all those years. This doesn't mean we don't have healthy, spirited discussions. Indeed, we have great and sometimes lengthy debates.

However, because we have carefully constituted that board to be united around our mission to be "a global force for producing and distributing high-quality content that satisfies human curiosity," we always find common ground in making decisions that advance our purpose.

Chapter 21

Digital Dreams

Civilization advances by extending the number of important operations which we can perform without thinking of them.

—ALFRED NORTH WHITEHEAD

It was 1993. The dawn of a new era.

"Rupert has to see this," John Malone said to me at the end of the demonstration.

"I agree. Fox is the only one not participating in the test."

A few weeks later, John Malone and I arrived at Twentieth Century Fox Studios in Los Angeles. We had come to show Rupert Murdoch the future of television.

John Malone had started it all. And indeed, it seemed as if his entire career had brought him to this moment: engineering and economics degrees from Yale, a Ph.D. in operations research from Johns Hopkins, then Bell Labs when it was the cradle of communications innovation, then management training at McKinsey & Company. In 1970, Malone was named group vice president at General Instrument Corporation (GI) and soon thereafter he was named president of Jerrold Electronics, a GI subsidiary. Three years later he was hired as president and CEO of TCI—and then built that company into the cable television industry's largest and most important distributor.

If the cable industry had a wizard, it was John Malone.

A Five-Hundred-Channel Universe

By the late 1980s Malone realized that television distribution would be dramatically more efficient if its analog signals were converted into digital transmissions that could be easily manipulated and compressed for efficiency. Specifically, in the same 6 megahertz (MHz) of spectrum required to send just one analog television channel feed, you could send as many as ten digital channels.

Meanwhile, the U.S. government was poised to adopt the Japanese MUSE analog standard for high-definition television. By doing so, the U.S. government not only would be surrendering leadership in television equipment manufacturing to the Japanese, it would also be enslaving itself to a "spectrum wasteful" form of analog communications for the indefinite future.

When John Sie learned of this he was horrified, as was his boss, John Malone. Sie went to hearing after hearing in Washington, explaining the folly of adopting an analog transmission standard in the age of computers. Slowly, he got converts—and in 1987, the FCC adopted a digital transmission standard. Through his tireless efforts, John Sie had almost single-handedly derailed the U.S. government's adoption of an obsolete television standard—and deservedly earned his title as the "father of digital high-definition television."

Throughout John Sie's fight for digital television, he was on my board at Discovery, advising us on the potential of the technology. By 1990, John Malone began to attend our Discovery board meetings alongside the principals of each of our major cable shareholders, and between the two men they educated us on the power of digital. It proved to be a powerful head start.

It wasn't until a cable trade show in Anaheim in late 1992 that John Malone famously coined the phrase "five-hundred-channel universe" to describe the digital future of television wherein 50 analog channels could potentially be converted into 500 digital channels. It had been a simple description of the 10x power of digital over analog, but John's catchphrase caused a media firestorm.

The word was now out about our digital television future. And thanks to our early heads-up from Malone and Sie, while other programmers were just starting to take note of digital transmission, we at Discovery were already deep into planning its implementation.

Your Choice TV

I can honestly say that my initial fascination with digital quickly turned into outright obsession. In my mind's eye I could already see what digital transmission would mean for the future of television and media.

In late 1991, I presented a white paper to my board outlining a future of menu-accessed—rather than channel-accessed—television. Then, over the year that followed, I continued to refine this vision of digital television in which viewers could watch what they wanted, when they wanted.

It seemed to me self-evident that consumers would migrate to such a platform, which I dubbed "Your Choice TV." And so, even without a lot of proof, I set to work with a team designing an entire "on-demand" system, complete with handheld remotes, set-top converter menus, and digitally compressed satellite transponder feeds of individual shows from all the major cable and broadcast networks. We even demonstrated the ordering of airline tickets and seat selections from a TV set.

We even made the argument, which proved prescient, that cable operators would at last be able to deliver advertising "addressed" to each consumer based on their interests and demographics. There would also be, we argued, abundant choices of movie selections and many new digital channels, like a Science Channel, paralleling the many popular special-interest magazines found at newsstands.

By late 1992, I was ready to test Your Choice TV. The idea was to take popular shows, such as NBC's *Saturday Night Live* and CBS's *60 Minutes*, and put each of them on their own channel to run continuously for up to a week. Viewers could then watch the show when they wanted.

It wasn't quite the modern video on demand (VOD). A consumer couldn't start the show from its beginning, but at least that show, say NBC's *Seinfeld*, would start at the top of the hour, every hour, for up to a week on its very own channel. That alone would be a huge breakthrough. We were creating near video on demand (NVOD).

I wanted to test twenty-four top shows running on twenty-four different channels. But how would I ever secure all of the broadcast rights to those shows? Or, indeed, all of those cable channels?

It was John Malone who gave me a solution path to the second question. "You can find systems that have been overbuilt with two cables and one cable is dormant," he told me when I discussed my test plan with him. "We have a system like that in Mount Prospect, Illinois. You can test there, and I'll bet other operators can find other systems for you."

Malone was right. Within weeks, seven other cable operators searched their systems and found cable plants with dormant capacity that I could use. Those eight test systems served a total of twenty thousand cable customers across the nation. We selected Comcast's cable system in Palm Beach County, Florida, as the initial test site.

With the test systems lined up, I needed the rights from the networks to test their hit shows. Through a mutual friend I was introduced to Larry Tisch, who controlled CBS. Larry in turn recommended that I speak with CBS president Howard Stringer. After a series of meetings, Howard agreed to join the test—and offered us numerous shows, including *60 Minutes* and *Dr. Quinn, Medicine Woman*.

Next, Tom Rodgers at NBC got clearance from Bob Wright to use *Seinfeld* and *Saturday Night Live*. Following a meeting with all the top brass at ABC, including Tom Murphy, Dan Burke, Bob Iger, and Roone Arledge, ABC offered up *20/20* and the soap opera *All My Children*. PBS agreed to participate, as did HBO and the leading cable networks. Fox was the only major network that declined to participate after our initial round of meetings.

Meanwhile, two of my Discovery staff members, Bob Liguori and Gil Cowley, had devised a clever way for me to use a laser disk to demonstrate my television menu system. I could step through all the menus of choices (movies, hit TV shows, new specialty channels, sports programs, interactive shopping, and high-definition shows) and demonstrate how the consumer could order a particular show for prices ranging from $.79 to $.99 each.

The presentation simulated what today we all experience via menus on advanced digital cable and satellite systems. But in 1993 it was a revolution to viewers. By the same token, on the Your Choice TV remote control I had designed a four-directional set of control buttons with a center "select" button—also a first for the industry.

Now, with the network agreements in place, I could add the CBS, ABC, and NBC shows to the demonstration. I flew out to

Denver to show this version of the demonstration to CableLabs (a nonprofit research and development consortium founded in 1988 by cable operating companies), as well as to Malone and his technology team at TCI. It was after seeing this latest update that John Malone proposed that we meet with Rupert Murdoch.

Meeting a Giant

John Malone and I arrived at Rupert's office at Twentieth Century Fox Studios in Los Angeles accompanied by a very excited Bob Liguori. Bob set up the laser disk presentation in Rupert's office and then stepped outside, leaving the three of us alone for what turned out to be a wide-ranging, two-and-a-half-hour discussion on the future of television.

Not surprisingly, given that he was one of the most successful media giants of the twentieth century, Murdoch quickly saw the promise of digital compression and the value to consumers of accessing programs on demand. However, after noting digital's potentially massive disruption of advertising-supported television delivered through affiliated broadcast stations, Murdoch began peppering us with very smart questions. How will you split up VOD revenue with the affiliates? What will happen to live viewership if consumers lose the urgency to show up to watch programs on their initial air date?

(That last question had also troubled Howard Stringer at CBS—until David Poltrack, the head of research at CBS, pointed out that CBS only received a penny per viewer from advertisers on the network; in comparison, CBS would get a half share, or 50 cents, for each paying viewer of Your Choice TV.)

The three of us also discussed the coming world of high-definition television (then almost eight years away) and the extra channel capacity created through digital compression. It was obvious that Malone and Murdoch had a history of strategic discussions about television, and about global cable and satellite distribution. They seemed to enjoy each other's company and they made me feel like a welcome addition to their discussions.

By the end of the meeting, Rupert was intrigued by Your Choice TV, but he still declined to participate—it just seemed too disruptive to the current broadcast distribution system in which his Fox Network was then growing and thriving. Still, it was a fascinating couple of hours exploring television's future with two of the brightest minds in global business.

Bombshell

Now I anxiously awaited the first results from the Your Choice field test. How would these twenty thousand homes react? I already sensed that they were ready to spend extra for content that they could control. After all, at Discovery, hundreds of thousands of consumers were already sending us $19.95—almost the equivalent amount of their monthly basic cable bill—just to get a VHS copy of a single show they had missed.

The test results, when they came in, stunned us. Consumers responded even more enthusiastically than we had expected. We learned to our amazement that women were coming home every day after work and paying $.79 to watch that day's episode of *All My Children*. They could, of course, have taped it with their VCRs—but, as they told us in focus groups, that was "just too much trouble." Other people ordered *Saturday Night Live* episodes on the following Sunday through Wednesday because they were now free to go out on Saturday night.

We had clearly proven that people would pay for more choice

and more control. Ironically, however, those same test results confirmed the disruptive nature of Your Choice TV that Rupert Murdoch, Howard Stringer, and others had worried about.

Meanwhile, the network affiliates went ballistic. They contended that Your Choice TV was an "end run" around the same network affiliates that had made *Seinfeld*, *20/20*, and other broadcast shows hits in the first place. Even though we tried to design a payment stream for those angry affiliates, they would hear none of it.

So, in the end, Rupert was right. Your Choice TV, if implemented, would be enormously disruptive to the current broadcast system. It was too soon. It would take another decade to realize. One by one, the major networks withdrew their content from Your Choice TV.

Entrepreneurs always worry about being too late to market. I had now been taught that it's just as dangerous to be too early.

The Electronic Book

At home one quiet evening in December 1992, I found myself pondering the other forms of content that might be delivered in a digital format. Soon I turned to books.

What if books were delivered via cable to households in a secure, encrypted digital data stream, originating at a national file server? The digital books could then be wirelessly transmitted by the cable set-top box to a portable handheld reader. Since not all consumers had cable, I imagined that the book delivery and portable reader system would alternatively use telephone and cellular delivery technologies.

By now my curiosity was fully engaged. I constructed a menu system that would be resident on the reader but updatable from a central server with the title, description, and pricing of books to order. Consumers would be able to register their credit card and the system would need to securely process this sensitive information. Finally, I designed how the book could be read on the portable reader and how pages could be turned and bookmarked. Gil Cowley, a designer on the Discovery staff, took my drawings and constructed models of this portable book reader.

About this time I became acquainted with a digital communications visionary named James Phillips. Early in his career, Jim Phillips had been president of National Satellite Paging. He changed the company's name to SkyTel and built the nation's largest messaging business.

When I met Jim he was a senior executive at Motorola, having joined that company in the wake of Motorola's purchase of SkyTel. At Motorola, Jim participated in the launch of its digital cellular and multimedia services, and helped bring the cable modem to market. In addition to discussing the potential of digital cable, Jim introduced me to a fascinating start-up company in Tennessee called Interactive Pictures Corporation (iPIX). Discovery had made an investment in iPIX, along with Motorola, and I served with Jim on its board of directors. Today Jim is chairman and CEO of NanoMech, a leading global manufacturer of nano-coatings and nano-lubricants. Jim was always cutting-edge.

In 1994, I showed Jim Phillips my proprietary designs and models of the portable book reader and its delivery system. Once he saw them, Jim was adamant that I show them to Christopher Galvin, president of Motorola. I agreed to meet with Chris and Jim at the Motorola headquarters in Schaumburg, Illinois.

Before my trip I talked at length with Alberto Vitale, then chairman and CEO of Random House, one of the world's largest book publishers. Random House was then owned by the Newhouse family. My Discovery board member and Newhouse family member, Bob Miron, asked Alberto to study my invention and then meet with me.

Alberto was intrigued over the invention but was concerned that the major bookstore chains would view it as a way to bypass their stores and go directly to consumers. Alberto counseled that my e-book would be too much of a shock to the current distribution system—and predicted that its day would come, but only well into the future.

In my meeting at Motorola, it became clear that Chris Galvin was also enthusiastic over my electronic book. He had even assembled a team of senior staff members and engineers to evaluate its market potential.

At that time, Chris was focused on making Motorola a leader of the digital age—and he had succeeded in both cellular technology and digital cable communications. An electronic book could only enhance this strategy. Unfortunately, after a more comprehensive review by Motorola's engineers, it became apparent that powering the portable reader would require a big, heavy battery pack or a power cord to a wall outlet. In other words, it could not be truly portable.

In the end, the resistance by publishers to explore an "end run" around their traditional distributors, combined with the weight challenges of a battery, killed my electronic book project—for the time being. Here, in the age of the Amazon Kindle and the Apple iPad, we now know it would take another dozen years. As for me, what I learned from the experience was that an electronic book would be a powerfully disruptive technology and would forever change book publishing.

And it has done just that. It is both ironic and satisfying to me that this book will also be published as an e-book.

Even though the electronic book would have to await advances in battery technology, my meetings at Motorola with Galvin and

Phillips were invigorating. All three of us were convinced that nothing could stop the miracle of digital sweeping through every corner of the personal and mass communications worlds.

Chris Galvin would go on to build Motorola into a global leader in digital communications with such innovations as the RAZR cellular phone. By the time he left Motorola in 2004, Motorola had achieved a $30 billion run rate in annual revenue.

Making Book

Our legal team had shrewdly hired patent counsel when they realized I was breaking new ground, not only in video-on-demand technologies, but also in menu designs for set tops, remote controls, and addressable advertising. Thanks to that decision, Discovery now owned the first invention of an electronic book reader, along with an associated book content purchasing and delivery system. Patent applications were quickly filed.

Discovery had spent a considerable sum in research and development on the Your Choice TV project, but we soon began recovering our investment through the sale and licensing of our patents. That same R&D experience also helped us to make smart—and rewarding—investments in new technologies.

A consortium of cable operators, anxious to use this patented Your Choice TV technology, ultimately paid Discovery more than $20 million to purchase those patents. We held on to the world's first electronic book patents and today they are being licensed to companies that offer affordable book-reading devices. Internally, our Discovery Education division has continued our electronic book patent legacy by producing our revolutionary *Science Techbook*.

TiVo and the Dawn of the DVR

In 1999, Jim Barton and Mike Ramsay developed a revolutionary new set-top device that enabled consumers to record digitized video onto a hard disk. They called their device TiVo and it became an instant sensation.

At Discovery, after our Your Choice TV research experience, we were confident in the success of TiVo. So we invested early in TiVo and profited from its success. I joined the TiVo board of directors and, during my term, had the pleasure of sitting through some wonderful discussions about the future of television. These discussions included fellow board members and friends such as David Zaslav of NBC and Sir Howard Stringer, who by then had left CBS to become president and CEO of Sony.

TiVo ushered in the era of the digital video recorder (DVR), which dramatically altered the way television was consumed. DVRs enabled consumers to easily "time-shift" their favorite shows, as well as to fast-forward through commercials.

Commercial skipping, of course, posed a challenge for networks and their advertisers. It still does. Networks continue to grapple with the threat posed by DVRs to the critical advertising stream that underpins the financing of television programming. Looking ahead from the present, I can see that digital technologies, implemented through cable and the Internet, will likely allow consumers to access television programs on-demand with a choice between two prices: (1) a free or low price (perhaps 5 cents) if the program contains advertising; and (2) a higher price (perhaps 50 cents) if the program is commercial-free. That in turn will make consumers increasingly more aware of the value of advertising in subsidizing the cost of television.

A Multichannel Network Company

The Your Choice TV project changed us. We at Discovery had seen the future and, while others dreaded a world full of new competitive choices, we had embraced that new reality. And now we raced to capture the opportunities that were about to emerge.

While Discovery was working on a content plan for digital, John Malone was busy building the nation's first satellite uplink and transmission system capable of delivering an abundance of new digital channels. He called this system a digital "head-end in the sky."

In 1995, Malone's TCI completed this new system—and began raining down new digital movie channels across the nation. Discovery was the first cable programmer in line, ready with new specialty channels that we had custom-designed precisely for this new TCI platform.

Malone's platform was open to any cable operator who wanted to downlink and distribute the new digital channels. That was great news for us, because soon, all across the nation, cable customers were signing up for the new digital set-top converters that brought six new digital Discovery channels into their homes along with numerous movie choices.

So, in 1996, thanks to the miracle of digital television and our aggressiveness in exploiting its potential, we were transmitting a total of nine networks, more than any other cable programming company in the world. Our three analog networks (universally available on both analog and digital platforms) were Discovery Channel, TLC (acquired in 1991), and Animal Planet.

Our six new digital networks (available only in homes with digital converter boxes) were Discovery Science, Discovery Kids, Discovery Civilization, Discovery Health, Discovery Wings, and

Discovery Living. Soon we grew to eleven networks with the addition of Discovery en Espanol and the Travel Channel. (We acquired the Travel Channel in 1997 and sold it to Cox Cable in 2007 as part of our buyout of Cox's equity interest in Discovery.)

Discovery was no longer just a channel but a full-blown multi-network media corporation. We had joined the ranks of the television giants I had so admired as a boy.

High-Definition and 3-D Television

Digital television's efficient use of the electronic spectrum certainly contributed to the rollout of high-definition television in the United States. However, as late as 2002, no network had taken the risky plunge into HDTV.

Among consumers, there were a few early adopters who had purchased HD television sets just for the small amount of HD content on the air. But most consumers were waiting for the airwaves to fill with HD—even as the broadcasters were waiting for the consumers to buy enough HDTVs. It was a classic stand-off, with nobody willing to go first.

Somebody had to make the first move. And we decided it would be Discovery. So we launched Discovery HD Theater in June 2002. Soon retailers such as Best Buy and Sears were showcasing our shows, and those of other pioneers such as HBO and ESPN—and the consumer adoption of HD television began.

And thank goodness—a year before HD distribution commenced I had taken a major risk by investing heavily in a major HD production. If HDTV hadn't taken off, we would have squandered millions of dollars. Instead it became one of the biggest programming events in Discovery history—and the greatest advertisement imaginable for HD.

The high-risk decision I'd made dealt with the choice of camera technology to be used in filming a new series called *Planet Earth*. The series, a coproduction between Discovery and the BBC, was the next major project by Alastair Fothergill, whose previous groundbreaking work at the BBC's Natural History Unit had included *Blue Planet* and the *Trials of Life*.

As the filmmaker responsible for undertaking the world's most expensive documentary project, working in extreme environments, Fothergill understandably wanted to use well-proven film camera technology in the field. And, with no high-definition television yet in the British market, the BBC naturally resisted adding substantial HD production costs to an already expensive project.

Confident that HD television would be well penetrated in the U.S. market by 2007, the expected air date of the five-year production, I insisted that *Planet Earth* be produced in HD. After weeks of agonizing stalemate, the BBC finally relented.

As we all know, in the end Alastair Fothergill and his dedicated HD camera crews created an epic series that enchanted audiences in the United Kingdom, the United States, and around the world.

In America, Oprah Winfrey fell in love with the series and her promotion of *Planet Earth* on her popular daytime television show helped drive Discovery's viewership of the eleven-part series to historic levels. Alastair and members of his crew even appeared on her show to explain how they had managed to capture sequences and situations in nature that had never before been seen. Meanwhile, Americans rushed out to buy HDTVs to see the series as it had been captured—in full high-definition resolution.

At Discovery, we believed that consumers would continually migrate toward television platforms—such as HD—that offered an ever-closer-to-reality viewing experience; 3-D television was next.

And in order to stimulate the rollout and adoption of this next technology, Discovery joined forces with Sony and IMAX to launch the world's first full-time 3-D channel—"3net"—on February 13, 2011.

In the not-too-distant future, perhaps within a decade or two, the resolution quality of television will increase to a point where pixel density and imaging technology will match the fine resolution power of the human visual system. In other words, viewing a television monitor will be like looking out a window or through a doorway into the next room. I call this endgame for viewing resolution "Retinal-Definition, Three-Dimensional Media," or simply RD3D Media for short. It is surely coming. It will cause a sensation. And you can count on Discovery to help pioneer it.

Discovery Education

At Discovery, we never forgot that our very first viewer call came from a teacher in Kansas. That teacher's inquiry, concerning the use of our programming in the classroom, foreshadowed our remarkable Discovery Education division.

Following the introduction of *Assignment Discovery*, we began to accumulate an enormous digital library through acquisitions and the careful editing of our own content. This new digital library was custom-designed for interactive use—and once it was completed in 2001, we began to stream the content to the nation's schools both through the Internet and through cable's broadband infrastructure.

The revolutionary subscription service, called Discovery Education Streaming, became the nation's leading educational multimedia resource. Today it is used in more than half of America's schools—and is playing a crucial role in bringing classrooms into the twenty-first century.

A more recent innovation by Discovery Education has been the creation of the world's first digital K–8 science textbook. Known as the Discovery *Science Techbook*, it was announced in 2010 and rolled out to the nation's schools in 2011. It features interactive glossaries, explorations, informational text, and hands-on and virtual labs that support the teaching of biology, chemistry, earth and space science, and physics.

Even as states and their school districts began adopting the *Science Techbook*, Bill Goodwyn and his team were creating a similar textbook for social studies. Discovery now leads the world in these digital textbooks, with science and social studies *Techbooks* for both middle schools and high schools.

The Tablet and Personal Media

The landmark Apple iPad pioneered a new form of personal media that is likely to reach 1 billion global users within a decade. Better yet, this new platform seamlessly integrates and presents all forms of media. And since these tablets are constantly connected to the world's vast information resources through the Internet, they offer consumers a hugely appealing tool for personal exploration and discovery.

At Discovery we have always defined our business as being independent of technology delivery. Rather, we are in the business of satisfying curiosity and we will do that on all important forms of technology as those forms evolve through time.

That's a crucial distinction, not just because technology advances so quickly, but because it is almost impossible to predict which path it will take—who saw the PC or the iPod coming? You need to be technologically agnostic—open for any emerging new technology, but wary—and then be prepared to pounce when the moment is right.

Just such a moment occurred at a board retreat in August 2010, when I presented a plan to create a new company division, called MyDiscovery, that would develop new content forms for tablets and other future personal media devices. The board agreed—and today the MyDiscovery unit is busy developing new ways in which people can use the tools of social media to create and share "interest zones." Through these interest zones, tablet and computer users can access a rich and trusted source of multimedia content organized around popular categories of human curiosity.

Internet Television

I first heard about the Internet at a 1985 meeting that Harry Hagerty had arranged. Harry wanted me to meet his old Army buddy Jim Kimsey.

Jim Kimsey had been a consultant to Control Video Corporation, which was at that moment was being reorganized as Quantum Computer Services with Jim as its new head. The company was based in northern Virginia just around the Beltway from my Discovery offices in Landover.

By then, Discovery was already on the air, but I was looking for investors for a second round of financing. Harry thought Jim could recommend potential investors, and he also thought I'd be interested in Jim's company. In the meeting, Kimsey explained his company's history of providing downloadable games via phone lines and modems to Atari and Commodore game consoles.

When I began asking detailed questions, Kimsey called in his new vice president for marketing to help explain. When the young head of marketing entered the room, Jim casually said, "This is Steve Case."

Case outlined a future market of interconnected computer and game users: a new "community" online in which members could share experiences. At that point, Case made reference to government agencies and universities already using shared networks of computers. It was my first introduction to the DARP/ARPA/Internet.

I then explained what I was up to at Discovery. Jim offered a few suggestions about potential investors, and Harry said he would follow up. The meeting ended and I headed back to Landover. Not much came out of the meeting—and yet everything did.

On the way back, I thought about that interconnected "network of computer users" being run by the government. Steve Case and Jim Kimsey were confident that a similar interconnected network would develop at the consumer level. Interesting. I filed that notion in the back of my mind.

Within a decade, everything Case and Kimsey had predicted came true. They went on to create America Online (AOL). The Internet exploded once browsers, notably Netscape Navigator, were developed to provide an easy-to-use, common access portal to the addressable portion of the Internet, the World Wide Web. And once that capability was available to consumers, as we all know, the world turned upside down.

Once again, by identifying early the emergence of the Internet—and especially noting how it was being used to satisfy curiosity—Discovery was already well on its cyber-way by the time the Web exploded. We began as early as 1998 to add video clips to all of our network websites. And, by 2006, we were looking for ways to dramatically accelerate our presence on the Internet through the acquisition of hot new content enterprises. One of those companies was HowStuffWorks—which, by 2007, when we acquired it, had tens of millions of annual visitors. HowStuffWorks was headed by Jeff Arnold, an Internet pioneer who had previously founded

WebMD. We quickly began adding video resources to its website. A Compete.com survey reported that the site attracted more than 58 million visitors in 2008.

We also made a significant number of acquisitions to increase our online video presence, most recently our acquisition of Revision3. Revision3 produces and distributes Web television shows on niche topics. The company was founded in April 2005.

A year later while checking out YouTube (this is where surfing the Web is valuable), I first ran across the creative and endlessly clever Philip DeFranco, who hosts his own daily Internet show. To me, DeFranco's daily episodes about politics, pop culture, and world news stood out from others for its wit, respect for the audience, and high production values. It wasn't long before Revision3 became the new home for programming innovators like Philip DeFranco.

By early 2012, Revision3 enjoyed more than 23 million unique viewers monthly across 27 digital channels, and was one of the ten largest networks on YouTube. That spring, when Jean-Briac "J.B." Perrette, our chief digital officer, proposed that Discovery acquire Revision3, we jumped at the chance.

Today, Discovery is navigating through a tricky new world in which television shows can be delivered both by traditional cable distribution systems and by the Internet. We learned from our early work on the Your Choice TV project that consumers will not be stopped in their never-ending quest to watch what they want, when they want, and where they want.

Fulfilling that desire has defined Discovery from our very first day. And it has never done less than fully engage our curiosity. How can we deliver individual programs directly to the consumer via the Internet while still preserving the revenues that make those programs possible in the first place?

Sound familiar? It's just the latest incarnation of the challenge we faced in the Your Choice TV project. Internet television may soon make an end run around Discovery's cable affiliates the same way that Your Choice TV in 1993 was viewed as circumventing broadcast network affiliates.

What's scary is that we never could solve the Your Choice TV puzzle. But now we *must* solve the puzzle of Internet-delivered television. Yes, it is disruptive. But it is also unstoppable, because the consumer demand driving it is just too strong. That means we have no choice but to invent a way to preserve real-time television in an on-demand world. We can't run away from it; we can't fight it; we must *embrace* it.

Believe me, we are working on it—and loving the challenge.

It's what we live for.

Chapter 22

Programming for the Planet

In any moment of decision, the best thing you can do is the right thing.
The worst thing you can do is nothing.

—THEODORE ROOSEVELT

We produce content. That is our product and our purpose. So, to understand Discovery, one must first appreciate the critical decisions and choices we make that ultimately find their way onto the television screen.

Enchanting and informing viewers worldwide depends upon sparks of imagination and insight that are hard to manage, let alone predict. Our goal is to be open to these "sparks of imagination" *wherever* and *whenever* they arise. Sometimes that is an immense undertaking. Other times we just go off on a retreat and get lucky.

Shark Week, the most popular and enduring creation in our history, is an example of the latter.

In the early spring of 1987, Ruth Otte and I decided to treat our small team of programmers and managers to a two-day brainstorming session at the Hay-Adams Hotel in downtown Washington, D.C. We arranged to have our small band of senior employees, about fifteen in all, meet in the living room setting of a suite overlooking the White House. Given that our company headquarters at the time was ten miles away in a nondescript industrial park in Landover, Maryland, we had hoped this offsite trip to a famous Washington landmark hotel would prove inspiring.

On the second day of this retreat, we went around the room soliciting breakthrough content ideas from everyone. I made it clear that there were "no bad ideas" in hopes that people would blurt out any random thoughts. We soon found ourselves discussing novel ways that we could package stand-alone documentaries into branded anthologies that resembled series. That was when Steve Cheskin, our scheduler, spoke up.

"Do you know," he asked, "how local independent broadcast stations theme their movie weeks around movie stars like John Wayne, Marilyn Monroe, and Jimmy Stewart?" Everyone nodded. We all knew that themes gave viewers a daily destination to experience a favorite movie star. And for the broadcast stations, movie theme weeks provided attractive sales packages to local advertisers.

Steve then blurted out his idea: "Well, what if we created *Shark Week*?"

The room erupted with that rare laughter that comes with encountering a brilliant new idea.

We spent the rest of the session debating how to best implement Steve's idea. We simply could not wait to get *Shark Week* on the air.

Shark Week premiered on July 17, 1987, and it has been a fixture on Discovery Channel's summer programming schedule ever since. In the interim, it has become a cultural phenomenon and has featured well-known hosts, such as *The Late Late Show*'s Craig Ferguson and the comedian Andy Samberg. Every few years during *Shark Week* our headquarters in Silver Spring is decked out with massive fin, head, and tail balloons that create the appearance of an enormous shark swimming inside our eleven-story office structure. We call him *Chompie*.

Shark Week is an ongoing reminder that many of the best programming ideas come out of left field, and to always be ready to catch the sparks—and use them to start a fire.

Programming Within a Revolutionary Media Environment

I take tremendous pride in the fact that no government, nonprofit organization, or media company on the planet provides more households with television programming than Discovery Communications. But I also recognize that being the leader also entails enormous responsibilities.

Today, Discovery provides 1.8 billion cumulative subscribers in more than 215 countries and territories with programming on more than 150 worldwide networks delivered in 45 languages. Our 28 network brands appearing in markets throughout the world include Discovery Channel, TLC, Animal Planet, Investigation Discovery (ID), Science, Military Channel, Velocity, OWN, Discovery Fit and Health, Destination America, The Hub, DMAX, Discovery Turbo, Discovery Real Time, Quest, Discovery History, Discovery Travel & Living, Discovery Civilization, Discovery Familia, and Discovery HD. From New Zealand to Sweden and all points in between, Discovery Networks have become must-have television for the world's viewers.

So much of life is about the choices we make. At Discovery, we have attempted to make programming choices and decisions that meet the demands of our worldwide market. We develop programs to satisfy the many curiosities of our viewers, and we distribute these shows and series on networks themed to reflect the major categories of nonfiction content.

In doing so, Discovery has become a major participant in what I see as the second and third evolutionary steps of television. Because each step has provided a revolutionary new benefit to consumers, I believe it is appropriate to simply call this history the "Three Revolutions of Television."

Revolution 1: Television on Demand

With the invention of the medium, its distribution via broadcast transmission in the mid-1940s, and a drop in TV prices due to growing production, the world experienced "Television on Demand."

With a flick of a switch, we could turn on a television set and enjoy what broadcasting network programmers chose for us to watch at that particular hour. The three major broadcasting networks (ABC, CBS, and NBC) controlled when we could watch the news or a movie or a documentary—and, if we missed a broadcast, we might never see it again.

We had the mighty new medium of television, but only on its terms. By the mid-1970s, the world was poised to welcome the second revolution of television.

Revolution 2: Genre of Television on Demand

Cable network television was a stunningly simple—but earth-shaking—proposition. It began when HBO transmitted its first satellite signal to cable operators and their customers in 1975. HBO's consumer promise was to deliver a particular category or genre of content (movies) all day long. After that, television could never go back.

Maintenance

749-6300

In the industry we refer to the early days of cable network programming as the "truck-chasing era." Homeowners across the country would literally chase and flag down passing cable installer trucks and beg for a hookup. The age of "Genre of Television on Demand" had dawned and would-be television entrepreneurs— like me—began pondering what other categories of themed content might be welcomed by consumers.

It all seems so obvious now, but great ideas always do in retrospect.

In addition to movies, it was apparent even in 1975—or at least it was to those of us looking closely—that consumers would equally welcome separate cable channels devoted to news, sports, documentaries, children's entertainment, movies, or music. In time, multibillion-dollar enterprises—like ESPN, Discovery, MTV, CNN, and Nickelodeon—would emerge from entrepreneurs outside the mainstream television industry who shared that vision. And they would lead television's second revolution.

To this day, it amazes me that the three major broadcasting networks (ABC, CBS, and NBC), even after seeing the success of HBO, didn't rush to capitalize on this obvious next step in television consumption. Unlike us, they had the money *and* the content.

With a brand like ABC's *Wide World of Sports*, it would have been simple for ABC to launch an ABC Sports Channel in 1976— and keep ESPN from ever existing. And how easy would it have been for CBS to devote its considerable news infrastructure to the task of delivering a 24/7 CBS News Channel? Goodbye, CNN. ABC would, of course, eventually acquire ESPN, but at an enormous sum—the price of being late to the game.

There is a big lesson here for established businesses. So many businesses fail to exploit significant opportunities incubating in their own industries simply because they have failed to correctly define themselves.

Most often this failure stems from companies mistakenly identifying their core business with a currently popular delivery or distribution technology. A business that defines itself as a "railroad" company will likely miss the opportunities of overnight air express delivery. By comparison, a company self-defined as being in the "transportation" business would more readily realize that *all* the alternative delivery technologies to railroads—air, highway, and shipping—are within their scope.

In 1975, America's Big Three networks considered themselves to be in the "broadcasting" business. In fact, they were in the "television entertainment" business. Had they understood that simple fact they would surely have leapt on the new television distribution system of cable.

Instead, they were asleep at the switch. And, speaking for myself, I'm glad they were. And I'm obsessed with not making the same mistake.

Today, if you stop and ask a Discovery employee what business we are in, you will hear that we are in the "business of satisfying curiosity." By not tying ourselves to a particular distribution technology—even to a particular content form—we hope to remain nimble and poised to exploit all content development and distribution opportunities worldwide through cable, satellite, DVD, Internet, computers, tablet applications, mobile platforms, social media, cinema, publishing, radio, broadcasting, and through technologies yet unborn.

Revolution 3: Television Programs on Demand

One reason I still find the television industry endlessly fascinating and exciting is that Discovery, like the other "second revolution" companies, is now being challenged by a third revolution.

The same, unceasing consumer demand for more choice and control over television, the demand that created the second revolution, is now greater than ever before.

Ever since the introduction of TiVo, television's third "on demand" revolution has been under way—and it has been picking up speed now that cable operators have been providing ever-more content on demand, including menus of hundreds of movies and entire television series.

The Your Choice TV tests had long ago taught us that there was an enormous consumer demand for shows on demand. That's why we invested in TiVo. And it wasn't long before the major suppliers of converter boxes to the cable and satellite industry were hard at work competing with TiVo. Cable operators purchased digital video recorders by the millions for their eager subscribers. Viewers not only wanted to time-shift shows for convenient viewing, but—more menacing to content providers—they also wanted to skip commercials.

Concurrent with the digital set-top box rollout, cable operators also began investing in large digital file servers at their operational "head-end" facilities. These were used to deliver stored programs on demand to subscribers equipped with the new digital set-top boxes. Now digitally equipped customers of Comcast, Bright House, Time Warner, Cablevision, Cox, and other large cable distributors could not only time-shift their favorite broadcast and cable shows, they could also enjoy watching other top content on an on-demand basis from the local file server. Video on demand was a huge step forward for viewers. Consumer demand quickly intensified for even more on-demand product, with viewers clamoring for more movies and shows on demand, with commercials deleted or easily skipped.

The opportunities and threats of this third revolution in television today are just as great as those faced by the old broadcasters when they met the full force of the second revolution. The consumer demand for "Television Programs on Demand"—the third revolution—will not be stopped. Consumers will migrate to any new platform company, such as Netflix, that offers a substantial choice of commercial-free content at a viewing time of their choosing.

At Discovery, we have chosen not to stand on the sidelines of this next revolution in television; we *will not* stick our heads in the sand the way broadcasters did in the mid-1970s and just wish the threats would all go away. They are not going away.

On Demand

While this revolution in the delivery of television to consumers has been taking place, a second—less celebrated but equally important—transformation has been taking place at the heart of the industry.

While almost no one outside the cable world was watching, the nation's cable infrastructure was upgraded to provide on-demand program delivery with an efficiency as good as, if not better, than the Internet.

As a result, cable operators now enjoy a competitive advantage in that they can not only deliver on-demand programs stored locally on their file servers, but also deliver on-demand "streamed" content through fast broadband connections to the Internet.

The full force of this third revolution of television is bearing down on every player in our industry, including Discovery.

As I described in the previous chapter, this is an intellectual challenge. How do we participate in this third major revolution in television while preserving the economics we have built in the second revolution from basic subscription fees and advertisers? Can we be as aggressive in exploiting video on demand as are the new market entrants who are not encumbered by the need to protect legacy revenue streams? How can we forge new distribution alliances with those cable and satellite distributors who, after all, brought us to the dance? Can Discovery, together with our current distributors, craft new, streamed VOD offerings that will unleash greater spending by eager consumers?

One of our obvious advantages, accrued over the course of a quarter century, is that Discovery has tens of thousands of hours of digitized content that can be streamed through the advanced broadband infrastructure built by cable. Today, consumers send us $19.95 just to buy one of our shows on DVD. Imagine a premium Discovery on Demand streaming video service, with easy-to-navigate menus, delivered through cable and available only to Discovery's basic cable subscribers. And through that pipeline, connected to a massive cloud server, consumers can stream 30,000 shows of history, science, technology, nature, health, travel, human adventure, how-to, and self-help programming. Wouldn't Discovery fans eagerly spend $6 to $8 per month for that service?

Those of us in cable have the power right now to invent valuable new content subscription services that can produce new revenue streams shared equally between content creators and content distributors. Our task in the decade ahead is to continue to delight and surprise viewers on a daily basis through our existing real-time networks while also affording them an opportunity to dive deep into our multibillion-dollar content archive.

Ultimately, our goal is to generate incremental revenue from new distribution outlets in a fashion that nourishes our existing fan base. Yet we also need to promote and reinforce the value of the basic cable and satellite channels that present our new and premier productions. This is the "delicate dance" of the next decade.

It's a long way from just trying to acquire a few shows from the BBC back in 1984 . . .

Bedrock Assessments on Consumer Behavior

Content and technology aside, the heart of our business—frankly, of any consumer business—is the ability to discern fundamental trends in consumer behavior. Shifts in these trends will either drive or retard the growth of new and existing products and services.

For that reason, every consumer-oriented company needs to develop what I call "bedrock assessments on consumer behavior," on which planning for growth can be reliably based.

At Discovery, we have seven of these assessments on which we base our growth investments. I share them with the reader both to help you understand how we at Discovery operate, and in hopes that our process of establishing bedrock assessments will be useful to you in your enterprise:

1. Consumers will migrate to distribution platforms that offer *more content* choices.
2. Consumers will migrate to entertainment platforms that offer viewers the *opportunity to control* viewing choices, so that they can watch what they want to watch and at a time of their choosing.
3. Consumers will migrate to entertainment platforms that offer a *closer-to-reality* viewing experience.
4. When consumers secure a viewing platform that allows them to watch their favorite content at times

of *their choosing*, the demand for alternative, poorer-quality content will always diminish.

5. Consumers will migrate toward services and platforms that offer content *free* of commercial interruptions.

6. In a world of overwhelming content choices on the Internet and on television, consumers will increasingly rely on *quality brands* as an important editorial filter.

7. Last, consumers *worldwide* will demonstrate these behavioral trends.

These seven bedrock assessments on consumer behavior guided Discovery to invest with confidence in HD and 3-D content, on-demand video services, and global distribution. They will continue to guide us into the future.

To be sure, some of these assessments are troubling—such as assessment number 5, which presents us with the challenge of keeping our advertising revenue streams intact in the face of an indisputable consumer preference for content without commercials. We might wish that this were not the case. However, it would be irresponsible of us not to recognize this consumer trend—and then aggressively address it in our long-range strategic plans.

Multiple Brands to Serve Multiple Interests

The very first bedrock consumer demand is that viewers always want more content choice.

That's why over the years we have consistently created two types of specialty networks. The first are subcategories of the original, broad Discovery Channel mission (e.g., Science Channel); the second are new networks that supplement and expand our original Discovery mission (e.g., OWN, The Hub, Velocity).

Our development into a multi-network media company began in 1991 when we acquired The Learning Channel (TLC). Five years later, we launched Animal Planet for widespread "analog" cable and satellite distribution. Also that year we began to uplink an array of new channels designed for "digital" cable and satellite distribution.

Knowing that digital would be the technology of the future, we made the strategic decision in 1996 to seize the digital shelf space. We preemptively launched six digital channels on satellite before most other programmers had even begun to contemplate digital programming. These channels were given brand names: Discovery Science, Discovery Kids, Discovery Health, Discovery Wings, Discovery Living, and Discovery Civilization.

To be sure, there was a certain amount of risk in being so premature. At first we reached only a handful of cable customers: just the few early adopters who requested the installation of a new digital set-top box. However, even then there were payoffs—we secured shelf space and we received accolades from our distributors for being cutting-edge. They recognized that we were going to help drive digital set-top penetration. And ever since they have looked to us to be the industry's technical innovator in programming.

Frankly, some of our six digital channels served as placeholders until we ultimately determined the themes of content most desired by subscribers.

For example, we launched a channel called Discovery Civilization that we later, in 1999, contributed into a 50–50 partnership with the *New York Times*. Together we rebranded the channel as Discovery Times. But the audience failed to materialize for Discovery Times, so, in 2006, we bought back the interest held by the *Times*. By the time we regained full control of the channel, we realized that there was an enormous consumer demand for factual crime programming featuring forensic science and real-life detective stories.

So, in 2007, we again rebranded the channel. Discovery Times became Investigation Discovery (ID). ID has become a runaway success, outpacing the ratings growth of all other networks on television from 2008 through 2011.

The story of ID is yet one more reminder of why we at Discovery have always prided ourselves in being nimble, in staying "flexible" in our thinking. This allows us to respond swiftly to changing consumer demand as well as to unique partnership opportunities. It is also how we survive bad decisions—and we have had our share of those; they come with competing in a high-risk industry.

As Discovery CEO since 2007, David Zaslav has had to learn how to move quickly to reinvent struggling services and to seize fruitful partnership opportunities. Discovery Kids stalled until David created a 50–50 partnership with Hasbro, in the process launching an exciting new service called The Hub. When interest in Planet Green waned in 2011, David led the management team in redefining and rebranding the channel as Destination America. Destination America launched its new slate of programming on Memorial Day 2012. Today ratings are already up, and the channel is becoming a hit with sponsors. And, as we'll see, it was David's idea to partner with Oprah Winfrey in one of the biggest deals in our history.

Our basic tactic in pursuing global multi-network distribution is to develop specialty channels with strong themes that create a common appeal to an enormous number of viewers with otherwise divergent interests.

For example, a viewer interested in particle physics can watch an episode of *Through the Wormhole with Morgan Freeman* on the Science Channel. A parent with a young child to entertain can tune to The Hub or to a nature show on Animal Planet. An individual seeking inspiration can watch an episode of Oprah's *Master Class* on OWN. A veteran and his family may want to watch a series about the Gulf War on the Military Channel. TLC's *Cake Boss* might be the choice for a family excited by the next big challenge for bakery entrepreneur Buddy Valastro. Those interested in a crime mystery might want to curl up on the sofa to watch the latest episode of *On the Case with Paula Zahn* on ID. And it seems that most people in America, from every walk of life, want to see how the miners on *Gold Rush Alaska* are faring in their inspiring quest for the precious metal.

When we do our job right, each of these populations of viewers will turn to one of those Discovery channels with the happy expectation that they will find either the show they love or one that is philosophically or thematically related to that show. As such, each channel presents a *comfort zone*—one that the viewer can trust to always fit with his or her interests.

Needless to say, creating those environments doesn't come easily. You first must understand that audience—and then either dial in existing productions or create new ones that fit the profile of that viewer.

Sometimes you simply miss the target—or, just as commonly, the target moves. Interests change, fads die, situations evolve. And then you must be clear-eyed and honest enough to accept that fact and move on to something new and more appealing. That's what happened with Investigation Discovery. And I suspect it will happen even more often in the future as the pace of daily life accelerates.

A Mission and a Loss

I must confess that I am partial to the big-subject documentary shows and series in the tradition established by *Cosmos*, *The Civil War*, and

The Ascent of Man. One of the great satisfactions of my career is that Discovery has continued and expanded television's role in telling big stories on significant subjects. My own favorite Discovery landmark projects have been with the BBC: *Blue Planet*, *Planet Earth*, *Life*, and *Frozen Planet*. Our own production of *North America*, an epic eight-part series about the incredible landscapes and wildlife of our amazing continent, is going to dazzle viewers in 2013.

In the past, we have invested in series that have told stories about dinosaurs, human evolution, ancient civilizations, space travel, and the conflicts of modern society. Internally, we refer to these big subjects as "mission programming": programs and series designed to convey the details and intimacies of a significant topic.

As you might imagine, these are *very* expensive endeavors; in television, "depth" is tough. That's why most television is shallow. Our viewers tell us that they are grateful for the difference, but frankly, even if they weren't I'd still do mission programming. Sometimes you need to follow your heart.

In addition to these periodic landmark series, we also consider many of our regular weekly series as another type of "mission programming." These weekly series help viewers explore their world and satisfy their curiosities—the twin components of our brand promise. I consider weekly series such as *Mythbusters* on Discovery, *River Monsters* on Animal Planet, *How It's Made* on Science Channel, and *Master Class* on OWN as informative, engaging, and entertaining content that supports our mission.

For many years on the Discovery Channel and on Animal Planet, Steve Irwin charmed and educated our viewers. He embodied our mission to provide informative content in an entertaining and engaging fashion. Irwin's excitement and knowledge about wildlife poured from the television screen as he breathlessly taught viewers about the natural world.

Steve, his talented wife, Terry, and his adorably bright daughter, Bindi, became Discovery's nature ambassadors. They helped millions of our viewers worldwide to understand the intimate details of life in the wild and growing threats to natural habitats.

One of the saddest moments of my life was when I was awakened in the early morning of September 4, 2006, by a call from Billy Campbell, then president of Discovery Networks. Struggling to restrain his emotion, Billy's voice was terse and tight. "Steve Irwin is dead," he told me.

At first I didn't believe it. Nobody that full of life could be gone so quickly. But then Billy told me what little he knew: While filming underwater, Steve's chest had been pierced by a stingray barb. The crew tried to save him, but it was one of those awful, unlikely events that occurred far away from the kind of world-class medical attention that even then might not have saved him . . . and he was gone in a matter of seconds.

In addition to being stunned almost speechless by this devastating news, Billy and I were also in anguish (as was the on-location producer in Australia) over being unable to track down Terry, who had taken Bindi and baby Bob with her to Tasmania for a walking tour. Finally, after hours of searching, she was reached with the gut-wrenching news. Soon the world was in mourning.

If ever a company of people was heartbroken, it was Discovery. On that day in the waters off the coast of Australia, the natural world lost its most passionate voice. As the years pass it is only more obvious that we can never, ever replace Steve Irwin. But we can console ourselves by redoubling our efforts to carry on the spirit of his work.

Going Deep

In 2009, I began working with David Zaslav and our programming team on a new series that was designed to further focus our mission of satisfying viewer curiosities. The series would cover a wealth of topics including medicine, space travel, nanotechnology, consciousness, human behavior, and ancient civilizations. No skirting the issue this time; I was going to make manifest what had brought me to this point. That's why I named the series *Curiosity*.

I next enlisted the support of a number of major universities—including Princeton, Syracuse, Georgetown, Maryland, Virginia, and Cornell—to help us identify and define the major questions that each episode would tackle. Intel, Nissan, and the University of Phoenix stepped up as initial sponsors.

In describing the project, the *New York Times* quoted chancellor Nancy Cantor of Syracuse as calling the project "a refreshing development for all of us in higher education." That was gratifying—as was the end of the piece: "Mr. Hendricks said that such programs had value beyond ratings. 'They solidify you emotionally as a brand for your viewers,' he said."

For Discovery, *Curiosity* is the ultimate "deep" production—and it is destined to be a long-running series brand that will define us the way *60 Minutes* did CBS.

From the start, we had no shortage of talented celebrities eager to help the series find its audience: Martin Sheen, Samuel L. Jackson, Robin Williams, Maggie Gyllenhaal, Michelle Rodriguez, Brendan Fraser, Mike Rowe, Adam Savage, Morgan Spurlock, and Eli Roth. Each hosted an episode of the first season of *Curiosity*.

My goal for the future of *Curiosity* is that it will probe such complex subjects as consciousness, artificial intelligence, and nanotechnology. And I hope that, from time to time, we will present something truly sensational—as we are doing, as I write this, in our planned examination of the structural integrity and safety systems of commercial aircraft during crashes.

For this *Curiosity* episode, we actually bought an old Boeing 727, loaded it with HD video cameras, crash dummies, and sensitive G-force measurement equipment, and then crashed it into a remote desert in Mexico. The preparation for this landmark crash, which was controlled by remote controls from a chase plane after the pilots bailed out, is a story in itself. As for the airplane crash— itself a master class in flight dynamics, structural engineering, and human tolerance for G-forces—it is must-see television.

Rethinking Reality

Documentary television and nonfiction entertainment have always been about the real world.

Walter Cronkite, Carl Sagan, Ken Burns, James Burke, David Attenborough, and others have used television to help us better understand the reality of our world and the universe beyond. However, the term *reality television* has come to take on a new meaning during the last two decades. "Reality," it seems, is being redefined.

At Discovery, we first encountered the allure of this new form of reality television when we saw the success of *Changing Rooms* on BBC TV in the late 1990s. Based on the same format—two couples exchange homes for a redecorating project of their choosing—we created *Trading Spaces* in 2000 for TLC.

The series became a runaway hit. Cable had never really seen audience levels like those generated by *Trading Spaces*. Indeed, the entire television industry took note of the success, and ABC became the second to develop a series similar in concept. One of our original carpenters on *Trading Spaces*, Ty Pennington, jumped ship to host a new ABC show, called *Extreme Makeover: Home Edition*.

Even earlier, in 1996, we aired televised coverage of an adventure race called *Eco-Challenge*. With race settings in exotic locations in countries such as Morocco, Argentina, and Australia, this series grew to be a favorite of Discovery viewers, and of industry experts: it won an Emmy Award.

The millions of viewers of *Eco-Challenge* and *Trading Spaces* were telling all of us in television that there was a huge audience for this type of programming: shows that captured the dramatic outcome of novel competitions or the final "reveal" of a contrived situation or predicament. The surprised faces on the victims of a botched decorating job on *Trading Spaces* were the payoff to viewers.

No one realized the opportunity for this new reality television format more than *Eco-Challenge* producer Mark Burnett. Mark quickly went to work on a new series concept that he called *Survivor*. And he offered it to us.

In a decision that is still debated within the halls of Discovery, we declined Mark's invitation—and missed one of the great breakthrough series in television history.

Why did we pass? The short answer is that although *Survivor* was, and still is, a masterful concept in pitting contestants against each other in dramatic situations, the series just seemed a bit too contrived for the real-world brand we'd cultivated for Discovery.

Sure, we were willing to experiment on the TLC brand with invented situations, such as those predicaments in *Trading Spaces*. But *Survivor* was just one bridge too far. Sometimes you just have to defend the brand, even in the face of appealing opportunities—and this was one of those moments.

Looking back, I think we made the right decision—but that doesn't keep me from grinding my teeth a bit whenever I think about it.

Cupcakes

As an example of entrepreneurial passion born of daydreams, I have to tell the story of Georgetown Cupcake. If you have not tasted a cupcake from this establishment, well . . . you just have not lived a complete life.

Georgetown Cupcake was founded in February 2008 by sisters Katherine Kallinis Berman and Sophie Kallinis LaMontagne. Prior to their entrepreneurial venture, these two sisters (still in their twenties) were busy in their separate careers. Katherine was an event planner for Gucci, and Sophie worked in private equity. Yet they shared a daydream that simply would not go away. It was a very persistent daydream about opening a business together, in which they could fully unleash their love of baking.

They had first experienced this passion and joy for baking with their Greek grandmother when they were little girls in Toronto. Their grandmother would let the girls pour leftover cake batter into tiny cake pans, one for Sophie and one for Katherine. The little granddaughters loved to watch as their miniature cakes baked and rose next to the larger one in the oven. It was a love that never died.

Sophie and Katherine listened to their daydreams and, in 2007, they decided to quit their jobs and set out to create the very best cupcakes in the world. Their passion for baking excellence produced a sensation in the Washington, D.C., area. Lines formed outside their first "cupcakery" in Georgetown and, yes, I must admit to personally waiting in line for their creations at their shop in Bethesda, Maryland. I am a victim of two of their flavors, peanut butter fudge and German chocolate.

TLC producers, always on the lookout for inspiring stories with series potential, discovered the sisters. The young women then put their entrepreneurial instincts and phenomenal work ethic on full display in the TLC hit series *DC Cupcakes*. The sisters and their staff bake more than ten thousand cupcakes daily. When I read Malcolm Gladwell's book *Outliers*, in which he attributes success in any field to a devotion of ten thousand hours to practicing the task, I thought not only of Gladwell's examples of Bill Gates and the Beatles, but also of the cupcake sisters.

Real Personalities

On TLC, many viewers first discovered the real-world drama of hospital emergency rooms when we aired *Trauma: Life in the E.R.* The series, produced by New York Times Television, debuted in 1997. *Trauma* was the nonfiction counterpart of popular network shows such as *ER*, then a hit drama series on NBC. Viewers flocked to the series. Actress Jennifer Aniston told Jay Leno on *The Tonight Show* that she had become addicted to reality TV, her favorite being TLC's *Trauma*.

One of television's most engaging personalities is Mike Rowe. His initial work with us was as a narrator/host of 2004's *Egypt Week Live!* Originally from Baltimore, Rowe has done everything from singing professionally with the Baltimore Opera to serving as one of shopping channel QVC's most entertaining hosts. From 2001 to 2005, he hosted *Evening Magazine* on KPIX-TV in San Francisco.

Mike's warm, authentic, and humorous connection with fellow show participants, as well as with the audience, made him the perfect host for *Dirty Jobs*, a series produced for us by Pilgrim Films & Television. *Dirty Jobs* was one of Discovery's most highly rated and successful series, with original episodes airing from 2005 through 2012. Viewers, it seems, could not get enough of watching Mike's relentless attempts to work alongside real-world employees in tasks involving every imaginable hazard, discomfort, and repulsiveness. Not only was the series fun to watch; it offered viewers an inside look at the valued work of unsung blue-collar employees and laborers delivering products and services we can't live without. In my mind, this is "reality TV" at its best—and despite his casual style, Mike took the series very seriously: he's even created a nonprofit foundation to help raise appreciation of America's blue-collar workers.

Rowe is also the narrator of our reality series *Deadliest Catch*, which has come to define authentic reality television. The fascination of witnessing men at work off the coast of Alaska, in one of the world's most challenging and dangerous professions, has made *Deadliest Catch* one of our most successful television series. Viewers connect with the hardworking captains and crew members whose true characters emerge under extraordinary pressure, and keep audiences tuned to each episode.

The brilliant nonfiction television producer Thom Beers created *Deadliest Catch*. His company, Original Productions (now a subsidiary of FremantleMedia), was also responsible for Discovery's earlier hit series *Monster Garage*. *Deadliest Catch*, which debuted in 2005, broke new ground in television as it faithfully chronicled the triumphs and tragedies of men passionately engaged in a hazardous occupation.

The *Deadliest Catch* camera crews take great risks themselves to capture all the action. It is a job that occasionally requires a high degree of sensitivity, particularly in situations where there is an injury or loss of life. Only seldom do our film crews stop filming, but it is necessary when there is an issue of privacy or family respect.

The most difficult period in the history of *Deadliest Catch* came in 2010 during the filming of season six. One the series' most beloved characters, Captain Phil Harris of the *Cornelia Marie*, complained of being excessively tired and, after going to his stateroom for pain medication, he collapsed. When discovered by second-year engineer Steve Ward, Captain Phil had managed to regain consciousness, but his left leg and left arm were paralyzed.

It would soon prove to be a fatal stroke. Yet Captain Phil insisted that his ordeal be filmed. The result was one of the most emotionally shattering segments ever presented on American television. The crew remained with Captain Phil and his sons until the end. I, along with many other viewers I suspect, choked up while watching the end of Captain Phil's final episode. It closed with the mournful Johnny Cash song "Redemption Day." This was real reality television.

I had gotten to know Captain Phil from his visits to New York during our annual promotional event for advertisers. When Discovery Communications became a public company on September 18, 2008, Captain Phil stood beside us on the NASDAQ podium as we rang the opening bell. He was a tough man with a most generous spirit. He had always been so supportive of our efforts to show the world the work he loved.

Controversial Content Choices

I have learned that it is incredibly difficult to explore certain topics without offending some groups, no matter how much sensitivity and care we bring to a production. Religion and politics, which play such enormous roles in our culture, inevitably engender controversy—and even hostility—from some viewers. You only need to scan my emails.

When producing content on controversial topics, we always demand of our filmmakers that they fairly present both sides of a conflict. However, in some instances, a filmmaker will ask to take a particular point of view. In those cases we make that bias known, usually by presenting the documentary as a "personal essay."

Here are some well-known—and controversial—examples of this genre:

From Beirut to Bosnia

In 1993, we undertook the challenge of exploring the roots of the Muslim conflict with the Western world. It was an explosive topic with an equally explosive host: the distinguished British war correspondent Robert Fisk.

From Beirut to Bosnia was a comprehensive, thought-provoking, and revealing three-part documentary series. It aired on the Discovery Channel in the United States and on Channel 4 in the United Kingdom. The representations made then by Fisk about the seeds of Muslim hatred toward the West proved eerily prescient when viewed after the terrorist attacks of September 11, 2001.

However, at the time, certain organized groups that supported Israel and Jewish causes targeted Discovery—as well as me personally—for choosing to air the controversial series. This became the first time our company had experienced the full force of an organized backlash. These well-funded advocacy groups easily mobilized legions of members in protest.

Noting that American Express had been one of our sponsors, both AmEx and Discovery began to receive mail containing American Express credit cards cut in half by angry protesters. A letter I received on June 16, 1994, from Sidney Laibson, president of PRIMER (Promoting Responsibility In Middle East Reporting) was typical of the scolding I received. Laibson wrote: "By airing *From Beirut to Bosnia*, The Discovery Channel has provided the purveyors of insidious propaganda an opportunity to spread their venom into the living rooms of America."

Although *From Beirut to Bosnia* could be considered in balance with many other programs we had aired on the Middle East featuring other perspectives, it was viewed by many in isolation from our other work.

Looking back, I realize that this should have been expected. Taken alone, the series—which focused principally on the grievances of the Muslim world—had indeed been one-sided. Our mistake was in not clearly labeling the series a "personal essay" and by not airing a panel discussion immediately following the program. A good debate forum could have addressed all sides of the contentious issues roiling the Middle East.

We took immediate steps to diffuse the uproar. I flew to New York to personally meet with Abraham Foxman, the national director of the Anti-Defamation League (ADL). Fences began to be mended.

Going forward, we weren't deterred from future "personal essay" documentaries. However, we also knew we had to do a better job in notifying viewers of the potential bias of such programs and by airing follow-up panel discussion shows. We have tried to follow those standards ever since.

The Lost Tomb of Jesus

Given our experience with *From Beirut to Bosnia* and other documentaries, I knew that an intriguing television project brought to us by the Canadian journalist and documentarian Simcha Jacobovici would surely provoke controversy.

Jacobovici had doggedly pursued an archaeological discovery made at Talpiot in the suburbs of Jerusalem. There, an ancient tomb, now known as the Talpiot Tomb, had been first unearthed in 1980. The tomb initially contained ten burial ossuaries dating back to the first century A.D. One of the burial ossuaries was missing, and so just nine were available to be examined by Simcha and his team of scientists and historians.

Based on those results, Jacobovici decided to tell the world in the form of a documentary. James Cameron, the famed filmmaker and an ardent supporter of the project, agreed to serve as executive producer.

The ossuaries, carved limestone boxes, originally contained the bones of the dead. After the initial excavation, the ossuaries were stored in a warehouse—where they remained until Simcha's reexamination of the inscriptions that were carved into the exterior sides. These inscriptions had been previously ignored and given little significance. A number of the ossuaries bore inscriptions with the same or similar names of the known family members of Jesus of Nazareth. One particular ossuary had the inscription "Yeshua bar Yehosef," which in Aramaic translates to "Jesus son of Joseph."

Although most of the inscribed names on the ossuaries were common in ancient Jerusalem, the familial relationships were not so common. The tomb even contained an ossuary written in Aramaic script bearing the name of "Maria," a Latin form of the Hebrew name "Miriam" or "Mary." Another had been inscribed with "Yose," a diminutive form of "Joseph." This name appeared in its Greek form, "Joses," in the gospel of Mark as the identity of one of the brothers of Jesus.

The tomb also contained the burial ossuary of what appeared to be another Mary, which was inscribed as "Mariamene e Mara," which in Greek could be interpreted as "Mary known as the master." Could this be Mary of Magdalene?

Based on this evidence, Jacobovici and his researchers wondered if the missing tenth box could be the "James Ossuary." The James Ossuary—which contained an Aramaic inscription that translated into English as "James, son of Joseph, brother of Jesus"—was in the possession of antiquities dealer Oded Golan. Golan claimed he was unaware of the meaning of the inscription until an expert epigrapher, André Lemaire, first made the translation while visiting Golan's apartment.

The existence of this James Ossuary was first announced at a press conference held by the Biblical Archaeology Society and the Discovery Channel in October 2002. A month later, *Biblical Archaeology Review* published an article on the find. And, in 2003, Discovery Channel aired the Cameron/Jacobovici documentary.

Although scholars were deeply divided on the interpretation of the archaeological findings in the Talpiot Tomb, we decided to air the film.

It wasn't a casual decision. We knew the team had used advanced chemical and DNA analysis, historical research, and various studies and interpretations by a number of experts. Most intriguing, they included an analysis of the mathematical odds of there being two or more families in first-century Jerusalem with the same names and family relationships as the ossuary inscriptions—odds that, depending on certain assumptions (that is, that one of the two Marys was a mother of others in the tomb), ranged from 600–1 to 1,000,000–1 in favor of it being authentic.

Given our experience with *From Beirut to Bosnia*, we were careful to add multiple on-air graphics to *The Lost Tomb of Jesus* to explain there was no consensus of expert opinions on the conclusions and interpretations presented in the film. Additionally, to provide a voice for experts who disagreed with Jacobovici's interpretations, we immediately aired a follow-up panel discussion.

Thus, after the film's premiere on March 4, 2007, Ted Koppel moderated an independently produced, hour-long panel dialogue with relevant experts called *The Lost Tomb of Jesus: A Critical Look*.

It proved a lively forum in which Koppel vigorously explored alternative opinions and beliefs about the Talpiot Tomb. One of the most fervent opponents of Jacobovici's work was Jonathan L. Reed, professor of religion at the University of La Verne, in California. Reed actually called the film "archaeo-porn" during the telecast. He certainly had his say—as did the others.

Sadly, our efforts to present strong counterarguments to the assumptions and interpretations of *The Lost Tomb of Jesus* did not stem an enormous backlash against Discovery from organized Christian groups. The film had obviously touched a nerve—especially in its suggestion that there might have existed earthly remains of Jesus. Although many progressive Christians believed strongly in a "spiritual" resurrection of Jesus and were comfortable with the thought of bodily remains, those Christians adhering to a strictly literal interpretation of the New Testament were deeply offended by *The Lost Tomb of Jesus*.

One fundamentalist organization that got involved in the controversy had a successful history of generating mass emails from its membership. And it took square aim at my email account. Although each of the emails contained the same message of protest, the sheer volume from several hundred thousand of their members crashed my Discovery email account.

Even stronger messages came my way. Anonymous phone calls and random emails sent to me from a handful of individuals contained language similar to that used before the murders of abortion clinic personnel. We took no chances; Discovery assigned twenty-four-hour security to my residence and my family until the furor subsided.

Oded Golan certainly did not escape reprisals. Following a significant effort by the Israeli Antiquities Authority to discredit the ancient artifact, Golan was formally charged in Israel in December 2004 with forgery of the inscription on the James Ossuary. After an investigation and a trial lasting for years, Golan was acquitted of all forgery charges in a verdict delivered in March 2012.

A month after the Oded Golan forgery acquittal, Discovery Channel aired a follow-up documentary film that captured Simcha Jacobovici's work in exploring an adjacent tomb at Talpiot. Simcha suspected that this tomb belonged to Joseph of Arimathea, a prominent individual referenced in the New Testament as having offered a temporary burial site for Jesus's body. The adjacent tomb, located under an apartment building, could be explored only through robotic HD camera systems.

The cameras revealed an ossuary bearing what James Tabor and others interpreted to be an image of Jonah and the Whale. This could have been an early Christian symbol of resurrection—one that eventually evolved into the well-known Christian fish. Curiously, even though this 2012 film contained potentially new evidence about the Talpiot Tomb complex and the family of Jesus, it did not provoke the outcry of five years before.

Jon & Kate Plus 8

Most of us parents know it's a challenge to raise just two or three children—endlessly coping with schedules of sports, dance classes, and countless other activities, not to mention the drama of the occasional mischievous behavior.

So when movies or television shows—*The Sound of Music*, *The Brady Bunch*, *Cheaper by the Dozen*—portray families with six, eight, or a dozen or more kids, we're riveted watching how these parents can possibly deal with such chaos.

So, it's not surprising that, as the Age of Reality Shows evolved, one of our executives set out to explore the fascination that viewers have with large families.

Eileen O'Neill first joined Discovery in 1990 as an unpaid intern while earning a graduate degree in popular culture from Bowling Green State University. Given her talents and her extreme work ethic, Eileen moved quickly through the ranks at Discovery, until, by 2005, she was managing the Discovery Health Channel.

In 2006, Eileen began experimenting with programming that featured what she calls "supersized families." On the Health Channel, Eileen introduced the world to Jim Bob and Michelle Duggar, whose family would ultimately grow to include nineteen children. The Duggars were first chronicled in specials on Discovery Health and later in a long-running successful series on TLC.

On May 14, 2006, Eileen aired a Discovery Health special titled *Surviving Sextuplets and Twins*, featuring the Pennsylvania family of Jon and Kate Gosselin. The Gosselins had eight children, consisting of fraternal twins (both girls) and sextuplets (three boys and three girls). The special garnered impressive viewership and the following year Discovery Health presented *Sextuplets and Twins: One Year Later*, a one-hour special that also rated well.

Based on the success of these two specials, Eileen commissioned the development, from Figure 8 Films, of a television series called *Jon & Kate Plus 8*. The television series launched on Discovery Health in 2007 but, given its popularity, *Jon & Kate Plus 8* moved in 2008 to our larger network TLC. Additionally, Eileen O'Neill advanced to become TLC's president and general manager that same year, so she was in a great position to shepherd the show to success.

Soon, viewers by the millions were drawn to *Jon & Kate Plus 8*. Audiences were mesmerized by the family's daily life and challenges. Although it appeared to viewers that camera crews actually lived with the Gosselins, taping sessions occurred only a few days each week, and just a few hours per session, so as not to put too great an imposition on the family.

Both Jon and Kate considered the media experience and associated field trips (and interesting people that the Gosselin children met) to be an overall enriching experience. The income earned from the television series also meant that college might one day be a possibility for all eight children.

Even though half of all marriages end in divorce, American audiences—and we at Discovery—were still stunned by the breakdown of Jon and Kate Gosselin's relationship.

On May 13, 2009, *People* alerted the news media and its online readers of its upcoming cover story about the marriage crisis:

> She's embroiled in a public scandal linking her husband, Jon Gosselin, to another woman, and Kate Gosselin tells PEOPLE in its latest cover story that she and her spouse have been privately struggling for months. . . .
>
> For the complete story on Kate and Jon—including how they're weathering the scandal and what their eight children think—pick up the new issue of PEOPLE, on newsstands Friday.

And so the very public saga of Jon and Kate and the breakup of their marriage began—and, thanks to cover stories in *People* and *US Weekly*, continued for months.

This led to a lot of soul-searching at *Discovery*. What were our responsibilities as the media company airing a popular and charming family reality series that had unexpectedly turned into the story of a divorce? Should we continue to air the series or should we suspend production?

All through May 2009, Eileen O'Neill regularly met with David Zaslav and me to update us about developments in the Gosselin marriage, the controversy in the press, and the welfare of the eight

Gosselin children. David and I supported Eileen's recommendation that we strictly follow the wishes of the parents so long as both of them were in agreement.

After Jon and Kate announced that they would be divorcing, we announced that the show would be in hiatus for more than a month to give the family time to regroup.

At the end of this hiatus, Jon and Kate Gosselin told us they wanted the taping sessions and episodes to continue.

Mindful that their children would someday view the episodes, Jon and Kate wanted to be very measured in their on-air appearances. For example, the couple's joint couch interviews had become a staple of each episode. Now all future couch interviews would be conducted with Jon and Kate individually.

As we proceeded with the series, these poignant interviews with real individuals involved in a real marriage crisis became must-see television for millions of people. Whether viewers were drawn by the well-publicized sensational aspects of the story or by the chance to learn something new about human relationships, the series continued to achieve historically high ratings records for cable. The highly anticipated fifth-season premiere of *Jon & Kate Plus 8* was seen by a record 9.8 million viewers, making it the most-watched show of that evening, including those on broadcast television.

As the Gosselins' family drama unfolded, many viewers and critics began to question the appropriateness of television that seemed to intrude into, and even perhaps influence, the private lives of a family in crisis.

Matters began to heat up considerably when Kate Gosselin's brother and sister-in-law, Kevin and Jodi Kreider, appeared on CBS's *Early Show* to claim that the series exploited their nieces and nephews. Gloria Allred, the well-known celebrity lawyer, accompanied the Kreiders on the CBS show to advocate for new federal laws and regulations to protect children and child performers on reality television.

Inside Discovery, we, of course, had direct knowledge of the tightly controlled taping sessions. We were satisfied that the children's interests were being protected, and yet we continued to closely monitor all aspects of the production as well as the deteriorating relationship between Jon and Kate.

The situation came to a head when the inevitable lawsuits were filed. At the same time, a contractual dispute arose between TLC and Jon Gosselin. We suspended production indefinitely when, during this period of litigation, Jon Gosselin indicated that he was no longer in favor of his children being taped. Kate, meanwhile, remained very supportive of the series and its economic benefits for her children.

Eileen developed a successor series for TLC entitled *Kate Plus 8*. It debuted in June 2010 and featured Kate as a divorced mom raising eight children. It ran for two seasons, ending in September 2011—bringing the total to 150 aired episodes of the original series and its successor.

There is no script for reality television and for networks like ours. *Jon & Kate Plus 8* taught us that Discovery must be poised to act responsibly when the unexpected happens. We did our best to manage our way through a difficult situation by steadfastly sticking to our guiding principle of following parental desires. We independently assessed the tight constraints on taping sessions that protectively limited the children's exposure to television production. We knew that we were a company that had to continually break new ground in television, but also that we had to act responsibly in delivering the provocative television that our viewers demanded. It also became clear during the Jon and Kate controversy that in order to protect the Discovery brand we would henceforth use TLC as our vehicle for taking controversial programming risks.

It didn't take long before just such a project walked through the door.

Sarah Palin's Alaska

Sarah Palin, the feisty former governor of Alaska, became a media sensation during her unsuccessful 2008 bid to become vice president of the United States. By 2010, opinions about Sarah Palin had divided along America's deeply partisan political lines. She was celebrated by conservatives and mocked by liberals. Americans, it seemed, either loved or hated Sarah Palin.

At Discovery, we knew we would risk alienating half of our viewers if we featured a show or series involving Sarah Palin. But the temptation of working with one of America's most talked about celebrities was just too strong. Many media outlets and producers tried, but it was the nation's most successful reality television producer, Mark Burnett, who at last scored Sarah Palin for a new series.

After securing Sarah Palin's commitment to host a travelogue series about Alaska, Mark immediately contacted Clark Bunting to see if Discovery Channel would take the project. Realizing the potential political controversy such a series could set off, Clark scheduled a meeting with David and me to get our thoughts.

By the end of the meeting, David and I concluded that we should not associate the Discovery Channel brand with the project. However, we also agreed it was still an interesting project worth pursuing. Eileen O'Neill, already up to speed on the project, eagerly embraced the opportunity for TLC.

Since this project would surely get a lot of press attention, we didn't want any of our board members surprised. David and I quickly scheduled a board conference call and they concurred with our judgment that we proceed with the series. As expected, our board members were supportive but, like David and me, they were apprehensive. All agreed with David and me that TLC would clearly be the best home for the series, not Discovery.

We reached an agreement with Mark Burnett in May 2010 and then raced to film the series during the warm summer months in preparation for a November premiere.

Sarah Palin's Alaska proved to be a remarkable production effort by a first-rate team that had to cope with the challenges of Alaska's rugged terrain and unpredictable weather. Palin and her entire family were fully supportive and engaged in the project.

There were many remarkable moments in the series. In one instance, the film crew captured an authentically frightened Sarah in a scary cliff climb. The cameras also recorded the family's candid and humorous moments as Palin persisted in keeping her teenage daughter's boyfriend safely downstairs and away from the bedrooms upstairs. Sarah also went on a caribou hunt with her father—and the crew caught her initial awkwardness with the rifle before she finally delivered a fatal shot.

In clearly the series' most contrived situation, Kate Gosselin and her eight children arrived in dismal, rainy weather to participate in the Palins' camping adventure. Kate's misery in the new environment and Sarah's annoyance at the concocted situation were clear to viewers. Although the insertion of the Gosselin family had been a dumb idea, at least this was honest television that didn't attempt to disguise the real reactions to an ill-conceived situation.

Even considering its shortcomings, I think the eight-episode series did a good job in introducing viewers to the magnificent scenic and wildlife wonders of Alaska. And Palin, the state's former governor, proved to be a remarkably unpretentious guide, unafraid to open up her private life, or to show her failings. The chief television critic for the *New York Times*, Alessandra Stanley, under the headline How's That Outdoorsy Stuff Working for Ya?, wrote:

> . . . to her credit, the governor who quit the job with more than a year left to her term doesn't use the camera crew to recast her image or pad gaps in her résumé. She doesn't pore over position papers in a book-lined study, phone foreign leaders or even watch *Jeopardy*. . . . The TLC program highlights her physical bravery, but the series' existence points to a different kind of courage: Ms. Palin is not afraid to be herself.

Even though television critics were generally complimentary about this unique reality television project, those with political axes to grind were horrified that we aired *Sarah Palin's Alaska*. Emails and letters poured in denouncing our decision to give airtime to an individual whom they considered an enemy of the environment. One viewer wrote, Sarah Palin is "a figure linked to many horrifying stories of cruelty to animals and ridiculous hunting practices."

In addition to objections we heard based on environmental concerns, others complained that we were unfairly and unwisely providing airtime to a potential 2012 presidential candidate.

Although we don't plan to shy away from politics in our future projects, we will continue to be mindful to always exclude political posturing and commentary from such content. This was not an issue in *Sarah Palin's Alaska* as Palin herself completely eliminated all politics from her commentary.

Still, it is a close call to provide television exposure to anyone with political ambitions. And when confronted with a future opportunity touching on politics, I'm sure we'll be just as nervous as when we were first offered *Sarah Palin's Alaska*.

Curiosity Episode One: Did God Create the Universe?

What would be the premiere episode of our flagship new series *Curiosity?*

Eileen O'Neill suggested we lead with an episode that addressed perhaps the most profound question of humanity: *Did God create the universe?* This would surely be a highly controversial topic made more so because our presenter for this topic would be one of the world's most preeminent scientists, Stephen Hawking.

I agreed, but I also knew that the choice of Hawking would be controversial. He had argued in his book *The Grand Design* that invoking God isn't necessary to explain the origins of the universe. Hawking contended that the Big Bang is a consequence of the laws of physics and nothing more.

His explanation wasn't simple: you have to read his book or watch our premiere *Curiosity* episode to understand the physics underlying Hawking's conclusion, which is that the universe could have spontaneously arisen from probabilistic quantum fluctuations acting to bring the negative energy of empty space—"nothingness"—into balance.

It had now been eighteen years since we learned from our mistake, with *From Beirut to Bosnia*, of not airing a concurrent forum. We would not make the same mistake with *Curiosity*.

We recruited David Gregory, the host of NBC's *Meet the Press*, to lead a post-episode panel. The panelists included two physicists, Sean Carroll from the California Institute of Technology and Paul Davies from Arizona State University, along with Roman Catholic theologian John Haught from Georgetown University. The forum also included additional video commentary from Jennifer Wiseman, NASA astrophysicist; William Stoeger, Jesuit physicist at the Vatican Observatory; and Michio Kaku, theoretical physicist at the City University of New York.

Gregory led the panel through a vigorous debate on the existence of God as First Mover. Most memorably, Kaku stated that Hawking's conclusion exceeded current evidence and predicted that, because God is a subject not answerable by science, people will still be debating the existence of God a thousand years hence.

Although we received a few letters from viewers who took us to task for blasphemy, there wasn't the outrage we'd experienced in the past. The panel discussion had done its task of enabling viewers to see their own thoughts expressed in a respectful manner. And Discovery showed it had learned a lot about making difficult choices in producing mindful television for the planet—most of all, to respect the intelligence and opinions of our viewers.

Hostage Crisis: Madman in the Lobby

When you start a company, you dream of one day seeing a glass office tower bearing that company's name. What you never imagine is an armed suicide bomber holding hostages in the lobby of that building.

I spent Wednesday morning, September 1, 2010, in my office reviewing the potential topics for the first season of *Curiosity*, the premiere episode of which was a year away. At 1:00 p.m., I was scheduled to videotape a message for supporters of the National Forest Foundation, a nonprofit organization that I chair.

A few minutes before the taping session, I walked down the hall from my tenth-floor office to our boardroom and the waiting camera crew. A minute after the taping began, we had to suspend recording due to a loud police siren just outside our building. It was quickly joined by other sirens.

At that moment, two executive assistants, Anne Gordon and Caroline LaMotte, entered the boardroom with Michelle Russo, our senior vice president of corporate communications. Security personnel had alerted them to the presence of a man in the lobby with bombs strapped to his body and brandishing a pistol. A shot had been fired and it was feared that hostages might have been taken.

The unimaginable had arrived.

I quickly ended the taping, gathered the staff around me, then ushered them down to my corner office. In accordance with our well-rehearsed emergency procedures, we locked the doors and awaited further instructions from our facility and security teams.

Within minutes, the security team activated the building's public address system. All 1,400-plus employees in the building were instructed to go into "lockdown."

Those employees who had children enrolled in our on-site daycare center faced the most grueling anxiety. The center was located on the same floor as the lobby, but on the opposite end of the L-shape building footprint. Thus, they were about one hundred yards away from where the perpetrator had entered.

For an agonizing twenty minutes, all of us waited in our offices. Many watched the unfolding news story on CNN, Fox, MSNBC, and local affiliates. And the news only got worse: there were now reports that a second gunman, this one armed with an automatic rifle, had entered the building.

We learned only later that this second armed "gunman" was in fact an off-duty policeman, Edward E. Paden Jr. Officer Paden happened to be passing by our building coming from a local gym at the very moment when the first urgent police radio call was made. He immediately ran into the building and took up position in a small telecom closet that opened into the lobby. (For his valor that day, Officer Paden was awarded the first Congressional Badge of Bravery, America's highest domestic award for bravery.)

At almost the same moment, our brave and quick-thinking lobby security guard Tom Fischer, recently hired after completing a tour in Iraq, smartly pushed a secure button to lock the doors separating the lobby from the rest of the building. Now no one could get in or out. Tom and two other TLC employees were soon taken hostage by the bomber.

As the situation became clearer and after massive police reinforcements arrived, our HR and Building Operations team led an orderly evacuation of our building—beginning with the precious occupants of the Discovery daycare center. International news footage captured what became the iconic photo of the whole ordeal: it showed toddlers in cribs being rolled across Colesville Road to the safety of a McDonald's that had been set up as a safe haven and parent reunion point.

On the tenth floor, my team was safely evacuated about thirty-five minutes after the situation began. When I reached the ground level, I was whisked off in an armored vehicle to a police command center bus that had been set up about a block away. There, coordinating and conducting the law enforcement and emergency response, were first responders from Montgomery County, the state of Maryland, and agents from the FBI. Outside, SWAT teams began assembling for an assault.

Having been immediately alerted to the hostage situation, David Zaslav, our president and CEO, was already en route back to Silver Spring from his meetings in New York. He was able to constantly monitor and supervise the successful evacuation process with the help of key employees onsite, including Larry Laque (head of facilities), Patrick Hawk (head of corporate security), Adria Alpert-Romm (head of HR), and David Leavy (head of communications and public affairs).

Over the next four hours, law enforcement officers repeatedly attempted to negotiate with the perpetrator for the safe release of the three employee hostages, but to no avail. At about 5:00 p.m., an officer came to inform me that the situation was coming to a head as the individual was becoming increasingly belligerent and had remarked that he "placed no value at all on the lives of the hostages."

Inside the building, the employee hostages could sense the rapidly deteriorating situation. Together—using hand and eye signals—they decided to make a run for the front lobby exit door while the man with the bombs strapped to his body was distracted looking outside. As they made their dash, the perpetrator suddenly wheeled around and aimed his pistol at the fleeing figures.

Unknown to the hostage-taker, a live video stream from our lobby security cameras was being monitored by a police SWAT team that had joined Officer Paden in the lobby telecom room.

The instant the perpetrator turned with pistol drawn, the SWAT team stormed through the rear door to the lobby and took the perpetrator down in a hail of gunfire. None of the hostages were hurt.

It was soon discovered that the perpetrator had been holding a "dead's man trigger" apparently attached to his home-crafted bombs, including propane tanks. Smelling the propane—and realizing that it signaled a gas leak—the SWAT team quickly confirmed the individual's death, then prudently retreated from the lobby.

For the next twelve hours, well into the night, robots carefully removed each bomb device—four in all—from the body of the dead man. The robots transported each bomb outside to a disposal canister where it was safely detonated. By the early morning of September 2, the lobby was safe for entry by detectives and the forensic team. The body was removed by 8:00 a.m.

The perpetrator of this shocking act turned out to be a very disturbed and delusional individual. His obsessive and anti-human beliefs included his advocacy for the sterilization of all humans and a ban on future babies. Apparently frustrated at the failure of mankind to listen to him, the man decided to commit a public act of terror at a media company to get maximum publicity.

This was not an experience one gets over easily. Our organization had been touched once before by terror. On 9/11 we lost a cherished employee aboard United Flight 93 (her story is relayed in chapter 29). Almost nine years after that horrific day, terror had again visited our company. This time it actually entered our headquarters and threatened the lives of our employees and many of their children.

I could not be more proud of the Discovery family for how it responded to such adversity. From the professionalism and emergency training of our personnel to the cool heads of the hostages, and through the bravery and skill of law enforcement officers, our company experienced no loss of life or injury to our employees that September day.

Remarkably, and in true Discovery fashion, there has been a lot to learn and a lot of positive that came out of this terrible situation. Our experience that day has become a case study used by professionals to teach emergency preparedness. The Discovery hostage crisis event offers valuable lessons in good business planning, building a cohesive organization, and communicating clearly and regularly the importance of emergency training.

The FBI has observed that the Discovery hostage event is the only suicide-bombing incident in history where the only loss of life was suffered by the perpetrator. If the bombs had gone off, the FBI estimated that the devices, given the propane tanks, would have created a four-story-tall plume of flame. The attack had been timed for our busy lunch hour. We got lucky.

David Zaslav and I are convinced that we emerged from the hostage event even stronger as a company. In the most remarkable scene, the very next workday employees began streaming in to work right on time. They included many parents who brought their children right back to the daycare center. The strength and resilience of the Discovery family was on shiny display that day. We were stronger than ever.

David and I tried to greet each employee as they arrived that morning, and we discussed the events of the previous day in an all-employee meeting before the workday started. The sheer sense of determination, common purpose, and loyalty to one another was palpable in that gathering.

When the meeting was over, we went right back to work on our peaceful pursuit of sharing knowledge and entertainment with the planet.

Chapter 23

Brand Guard

Character is like a tree and reputation like a shadow. The shadow is what we think of it; the tree is the real thing.

—ABRAHAM LINCOLN

When the idea of the Discovery Channel came to me in the spring of 1982, I had a clear vision for what I wanted the network to be. And on that plane flight, when I decided on the name "Discovery," that vision became even clearer as a *brand:* viewers would *discover* the past through history programs, *discover* the future through science and technology programs, and *discover* the world through nature and cultural programs.

After picking the brand, we needed a memorable logo—one that would enhance the Discovery message. I decided, from a visual perspective, to wed the typography with a globe. That image would convey that the Discovery Channel would help viewers explore their world.

The globe has been with us ever since. Through the years, every time we've hired a new marketing director or creative head, they want to change the logo. I'll bet that throughout Coca-Cola's history there have been scores of attempts to change the iconic script logo that we all know. Happily, the leadership of Coca-Cola has always resisted. And that's what I've tried to do at Discovery—keep our logo as consistent as our commitment to our brand promise in programming.

Staying on brand is particularly challenging for the cable industry. The broadcast networks are wide-ranging, entertainment brands not connected to viewers through a particular content promise. By comparison, cable networks do not appeal to the lowest common denominator. Whether it is Fox News, CNN, ESPN, or Discovery, we know that we are never going to appeal to the majority of television viewers. Rather, we have to fulfill our audiences' expectations.

Consider the Science Channel. As I learned all of those years ago, this channel is never going to appeal to more than 25 percent of television viewers, the information seekers. That means, over the course of a month, that of the 80 million households who receive Science perhaps 20 million will actually tune in. You can see that as bad news, but for me it is a positive: most companies can only dream about their product being useful to 25 percent of the entire population.

Like other cable networks, we have established our presence in the consumer mind through powerful brands. Consequently, consumers are loyal and dedicated to their cable channels in a way they are not to broadcast networks. They come back to cable because of the promise we have made about what they can expect—our *consistency*.

The temptation, always, is to drift from the core promise to chase a larger potential audience. But when you stray off brand, you may gain some new viewers, but they will not be the ones who are really attracted to your core programming. We've experienced it at Discovery, and I have seen it elsewhere: when a cable network drifts off brand, it may enjoy a short-term ratings bump—but then the numbers shrink again because the core audience has been driven away.

Once you are not predictable anymore, not true to your brand promise, your core audience tunes out. This was true in the world of fifty channels, and it is even truer in the world of five hundred channels. It will be absolutely crucial to stick to brand promises as we embark on the next phase in television's evolution.

Today, we are in a period of transition. Over the next couple of decades, the way we consume content will change. The current world of numerical channel surfing will evolve into menus of content. And it will be the predictable, quality brands that stand out and prosper on the menus.

As new platforms and delivery technologies emerge, we especially want to ensure that people seek out and trust the Discovery brand. We intend to remain a place where consumers can consistently find and enjoy quality content, no matter how they are viewing it.

Brand goes to the heart of the issues we face today in a world with Amazon, Apple, Google, Netflix, and whatever is coming next. As content owners, we certainly want the money that these new distribution channels promise. However, as we take advantage of these opportunities, we must never sacrifice long-term sustainability for short-term gain. It is a fatal attraction that's hard to resist in our fast-moving marketplace.

Since we first launched the Discovery Channel, I have consistently reminded our employees about the importance of *not* defining our service as a cable network. Rather, we are in the business of helping consumers explore their world and satisfy their curiosity. As we move to new distribution platforms and screens, it will be more important than ever that this philosophy is preserved. Otherwise, we will lose the connection we have worked so hard to establish with our audience. If we ever allow ourselves to become just a commodity, the vision that created Discovery will die.

Chapter 24

Enduring Company

If the highest aim of a captain were to preserve his ship, he would keep it in port forever.

—Thomas Aquinas

I believe that every entrepreneur dreams of building a lasting company, one that endures far into the future. However, given robust competition within a healthy free enterprise system, this is a challenge.

Although many companies are around long after their founders pass on—Ford Motor Company, Wal-Mart, General Electric—many others fail within a founder's lifetime. There are many reasons why certain companies fail to endure. Often it results from management's failure to recognize and adapt to a changing market environment. Sometimes businesses go under because of a systemic failure by company leaders to continually undertake bold but intelligent risks. In the end, business failure and business success are simply determined by the people in charge.

Company founders are passionate about the enterprises they create. Entrepreneurs are justifiably proud to have brought something new into the world. Nevertheless, this pride of authorship of a new business creation sometimes proves to be its ultimate undoing.

As I've explored in this book (and describe at length in appendix 1), entrepreneurs possess skill sets and emotional traits that are different than others. Although vital to the creation of a new business, the obsessive nature of an entrepreneur can nevertheless impede the development of good management processes and practices that facilitate long-term business sustainability. I have watched numerous entrepreneurs build a business with admirable zeal and fervor only to lose it because they could not transition the venture to a stable enterprise that takes maximum advantage of all human talents within the organization.

Entrepreneurs love every aspect of their creations but they simply cannot hang on too long to their micromanagement of operations. This is the fatal flaw of many entrepreneurs. The intense passion and single-minded obsession that was so necessary to overcome all the doubters standing in the way of a new business creation can prove deadly within a large organization searching to develop efficient operational systems that depend on disciplined analysis rather than wild-eyed optimism. The trick is to find a balance between the bold, optimistic risk taking of an entrepreneur and the intelligent management of resources by experienced business executives.

Entrepreneurs have to be very self-critical if they are lucky enough to find that their business creations are poised to become global corporations having thousands of employees and valuable product brands to grow and protect. A successful entrepreneur, more than anything else, needs an operational partner who has the skill sets and training to manage a large, complex organization that has grown far beyond the start-up phase.

The ideal partner for an entrepreneur is an individual who deeply shares the passion and purpose of the entrepreneurial brand but also brings something more to the table: an intense drive to achieve growth through discipline and intelligent risk taking.

Entrepreneurs, myself included, are somewhat "creation addicted." And because of our success in witnessing our dream come to life, we are often overly confident or optimistic in the potential market response to our next big idea. Entrepreneurs are guided by emotion—which is valuable, to be sure—but business sustainability and growth require that emotion be tempered by rigorous and thoughtful analysis. Again, it is a matter of balance—and, in my opinion, no entrepreneur can successfully embody both the "passion" and the "discipline" required to create an enduring company.

I am one of the lucky ones. I am an entrepreneur who understood that the skill sets and emotional traits that created my business are not the same ones that can grow and sustain a large, complex corporation. I needed a partner.

The Partner

In 1987, I met an extremely smart and energetic young lawyer who had been assigned by our outside counsel to help us on the daunting volume of programming and distribution contracts that our business had been generating. His name was David Zaslav. He worked for the New York law firm of LeBoeuf, Lamb, Leiby & MacRae under Richard Berman, lead counsel for Discovery.

David quickly found strategic solutions to our distribution and content challenges. I was impressed with both his enthusiasm and his intelligent insights. As I worked with David in 1987, I could easily see that he was becoming more and more attracted to our industry. David subsequently decided to leave his law firm and landed a job with Bob Wright at NBC. As I fully expected, David soared through the ranks at NBC and, by 2006, he was President of Domestic TV and New Media Distribution for NBC Universal.

While he was at NBC, David and I served together on the

board of directors of TiVo, the company that brought digital video recording to the world. My experience with him in the TiVo boardroom confirmed for me that David Zaslav was the most talented television executive in the industry. When Judith McHale resigned her post in 2006, I could not rest until David joined Discovery as president and chief executive officer. David is a remarkable leader. He has transformed the growth trajectory of our company with his passion, intelligence, and curiosity. He is the partner I needed.

Balance

When David Zaslav arrived in January 2007, he inherited a management team that contained several individuals with enormous talent and experience who would be part of his operational plan to build a thriving, growing global media giant. These executives included Mark Hollinger (international), Bill Goodwyn (education and distribution), Joe Abruzzese (advertising sales), Eileen O'Neill (programming), and David Leavy (communications and marketing).

To this existing pool of talent, David sought out the brightest leaders that could be found to round out a management team capable of achieving company growth long into the future. These new additions to our senior management team include: Bruce Campbell (legal and new business development), Andy Warren (finance), J. B. Perrette (digital media), and Adria Alpert Romm (human resources).

Endurance for a company is tied to the quality of people who are tasked to anticipate every market change and to respond accordingly. A "forever" company must stay true to its founding mission and purpose, but it must also intelligently adapt and take bold but smart risks. Although a company must be driven by the emotion of "cause," it must also be sustained by thoughtful analysis and discipline. The company must have balance. In the company of people we call Discovery, I think we have achieved this nimble balance.

Going Public

Throughout 2007 and the first half of 2008, David and the new management team got our organization prepared to become a fully public company. This is a big step for a company and involves an enormous investment in resources to transform a private entity into one that is fully compliant with all the rules and regulations of the U.S. Securities and Exchange Commission. Although Discovery as a private company had always been fully transparent in its financial reporting, the task was not burdensome as we had only three shareholders (Liberty Media, Newhouse, and Cox) in addition to myself for the greater part of our two-decade corporate history.

We had long resisted going public, and for good reason. In addition to the extraordinary new legal and accounting investments that we would have to make to remain compliant with government regulations in the wake of the Sarbanes-Oxley Act of 2002, the pressure on a public company to perform to meet short-term, quarterly earnings targets seemed anathema to our ownership group, myself included. We had built Discovery into a global media force over two decades by constantly reinvesting our ever-growing cash flow back into the company, which enabled us to expand internationally and produce better and better content. Never once did we pay a dividend to shareholders or make any decision based on a quarterly profit-and-loss projection. We sacrificed short-term cash rewards for the sake of investing for the long term. Since the time that the cable operator investors joined my cause in 1986, our vision was to grow Discovery to be as big and as influential on the world media stage as it possibly could be.

However, after two decades of strong organic growth around the world as a private company, we believed that going public could further accelerate our global expansion. For example, if we were a public company with marketable securities, we could make large strategic acquisitions utilizing our own stock for payment, rather than the cash we were investing back into our core business. Because of the strong financial record that we had achieved by the end of 2007, we had access to abundant cash through private debt facilities with many leading financial institutions. Becoming a public company would give us even more capital-raising flexibility.

Also, by 2007, our private shareholding structure had become a bit unusual in corporate America. We were a private company, to be sure, but our largest shareholding was held in a public company created by John Malone's Liberty Media for the specific purpose of tracking Discovery's increasing value. The public entity was called Discovery Holding Company, and the equity vehicle acted much like a tracking stock for the fortunes of Discovery Communications, a private company. Since we were privately held, Discovery was not obligated to issue detailed financial reports but it became increasingly awkward to not do so since many members of the public were buying shares in Discovery Holding Company. So, in order to better streamline the shareholding structure as well as to take advantage of stock payment options in future transactions, our Discovery shareholder group decided, in 2007, to take Discovery public. It would involve massive corporate transitions that would take until September 2008 to accomplish.

Nearly a year later, in the summer of 2008, after all the SEC registration filings were in order and the company's management was poised to operate and issue financial reports in full compliance with all regulatory requirements, September 18, 2008, was set as our target date for going public on the NASDAQ exchange. In our public registration statement, we described how we were creating three classes of stock: Class A (DISCA) that would have one vote per share; a preferred Class B (DISCB) that would have ten votes per share; and a Class C (DISCK) that would be nonvoting. Class C shares would be an ideal class of shares to issue as part of the payment for an acquired future asset as it would not affect corporate governance.

In what could be considered an unusual public registration, Discovery would not be issuing new shares to raise capital as we transformed into a public company. We were not a new company desperate for the cash that a typical Initial Public Offering (IPO) would raise. Little did we know that for all the planning, and for all our patience the past twenty-five years, we were about to go public during one of the worst financial crises in the country's history.

Monday, September 15, 2008, was three days before we were going public and the slow drip of Wall Street's exposure to toxic debt had become a full-blown tidal wave as Lehman Brothers filed for Chapter 11 and the Dow Jones closed down over 500 points, the largest single-day drop since September 11, 2001.

The markets continued to look very choppy, but the Federal Reserve Board announced an $85 billion rescue package for troubled insurer AIG on Wednesday, September 17. Although we knew this was not an ideal time to go public, we decided to forge ahead the next day. The thinking was pretty simple: because we were not raising cash through the initial public registration of our stock, our bankers and finance team were less concerned about the vagaries of the daily markets as we were the quintessential long-term-growth play. There really was no need to postpone our first day of trading as a public company.

It was a beautiful fall morning on September 18, 2008. David and I gathered with our senior management team at the NASDAQ exchange located right on Times Square for the ceremonial ringing of the bell (since NASDAQ is an electronic exchange there is actually no bell to ring, just writing your signature digitally on their board).

Despite the financial clouds, the mood was festive and upbeat. We invited many of the personalities that represent our brands around the world to join us for the historic occasion. The captains from *Deadliest Catch*, Emeril Lagasse, Terri and Bindi Irwin, and Stacy London and Clinton Kelley from *What Not to Wear* all arrived for the big day.

As the clock ticked to 9:30 a.m., the excitement was building and the team was clapping loud and cheering. I thought about all the many years of work building this company as we were about to take the biggest plunge yet.

It was 9:30 a.m. and I signed my name.

The actual mechanics of becoming a public company went off just like clockwork. Right at 9:30 a.m., NASDAQ CEO Robert Greifeld congratulated me and the team as the markets began to trade our stock smoothly. (Later, NASDAQ and Greifeld would not experience the same efficient and smooth initial trading experience that we enjoyed when Facebook held its IPO on May 18, 2012.)

The first few hours were exciting. It is natural, of course, for any entrepreneur to dream about how the public would respond and value your life's work.

Discovery's A shares opened trading at $18.53 and quickly rose to above $20. However, as the celebratory champagne breakfast wound down and we said thanks to our network talent, the word out of Washington was increasingly gloomy. The true depths of the crisis were finally coming into view. It quickly became known that Fed chairman Ben Bernanke and Treasury secretary Hank Paulson would be traveling to Capitol Hill later that afternoon to brief the congressional leadership on the dire financial situation in which the country found itself.

Our stock turned negative and ended up closing down nearly $5 at $13.81. Even though we rebounded to $17.29 the next day, DISCA would fall as low as $10.27 over the next couple of months.

What had become clear is that we had gone public on an historic day—and not necessarily the good kind. Bernanke and Paulson that night warned Nancy Pelosi, John Boehner, and other congressional leaders that if there was not a massive government bailout of the financial sector, the economy would contract to such a degree it would cause the second great depression. And this was the day we went public!

Although the nation and the world plunged into a deep recession over the next few months, what developed was one of the great stock buying opportunities of recent memory. Basically, the stock of corporate America was on sale at bargain prices.

As our stock drifted down toward $10 in October 2008, I became desperate to buy our shares. However, SEC rules prevent company insiders from trading in their own company stock, and rightly so, until quarterly earnings are released and the public enjoys equal knowledge about the company's financial performance. In the days immediately after our third-quarter earnings were released in early November 2008, I eagerly purchased additional shares in Discovery. Although I could not catch Discovery shares at their lowest level of $10.27, I did manage to add to my Discovery stock holdings at purchase prices averaging about $14.50 per share. A number of major investment firms who studied our financial performance also snapped up Discovery shares at bargain prices. Our employees who were granted stock options during this period also benefited from the setting of low exercise prices. Discovery's new public stockholders and employees together emerged from the winter of 2008–9 with an enormous financial growth opportunity. We were all aligned in the common goal of building Discovery value through accelerated growth within our already extensive global footprint. Within four years of going public, Discovery stock would climb above $60 per share. The confidence of our employees and our investors in our future continues to pay off—knock on wood.

Questions of Endurance

To endure over the long term, I believe companies must continually address and be mindful of key survival questions discussed in this and the previous chapter. Does the company's brand stand for a purpose or cause and is that brand carefully protected and guarded? Are the founding entrepreneur's passion, obsession, and zeal complemented by the recruitment of experienced and skilled management team leaders who bring the discipline required to steward corporate assets over the long haul? Does the company have ready access to capital and does it have publicly traded stock "currency" that can be used to acquire companies important to achieve economic scale and business leverage? Are the interests of shareholders, employees, executives, and board members aligned and incented to produce long-term revenue and cash-flow growth?

Finally, and most important, is the company constantly poised to undertake intelligent risks? To survive, explore, and prosper on the grand economic ocean of free enterprise, the ship's captain and courageous crew must never be afraid to leave port and set sail in their sturdy ship for places unknown.

Part Three

Reflections and Rediscoveries

Chapter 25

Oprah's OWN

The whole point of being alive is to evolve into the complete person
you were intended to be.

—OPRAH WINFREY

David Zaslav was calling from his New York office.

"Okay, I have this crazy idea," he said. "It's probably not going to work, but hear me out."

I love it when David starts out a conversation like that. What generally follows is an "outside the box" proposal that makes you stop and think.

This crazy idea had begun that morning during David's conversation with his wife, Pam.

It was late 2007, and David had been president and CEO at Discovery for less than a year. In that short time, he had already begun to transform the company.

When he had arrived at Discovery in January 2007, a number of major challenges were waiting for him. And with impressive energy and discipline, David had tackled them one by one.

One task was to unwind our partnership with the *New York Times* over the Discovery Times channel. Like its predecessor Discovery Civilization, Discovery Times could never find a strong audience, largely due to its lack of a singular theme or consumer promise. David took back full control of Discovery Times by buying back the 50 percent equity held by the *Times*.

Then Zaslav and his team, identifying forensic science and crime solving as a popular theme with viewers, rebranded the channel as Investigation Discovery (ID). He next hired a strong, passionate leader to run the reborn channel: Henry Schleiff, at the time president and CEO of Crown Holdings, and prior to that post, chairman/CEO of Court TV. Under Schleiff's direction as president and general manager, Investigation Discovery grew into one of America's top networks thanks to its fast-paced and provocative programming. Henry's pick of respected television journalist Paula Zahn to host *On the Case with Paula Zahn* set just the right tone and promise for Investigation Discovery.

David then turned to correct two of my mistakes.

I had pushed Discovery into bricks-and-mortar retail in 1996— just at the dawn of the Internet and online shopping. In retrospect, it was not a brilliant move. We bought The Nature Company, a 114-store chain of mall-based stores, to serve as the launch platform for our Discovery Channel Stores.

Soon, children across the country got their first telescopes and other educational merchandise emblazoned with a Discovery Channel logo, creating a powerful and lasting affiliation with our brand. However, we could never make the store chain profitable— and then we made the classic business mistake of hanging on way too long in hopes of turning the business around.

Fortunately, our *online* Discovery Channel Store had grown rapidly in sales. So David devised a way to exit all the mall leases, close down all the mall stores, and plow new resources and energy into our online retail business. His turnaround worked.

My second mistake, which David then turned to address,

proved more difficult. I had been responsible in 1996 for Discovery being first on satellite with an industry-leading number of new specialty channels—and it had proven to be a major revenue producer. But I had totally botched the revenue potential for one of those channels, Discovery Health Network. Overly optimistic about the potential for advertising by the large pharmaceutical companies—and overly eager to get widespread carriage for the new service—I had launched Discovery Health as a free service to cable operators.

In other words, despite my experience in the industry, I had launched a channel without the powerful economics of dual revenue streams from both advertising and subscription fees. Thus, even as Discovery Health grew rapidly in distribution, it nevertheless struggled to generate the revenue needed for programming excellence. Advertising revenue alone just wasn't enough.

Discovery Health required a bold and innovative solution that would convince our distributors to pay for carriage. And that's why David had called me that morning. He had an idea that would both address my mistake and, he hoped, create one of cable's most valuable new programming initiatives.

"So," David began, "Pam sits me down this morning and asks me to read her latest issue of *O* . . . you know, the *Oprah Magazine*. She wants me to go through all the sections. I do, and then we talk about how Oprah's passion to help people live their best lives just exudes from that magazine."

He paused, as if to prepare me, "The content promise of that magazine could be a channel, John . . . a great channel, an *incredible* channel. What if Oprah had her very own network?"

David continued, "We can use the eighty-million-home distribution base of a rebranded Discovery Health to launch it. You know that cable operators will pay for an Oprah Winfrey network.

Oprah could help people be accountable for their own personal fulfillment."

David didn't wait for a response, but plunged on: "It's a crazy idea, I know. But I think I need to get on a plane to Chicago and talk to her. It probably won't work. But what do you think, John? Should I go to Chicago?"

I knew a great idea when I heard one. "David, get on that plane," I told him.

Before David left for Chicago, we discussed the basic 50–50 structure of the joint venture he proposed. We would contribute the distribution base of Discovery Health, along with content rights and cash funding that we would recover out of the network's first profits. Oprah, for her part, would contribute content rights, a half interest in Oprah.com, and her leadership of the new channel.

In other joint venture channels, such as with the *New York Times*, Discovery had always insisted on editorial control. With Oprah at the helm of a channel bearing her name, we felt confident in her having total editorial and creative control.

Less than a week later, David landed in Chicago to pitch Oprah on the big idea. In our Silver Spring, Maryland, headquarters, I anxiously awaited his report by phone.

It arrived at last. "Okay, you're not going to believe this," David started. "I was in the middle of my pitch. Oprah stops me in mid-sentence. She just stopped me and took me to her office. I didn't know what was up.

"In her office, she shows me an entry in her journal from years ago in which she wrote down an idea about creating the Oprah Winfrey Network . . . OWN. She and Stedman [Graham] had talked about this a decade ago!"

"So, does she want to do it?" I asked.

"John, she's in."

I hung up and leaned back in my chair. Oprah, the most famous personality in America, was now part of Discovery. Imagine that.

Together, David and I briefed our board of directors. They were excited and intrigued by the idea.

David consulted the key Discovery players who would be needed to make the new channel a success in distribution and in advertising. Bill Goodwyn, Discovery's president of distribution, was confident we could convert the current distribution base of free subscriptions into paying subscriptions. If Oprah would participate in meetings with our largest distributors and personally describe what OWN would mean for their subscribers, it could work, Bill told me.

Bill, a veteran in solving difficult distribution challenges, knew that nothing could be more difficult than convincing cable and satellite operators to tear up a free deal and begin paying. However, he felt optimistic that it could be done, especially with Oprah involved.

Joe Abruzzese, Discovery's president of advertising sales, had taken our ad sales to more than $1 billion annually. It had been quite a coup when, in 2002, we recruited Joe from CBS, where he had been head of advertising sales for eleven years and recognized as the best in the business. Joe was now taking aim at $2 billion in annual ad sales for Discovery. In the first planning meeting about OWN, he all but shouted, "Are you kidding me? We can sell Oprah in a heartbeat!" He then set about making a list of prospective major sponsors.

As we proceeded toward the public announcement of OWN— scheduled for less than a month away, on January 1, 2008—David told me that Oprah wanted to invite our board members to a private dinner at her home in Santa Barbara, California. "She wants spouses to attend as well," David said.

Although we were still a private company in December 2007 (Discovery didn't go public until the next September), we were careful to keep any material development in our business confidential until it could be publicly announced. Our largest shareholding at the time was owned by a company whose stock was publicly traded. We did not want any information leaked about the upcoming dinner; it was important that nobody could trade stock with "insider information" about a potential deal between Oprah and Discovery. It was some secret to keep. Yet we all did, including our spouses.

Teacher

When we met in Santa Barbara in December 2007, Oprah and I had each been telecasting nationally for a quarter century.

My wife and I arrived, along with the other board members and their wives, at her elegant home in Montecito, overlooking the Pacific Ocean. After mingling a bit with the others, Oprah and I separated from the group and sat down for a conversation in her living room.

"You know," I told her, "Bill Baker always said that you and I should get together. He claims that he contributed to both our successes. He kept me on satellite and he put you on the air!" Oprah laughed and we reminisced a bit about our years in the business. I told her that Discovery's business is, at its core, simply about satisfying curiosity.

Oprah reflected a bit before she spoke, then said: "You know, John, after all these years, I have finally come to realize what I am. I know it deep down because it's my very first memory. I was just five years old, a little girl in Mississippi, and I had just learned something new—can't remember now what it was—but I am standing there and talking to my little friends who have formed a semicircle in front of me. I am telling them all about what I had learned."

Oprah paused and put her hand on my forearm.

"John, I'm a teacher."

With OWN, Oprah has a new purpose in life—one that will take her years to fully realize. She is passionate about teaching anything she has learned so that, in some way, it may empower others to live a more complete and meaningful life. It is her calling.

Now she has an entire television network to unleash that passion. And we at Discovery are honored to be her partner.

Chapter 26

Velocity

For my part, I travel not to go anywhere, but to go. I travel for travel's sake. The great affair is to move.

—Robert Louis Stevenson

The actor Dennis Haysbert was visiting with me in my Discovery office in Silver Spring. It was May 9, 2007, and Dennis was about to join me at the Tenth Anniversary Gala Celebration of the Discovery Channel Global Education Partnership (DCGEP).

DCGEP's charter is to use television to help educate children in the developing world. And Dennis had graciously agreed to serve as global ambassador for the nonprofit organization.

If you've ever seen him on television (*The Unit*, as the U.S. president on *24*, in Allstate commercials) or in movies (*Absolute Power*), you know that Haysbert has an imposing presence, especially with his rich baritone voice. In person, at more than six feet, four inches tall, he is even more imposing.

My family would be attending the gala with me, and so I invited them to join me in my office for some photos with Dennis. As Haysbert ambled around my desk to get into the shot, he spied on a nearby shelf a model Ferrari race car bearing the Discovery logo. It sat displayed along with some other plastic and wood miniatures of cars and airplanes. I had collected many of the models to commemorate shows we had done through the years. For example, a model of Amelia Earhart's Lockheed Vega aircraft rests atop my desk.

Dennis picked up the white Ferrari model and said, "So you like cars?"

"Yes," I replied, "I have to admit I like cars. Right now I'm fascinated by the potential of electric. Actually, I just ordered a Tesla Roadster, mostly to help support its development."

The actor's face quickly brightened into a surprised grin. "I'm thinking about ordering one, too," he announced.

"What number are you?" he asked, referring to the "Signature 100 Club" of the first one hundred individuals to purchase a Tesla.

"Number forty-two," I replied.

Shared Passion

Once again, as has happened so many times in my career, I had connected with someone who shared my passion for the science and engineering of cars.

Cars have always been important in my life. And that day, talking with Dennis Haysbert, I was rooting for the next great revolution in automotive technology, one that would finally help free the world from its reliance on fossil fuels.

Tesla Motors had been founded in 2003. By 2007, it still needed $10 million to bring the Tesla Roadster to market. Within three weeks, one hundred individuals each stepped forward with $100,000 deposits to purchase the new electric car, sight unseen. It was reported that George Clooney, Leonardo DiCaprio, and Arnold Schwarzenegger were among this Signature 100 Club.

The Tesla is an amazing little vehicle. Its battery fully charges in four hours and can power the vehicle for 300 miles (daily commutes in the United States average 25 miles). Since the electric engine applies tremendous instantaneous torque, the Tesla Roadster rockets from 0 to 60 mph in 3.8 seconds, faster than most Ferraris. When the physicist Michio Kaku visited me in Colorado, I put him behind the wheel of my "Signature Green" Tesla with me in the passenger seat. It was a delight to watch his startled face as he punched the accelerator after turning south on Highway 141. The Tesla silently pressed us both back in our seats, and we launched down the canyon highway.

The adrenaline rush of driving the Tesla only underscored a notion that had been growing in my mind: there just had to be a channel about cars and machines in motion. I had discussed the concept with my board several times in the past and all were supportive, particularly John Malone and Paul Gould.

Gould not only appreciated the engineering and performance aspects of cars; he also valued the great styling effort made by car designers through the years. A car collector, Paul believed that a car-themed channel would attract viewers to interesting stories about the people who labored to restore and bring classic cars back to life.

By the same token, I knew Malone had an interest in an automotive channel because of the evolving technologies involved in cars. "A great way to teach physics and engineering," John commented after I brought up the topic at a board meeting in 2006. Malone's words echoed in my mind as I watched my own son Andrew's growing fascination with cars.

From an early age, Andrew had been obsessed with how technology and engineering machines—especially automobiles—work. By the age of thirteen, Andrew could describe the intricacies of engine performance, transmission gearing, and the complicated workings of a car's rear differential. Cars had become the great passion of Andrew's life.

In his twenties, Andrew began racing, first driving in Grand-Am's Mustang Challenge Series. In Grand-Am's 2010 Continental Tire Series, Andrew and his Fall-Line Motorsports teammates drove their BMW M3 race cars to the season championship.

Auto-Revealing

In thinking more about the potential car channel, I reflected back on my own lifelong passion for cars.

At an early age, I discovered that cars reveal something very intriguing about the human spirit. Long before I succumbed to the sculptural beauty of the great Duesenbergs, Packards, and Auburns of the 1930s, I experienced cars as magic machines that provoked dreams of adventure on the open road.

As a five-year-old in 1957, I was already captivated by a world full of automobiles. Like many American boys of the era, I memorized the names, models, and years of every car I saw—and, as already noted, my father delighted in showing off my knowledge to his friends. To a child growing up in the mountains of West Virginia, cars represented adventure and exploration.

My imagination was also fueled by my father's beautiful old road maps from the 1930s. As a young man, Dad had traveled extensively in the western United States and he regaled me with stories of those trips. He still had his old maps and he used them to show me where those adventures took place.

I remember sitting behind the wheel of his parked 1952 Plymouth Cranbrook with well-worn Sinclair Oil maps of Colorado and Utah by my side, imagining myself driving across the country to the Wild West. For some reason, Provo, Utah, was a favorite fantasy destination. I guess I just liked the sound of the place, *Provo*.

In the summer of 1958 a friend of my sister came over for a visit. I'll never forget his car: a 1958 Corvette. My life changed that day as those glistening curves roared into my life. I simply could not stop touching every line and length of chrome. Even after all the gawking neighbors left, I remained behind, still admiring the marvelous machine.

Harley Earl and his design team at General Motors had produced this first true art experience for a six-year-old boy. Better yet, it was art that rolled and growled.

And then he took me for a ride.

I can still remember the warm wind in my face, the head-jerking acceleration, and being slammed tight against the door in left turns taken at speeds that would have flipped the Plymouth. I fell in love with speed and power and art all in one summer afternoon.

Like countless other boys across America, I devoted much of my childhood to model car building—and relished the successful completion of every Chevy, Ford, and Chrysler. In school, I perked up when the teacher told us where rubber came from, how friction stopped a car, or how a battery stored energy. Science, nature, history, and geography just seemed to sink in more when there was a car involved.

A Hot-Rod Heart

On my sixteenth birthday, I took possession of my first car, a gift from my sister and her husband. Rather than trade the nine-year-old car in on the new car they were buying, they generously thought of me. I couldn't have asked for more: the black 1959 Ford Galaxie 500 was a beast, complete with a 352-cubic-inch, 300-horsepower

Thunderbird V-8 engine. What my big old Ford lacked in design art was more than made up for in blistering performance. I instantly became the coolest kid in my neighborhood.

And that was only the start.

You simply cannot understand the allure of the first-generation Camaro unless you were a teenage male somewhere in America in the late sixties. For more than a year, I plotted with my father on how such a prize could be obtained. You've seen my love for numbers—but one number in particular is still etched in my mind: $82.17.

According to my father, that was the monthly car payment required for the purchase of a new Camaro with a sticker price of $2,575. It took endless hours of work, but between my after-school job at Budd's Men's Wear and my parents' generosity, I finally bought my Camaro. It was a white 1968 coupe that was the envy of my classmates. I still think of it with both love and awe.

One day in 2004, while I was talking on the phone with Walter Cronkite, I told him about my plan to create a museum in Colorado that would celebrate the engineering and style of one hundred years of American automobiles. I told him we would begin with a 1906 Cadillac Coupe and proceed through the years, featuring the great American automotive icons as well as "special" cars such as the art deco–styled Hudson Terraplane, which Amelia Earhart had famously endorsed.

"Will you have a Duesenberg?" asked Walter.

"Oh yes, we have to have a Duesey," I replied.

Walter sighed wistfully and said, "I remember first seeing a Duesenberg on a street in Houston. I couldn't take my eyes off of it."

"Well, you'll have to come visit us in Colorado," I said.

"Keep me posted and count me in," Walter replied.

In early 2005, I called Walter's office. He wasn't in, so I told his longtime chief of staff, Marlene Adler, about the impending completion of our Gateway Auto Museum, and told her that I'd promised to keep Walter updated.

"I'm sure he'll want to go," she told me. I then asked her to see if Walter would like to make a videotaped presentation about the history and engineering of cars that would be shown in the museum's entrance theater.

Within a few hours, Marlene called back. "He would love to do the museum videotape," she told me. "But he wants you to come up so that the two of you can go to lunch after the taping."

Marlene and I briefly discussed the development of a script over which Walter, the master narrator, would have final edit. I loved how he took such time to get things right.

I arrived at Walter's office at CBS just a bit early. Marlene came out to greet me and apologized that Walter would be tied up just a bit longer on a taping for another organization he supported. "I hope you don't mind us taking advantage of the crew that's already here for your museum taping," she said.

"Absolutely not. And I'm in no rush," I told her.

After another ten minutes or so, Marlene came to get me and I sat in on Walter's taping for my car museum. He brought every word to life in that voice I had treasured since childhood. In the end, it became a sweeping narration describing the key engineering, technology, and business milestones of the American automotive industry as only Walter Cronkite could deliver. To this day, our museum visitors are enchanted when their old friend Walter sets the stage for their tour.

Months later, I was astonished to learn what Walter and Marlene had been scheming that morning. Without my knowledge, Walter had taped an extremely generous video message about me. It was played as a surprise at Discovery's twentieth-anniversary event, held at the Washington Convention Center. Almost three thousand of our employees were in attendance, including many of our talented stars—even Steve Irwin, who had unexpectedly flown in from Australia. It was a special occasion made all the more so by Walter Cronkite's kind words.

Channel Switch

Like many men I knew, Cronkite had lit up when we talked about the history, engineering, and style of cars. That was a point in favor of a new Discovery car channel. So were the ratings for the car shows already appearing sporadically on Discovery, TLC, and HD Theater. Still, the idea for a car channel languished for several years, mostly due to my distraction with a number of other projects.

We also lacked an internal champion who could fully develop and implement the idea. And anyone who took the job would be facing an uphill battle: an extreme shortage of channel capacity among cable and satellite distributors meant that starting a new channel from scratch would be almost impossible.

Fortunately, the situation improved dramatically in 2010 after I brought up the idea with David Zaslav over lunch one day.

"Maybe we could reposition HD Theater as a car channel," David said—as always, thinking out of the box.

I had created and launched Discovery HD Theater in June 2002. The objective was to be the first cable or satellite television network in the world to transmit twenty-four hours of high-definition content each day. Discovery HD Theater quickly reached almost every household in America with a new HD television set.

However, in opposition to our network business strategy, Discovery HD Theater had no specific, distinguishing content theme. We had simply wanted to seize the initial HD "shelf space."

By 2010, all of the major broadcast and cable television networks, including our own, had obtained separate HD channels in addition to their analog channels. The technological novelty was gone.

Discovery HD Theater also began to be confused with the regular HD channel feed for the Discovery Channel. So, in 2009, we dropped "Discovery" and renamed it HD Theater. Still, the channel had no distinguishing theme—and that made it ripe for conversion.

Over that lunch, David and I discussed the challenges and opportunities facing us in creating a car-themed network. I was certain that automotive advertisers would be interested, and I offered to set up a meeting with Joe Abruzzese, our head of ad sales, to discuss the concept. David said he would talk to Bill Goodwyn, our head of distribution, to help iron out any conversion difficulties with our cable and satellite distributors. David seemed confident, not least because we already had enough automotive programming to fill the channel.

Joe Abruzzese and I met in our New York office. He too was optimistic. Like me, Joe was confident about sponsors. I suggested he set us up to talk with a leading automotive manufacturer and its agency. Joe suggested GM and scheduled a meeting. David was equally encouraged by his discussions with Bill Goodwyn about the likelihood of convincing our distributors to go along with our conversion strategy.

GM loved the idea and offered its support. When I reported the news back to David, he said he was already working on a management plan for the channel.

Fast off the Line

On October 4, 2011, Velocity launched on HD Theater's 40 million household distribution base. In the months since, viewership has remained strong and advertisers are responding with unexpected dollars in support for the network. It looks like we have another winner on our hands.

And people like me can tune in and feel like teenagers again.

Chapter 27

Facing Reality

Reality leaves a lot to the imagination.

—JOHN LENNON

The turn of the twenty-first century brought a new kind of programming to television—one that would eventually dominate all of prime time and transform both the content and the business model of Discovery.

"Reality" television—that is, non-news programming that features real people in real-life settings—had already been around for a couple of decades, famously beginning with PBS's *An American Family*. In the brief run of that series, the Loud family members lived out their complex lives—divorce, one son coming out as gay, and the many changes of seventies America—before a transfixed nation.

It was, in fact, Discovery that brought modern reality television to the U.S. audience—in the form of two shows: *Trading Spaces* (2000) and, earlier, *Eco-Challenge* (1995).

Trading Spaces, derived from the British series *Changing Rooms*, featured couples who redecorated each other's living spaces. It had a hugely successful eight-year run—and set off the reality TV trend of home decorating and restoration shows.

We premiered two new series in the 2003 season. Incredibly, given the short life span of television series, more than a decade later *both* are still in production:

> *Mythbusters.* Of the two pioneering Discovery reality series, *Mythbusters* was the closest to the soul of Discovery. That is, it combined pedagogy with entertainment, taking interesting and complex real-life questions about science (or science myth) and putting them to the test in novel and fun ways. An Australian production company brought us the series—and the show's stripped-down, ultimate garage laboratory feel proved perfect for an audience initially composed of techies, tinkerers, and high school robotics competitors (as did the Alameda, California, location, just across the bay from Silicon Valley). By tackling urban myths, much of them created by Hollywood, the *Mythbusters* team captured the imaginations not only of teenagers, but also of adults who might not otherwise watch "educational" television. Crucial to this, and a lesson we took to heart, was the choice of hosts: Jamie Hyneman and Adam Savage weren't traditional buttoned-down TV hosts; rather, they shared the sensibilities of their audience.

> *American Chopper.* The story of the Teutuls, Paul and Paul Jr., of Orange County (N.Y.) Choppers, was a much greater departure for Discovery—though just how great wasn't apparent at the start. What was obvious from the first was that this was a different kind of reality show, one that revolved around the design and creation of what was then an exotic product: artistic and themed motorcycle

choppers. What we thought was particularly compelling about the Teutuls was not just the unique and visually compelling nature of their creations, and the interesting insight into the building of the bikes, but also the relationship between father and son in a small, self-made business. What we couldn't anticipate was that *American Chopper* would suddenly turn into a riveting battle between father and son, with another conciliating son (Michael) caught in the middle, ultimately resulting in the shattering of both the family and the business. The schism between father and sons, and the lawsuits that followed, ultimately ended *American Chopper* in February 2010. And the insatiable curiosity of the audience to find out the fate of the Teutuls ultimately led to the return of the series, as *American Chopper: Senior vs. Junior*, that August.

I confess that, while I could rationalize *Mythbusters* in my mind as a valuable new direction for Discovery—one that planted our flag in the hot new world of reality television—with *American Chopper* I was seriously afraid that we had overstepped our boundaries and potentially undermined the business philosophy that had gotten us this far. Looking back, I'm embarrassed to admit that I was *culturally* blinded to the real story of the Teutuls. My staff was not—and I can still remember the stricken look on their faces when I dismissed this new kind of programming as "Tattoo TV." I was willing to trust their judgment on this, but that didn't mean I had to like it.

In the end, it was Mike Rowe who showed me the truth.

As I mentioned earlier in the book, Rowe began his career working for the nationally syndicated *Evening Magazine* in San Francisco. It was there that he created a segment called "Somebody's Gotta Do It." As Rowe tells it, after hosting an especially graphic segment on artificial insemination of cows, he was inundated with letters expressing "shock, horror, fascination, disbelief, and wonder"—a rare response for such an upbeat show.

Concluding that he had something valuable, Rowe sent the tape to the Discovery Channel—and we agreed. The pilot for *Dirty Jobs* was aired the same year as our other two big reality show experiments—and like them, it had a long run on the air.

Perhaps it is his naturally gregarious personality (the one you see in the Ford commercials) that enables Mike to engage in friendly conversation with anyone, or maybe it is his history as an Eagle Scout practicing woodcraft and other skills, but Rowe detected something important in his subjects the rest of us had long missed. It is captured in his familiar tagline, which has been stated in some form in every episode:

> "My name's Mike Rowe, and this is my job. I explore the country looking for people who aren't afraid to get dirty— hardworking men and women who earn an honest living doing the kinds of jobs that make civilized life possible for the rest of us. Now, get ready to get dirty."

What Rowe and the growing number of fanatical viewers who began to watch *Dirty Jobs*, *American Chopper*, and the numerous other shows that appeared on the Discovery Channel in the decade that followed—*Sons of Guns*, *American Guns*, *Auction Kings*, etc.— understood was that this country is filled with small, often family-run businesses. And that these little businesses not only often take on work that most people won't or can't do—they also take pride in their work. And that these individuals have a pride in their craft— and reach a level of mastery in what they do—that few of the rest of us ever know.

This has always been the case. But we quickly discovered that, in an era where big corporations get most of the attention from both the media and our elected officials, there was a vast, untapped audience of viewers who wanted to watch, and to celebrate, the lives of these hardworking individuals: men and women who had built their businesses from scratch, who had persevered and ultimately succeeded in the face of almost impossible jobs, and who ultimately had created livelihoods and careers for their children and grandchildren, not to mention for their employees and their families. As with the Teutuls, these shows were not just about a craft or a business—although those two factors were always important—they were about the lives, relationships, and dreams of the individuals and families involved.

Breakout

It wasn't until we were several years into broadcasting this new generation of reality shows that it suddenly hit me that, without noticing it, Discovery had quietly broken through the cultural barrier that had always defined the company. As you'll remember, that principle with which I had founded the company was that 25 percent of the population would be interested in "educational," as opposed to "entertainment," television. But, with these shows we had found a new formula: we were creating nonfiction television that could be *both* educational and entertaining.

Are these shows as information-rich as our science documentaries? No, but they are bringing an almost unprecedented amount of information to audiences that normally would never watch educational television. Having fulfilled, after three decades, our promise to the 25 percent, we were now heading out into open territory to provide the same service to the other 75 percent.

Needless to say, this didn't come without controversy. Some of our traditional viewers, as well as some critics, suggested that we were drifting away from our original charter and pandering to the mass audience and ratings. Well, it may have seemed that way to purists, but to me and my team at Discovery we were in fact continuing the quest that always had been at the heart of our network—bringing knowledge TV to everyone. Even if the subject was, most controversially, a little six-year-old Atlanta beauty pageant phenomenon named Honey Boo Boo.

That said, we have over the years learned that these two groups—what we might call the educational and the "infotainment" audiences—still remain comparatively distinct (though slowly converging), and for that reason we now typically premiere all of our new "infotainment" reality shows on TLC, while Discovery adheres more to our traditional content. TLC has fun exploring exotic and interesting lifestyles (*Breaking Amish* and *Honey Boo Boo*) while Discovery Channel takes viewers into the very heart of real-world occupations and exploits (*Deadliest Catch* and *Bering Sea Gold*) and educates viewers about the wonders of life (*Frozen Planet* and *Curiosity*). And our other networks, like Animal Planet under Marjorie Kaplan, exhibit both educational and infotainment content within their category promise.

If this market expansion has become self-evident to us, it hasn't been entirely acceptable to portions of our viewing audience. They see the growing presence of reality shows on Discovery as proof that we are putting profits over quality content.

I could not disagree more. Nor will I ever apologize for having built Discovery on good business principles. It is easy to forget now, when Discovery is a multibillion-dollar global corporation, that at the beginning we were a tiny start-up, with fewer than a score of employees, desperately trying to meet the next payroll. People were afraid to invest in us because they saw no way for us to survive against the mighty $400 million, government-subsidized national PBS network.

Today, less than thirty years later, public broadcasting is still the same size, while Discovery is many times larger than PBS in every way, including budget, hours of programming, networks, and audience. Why? Because we had to compete and survive in a tough industry; we had to generate revenues in ever-increasing amounts to afford the highest-quality productions, which were disciplined and shaped by a very demanding audience. And for those who worry that Discovery, with its much greater economic power, is threatening the survival of PBS—please note that the amount of annual taxes paid by our company and our employees to the federal government essentially underwrites public television in the United States. Free enterprise is a good thing.

Back to the Beginning

My second lesson in humility about reality television came almost a decade after Mike Rowe reminded me to respect and honor the workingman. In 2008, reality shows—the video descendants of the Louds, the Teutuls, and the men of *Deadliest Catch*—dominated television as much as westerns had in the 1950s.

And yet, as much as I had learned to love these shows, and to appreciate the talent and values of the men and women whose stories they told, I still remained only an observer. I still saw them only as marvelous characters doing unlikely work in curious locations.

It was only after the economic crash of 2008 and the long and devastating recession that followed that I began to see Discovery's reality "stars" differently. As the crush began on working Americans, columnists and bloggers began to notice that our reality shows offered hope and optimism to average folks at a time when they had little of both. These same essayists even suggested that Discovery's programming had become a last bastion of the American spirit of hard work and independence—and the last place to celebrate the achievements of the American entrepreneur.

Reading these articles was an epiphany for me. They taught me not only to see our work at Discovery in a new light—How many young people out there dreamed of designing products like Paul Jr.? How many middle-aged men and women found the courage to follow their entrepreneurial dreams from Cake Boss Buddy Valastro?—but also to look in the mirror at my own life. After all, what had I been in those first days of Discovery but a young entrepreneur, trying to build a business and feed my family, all the while betting everything to make my dream real?

In celebrating these entrepreneurs and their struggles to survive, weren't we also telling the story of Discovery itself? And weren't these tales of enterprise—filled with every human emotion and refreshed every few years with new technologies, new players, and new challenges—a fundamental type of human story that would never grow old?

I knew at that moment that no one will portray those lives better than Discovery, that their success will be our success, because we are cut from the same cloth, and that telling these stories will be part of our company's charter for many years to come. The future of Discovery is both real—and "reality."

I'm proud to say that I've come a long way from "Tattoo TV."

Chapter 28

In the Cabinet Room

Some people regard private enterprise as a predatory tiger to be shot. Others look on it as a cow they can milk. Not enough people see it as a healthy horse, pulling a sturdy wagon.

—Winston Churchill

I am, politically, an Independent. I have voted for Republicans and Democrats. Like many Independents I am "progressive" on social issues and "responsible" on fiscal issues.

In 1992, it seemed to me that Bill Clinton was most in line with my philosophy on good government. I financially supported his candidacy and voted for him on election day.

My only hesitation had come when he announced Al Gore as his running mate. Senator Gore had been a leading champion of the cable reregulation act passed by Congress in 1991. I had testified in Congress in opposition to this regulatory legislation. However, my neighbor David Ifshin, a friend of Clinton, assured me in the months leading up to the 1992 election that Bill Clinton would take a more thoughtful and competitive approach in developing regulatory policy.

In October 1995, while traveling, word reached me that U.S. secretary of education Richard Riley was on the line. I had previously met with Secretary Riley to discuss the potential of airing a national "town hall" meeting on education. In those discussions, I also shared my plans to use new digital compression technologies to offer more educational content, including a Science Channel.

After some pleasantries, Secretary Riley explained the purpose of his call: "John, I was just talking to the president and he wants you to come to a meeting at the White House to discuss educational technology. We really need to incorporate your thoughts in a new plan."

I was flattered at the thought, but I suspected that this would be a typical gathering of 100 to 150 people, some from companies and some from academia, in the East Room of the White House. I had attended meetings like this before. At some point the president would come in, address the group with some platitudes, and depart. Opinions would then be solicited from the crowd and there would be a promise to follow up. Still, how could I refuse a direct invitation from the secretary of education?

So, one morning during the following week, I arrived at the White House security gate at eight for the eight-thirty meeting. I expected to be directed to the large East Room after waiting in line for my security pass—and was a bit surprised to find there was just one man ahead of me showing his identification. When he turned, I saw that it was filmmaker George Lucas.

I had once met George in passing at a social function, but decided this day it would be best to reintroduce myself. After the usual small talk, we both professed to be a little puzzled that there was no one else with us at the security gate. At that moment, a White House security officer appeared and asked us to follow him to the Cabinet Room. George and I glanced at each other. I had never been in the Cabinet Room, nor, I think, had he.

I had met President Clinton on a number of occasions. David

Ifshin first introduced us in November 1991, shortly after Clinton had announced that he would run for president. Ifshin, who had become a Discovery consultant due his extraordinary connections, was Clinton's general counsel in the early days of the campaign.

I had been very impressed by Bill Clinton. He was a genuine student of government and economics. I had never met a politician with such a command of history as well as current trends in society. He also had an exceptional memory, as evidenced to me by his recitation, at that first meeting, of the complete Discovery Channel programming lineup.

As I entered the Cabinet Room, I tried to recall the famous black-and-white photo showing where each of President Kennedy's cabinet members and military advisers had sat during the Cuban Missile Crisis. President Clinton then walked in and greeted each of us personally. He took Kennedy's seat.

The president had convened the meeting to gather advice on how technology might be used to improve education—and, most important, how government policy could be shaped to encourage private sector investment in the infrastructure to deliver new interactive services to homes and to schools. In addition to myself, the small "think tank" assembled that morning included George Lucas, Ted Turner, Gerald Levin (CEO of Time Warner), and Ray Smith (CEO of Bell Atlantic). President Clinton also had Vice President Al Gore, Secretary Riley, and Secretary of Commerce Ron Brown seated at his side.

The president began the two-hour meeting with a series of questions to which he asked each of us to respond. George Lucas spoke about the use of interactive gaming in the classroom. Jerry Levin and Ray Smith outlined how a new competitive approach to government regulatory policies could stimulate investment by cable companies, phone companies, and others to build the fiberoptic and digital infrastructure needed for universal distribution of broadband Internet. When it was my turn, I explained what content would be useful to teachers based upon Discovery's experiences in *Assignment Discovery*, and how digital technology would someday allow a streaming of interactive content to the nation's classrooms.

At the conclusion of the meeting, President Clinton observed that government could not provide the staggering sums needed to build out the nation's new telecommunications infrastructure; rather, the private sector must be engaged and incented to make the investment. He let all of us know that he would be supportive of the bipartisan effort in Congress to craft a new regulatory scheme that would deregulate the telecommunications industry in a fashion that would promote new capital investments by unleashed competitors.

As we left the White House that day, none of us realized that we had just been part of what would soon be a regulatory revolution.

Frankly, if we felt any emotion, it was a combination of personal exhilaration and professional wariness. We entrepreneurs learn early on that government can either accelerate or destroy our dreams. Forever mercurial, government can be enlightened and act with wisdom, cooperation, and statesmanship to address the long-term needs of society; or it can be craven and foolish and serve only the short-term political interests of elected officials beholden to large, partisan interest groups. And because entrepreneurs operate at the heart of the free enterprise system, we often live or die by governmental policies that regulate business and impact capital formation.

Like other entrepreneurs, I had found my career defined by the capriciousness of Washington.

For example, satellite television networks were actually illegal prior to the 1975 Supreme Court ruling that struck down laws protecting the broadcast industry from competition. Even though satellite networks like HBO, CNN, and Discovery were finally allowed to emerge, the powerful broadcast lobby continued to exert its influence by crafting new regulations that restricted cable network distribution and limited their revenue potential through price controls. The resulting regulatory uncertainty from 1975 through 1995 severely depressed investor confidence and (as you've read in these pages) made capital formation for start-up cable networks like Discovery nearly impossible.

Thinking Smart

It was that meeting at the White House in 1995 that, although ostensibly about technology and education, proved to be a turning point in stabilizing the volatile cable industry. And, while our testimony that day was important, each of us had said the same things many times before. The difference was that this time we were talking to an enlightened leader who actually *listened*. The digital age wonders that we all now enjoy owe their origin to the liberating effects of the resulting Telecommunications Act of 1996.

I was fortunate that day to get a firsthand view into the way government should work to incentivize spending and free up competition. Smart government policy, I realized, could grow the economy and, at the same time, accomplish an important national objective: the improvement of education. Among other accomplishments, the new legislation broke down the regulatory barriers that had kept phone companies from providing cable service, and cable companies from providing phone service.

President Clinton signed the Telecommunications Act of 1996

into law in a ceremony I attended at the Library of Congress on February 8, 1996. Also in attendance were two congressional leaders I had come to know well through my testimonies and exchanges in the Subcommittee on Telecommunications and Finance of the U.S. House of Representatives. Jack Fields, Republican of Texas, and Edward Markey, Democrat of Massachusetts, were the subcommittee leaders who had collaborated constructively with the White House in leading the remarkably bipartisan effort to completely overhaul the Communications Act of 1934. I had a chance to congratulate Congressman Fields and Congressman Markey before the president arrived.

In his address at the signing ceremony, President Clinton commented on the benefits of legislation that fostered competition:

> . . . this revolution [in telecommunications] has been held back by outdated laws, designed for a time when there was one phone company, three TV networks, no such thing as a personal computer. Today, with the stroke of a pen, our laws will catch up with our future. We will help to create an open marketplace where competition and innovation can move as quick as light.

Then, after extolling the bipartisan support for the act in Congress, President Clinton concluded by describing the important role of government not just in developing regulations that protect consumers from abuse by monopolies, but also in shifting the burden of infrastructure investments to the private sector:

> Any truly competitive market requires rules. This bill protects consumers against monopolies. It guarantees the diversity of voices our democracy depends upon. Perhaps most of all, it

enhances the common good. Under this law, our schools, our libraries, our hospitals will receive telecommunication services at reduced cost. This simple act will move us one giant step closer to realizing a challenge I put forward in the State of the Union to connect all our classrooms and libraries to the Information Superhighway by the year 2000—not through a big government program, but through a creative ever-unfolding partnership led by scientists and entrepreneurs, supported by business and government and communities working together.

The Telecommunications Act of 1996 created a stable new regulatory framework wherein companies could finally have the freedom to create new communication services and price these services at what the market would bear, so long as consumers had a choice of providers.

By making new revenue streams available for all industry segments, the act unleashed hundreds of billions of dollars in investment by the private sector to build the nation's digital communications infrastructure and to program that infrastructure. As a result, wired and wireless communication services exploded. A multitude of video and interactive multimedia content began to stream into homes and schools through the new broadband systems constructed by cable and phone companies. The wealth of information and entertainment choices—which we now enjoy on our television sets, iPads, game platforms, smartphones, and computers—all ride on the broadband superhighway built by the private sector under the deregulatory provisions of the Telecommunications Act of 1996.

Looking back, I realize that I was fortunate to bear witness to the power of thoughtful, bipartisan government. The leaders in the White House and in Congress recognized the proper bounds of regulation, as well as the enormous investment potential of the private sector. Today I long for a return to this rational and constructive approach to government, one that is unimpeded by bitter, polarizing politics.

There is so much at stake in getting the balance right between government regulation and marketplace freedom—and yet our educational system increasingly fails to teach our young people the fundamental workings of the free enterprise system, the system of checks and balances that restrains government from abusing its power, and the crucial role of competition and capital formation to keep our economy healthy.

Sadly, instead of understanding the "referee" role of government, many people naïvely believe government itself can efficiently create, finance, and manage new products and services of value to consumers. Worst of all is the seemingly widespread ignorance among decision makers in government about how capital is really formed and deployed to create new businesses and enterprises.

We all need to pay taxes. It was Supreme Court justice Oliver Wendell Holmes Jr. who once remarked: "I like to pay taxes. With them I buy civilization." I would not mind paying even more taxes than I do now to a disciplined government that has eliminated wasteful spending and requires funds for projects impossible to undertake with private sector financing. However, in providing government with the tax resources needed to protect and enhance our society, we also need to be mindful of the creative value of funds left in the private sector.

Almost all of us who have created a business wince when we hear the latest call by a politician to "tax the rich" to stimulate the economy or cover a deficit caused by undisciplined spending. In my experience, the vast majority of affluent and successful people look for ways to *invest* in companies and in business start-ups. They may be motivated by a desire to increase their own fortunes, but these investments ultimately help form the capital necessary to create new jobs and new products and services. In other words, those investments drive the economy.

Writing for the *Washington Post* in an article titled "A Fierce Tax Debate, Without Much Light," columnist Glenn Kessler pointed out, "When it comes to federal income taxes, the wealthy already pay most of the income taxes." Citing statistics from the nonpartisan Tax Policy Center, Kessler noted that people who earn more than $200,000—just 3 percent of the population—were paying 60 percent of federal income taxes.

Democracy is civilization's most successful form of government and should be cherished and protected at all costs. But as the Founders feared, majority rule can target minorities for everything from restriction of freedom and denial of the vote to punitive taxes. Protecting the affluent 3 percent minority group is not a politically winning strategy, to be sure. Regardless of the adverse impact on capital formation for entrepreneurs, politicians routinely take aim at the discretionary resources of this 3 percent minority group in a "populist" appeal to the overwhelming 97 percent of society.

What is typically lost in this demagoguery is that if fewer funds were diverted from the private sector to the government, some of these funds would be used by the affluent to purchase new tangible assets that stimulate the economy. Most important, however, a large portion of the funds left in the hands of successful people in the private sector would be more thoughtfully deployed in company stocks, corporate bonds, and entrepreneurial ventures than it would by bureaucrats into government projects.

Entrepreneurs vie for these venture investments through a vigorous competition like the one I describe in this book. Indeed, the free enterprise system is all about competition and it starts with a fierce competition for private sector capital. It should be crystal clear that the private sector competition for capital, which involves a rigorous process for evaluating new business plans by experienced investors, is vastly superior to ham-fisted attempts by government to spur economic growth through ill-conceived initiatives. Government simply lacks the experience and knowledge base to make wise capital investments in business activity.

JFK

The leader who best understood this was someone whose economic thinking doesn't get much attention today, President John F. Kennedy. Kennedy presented his economic policy in a speech at the Economic Club of New York on December 4, 1962.

With the Cuban Missile Crisis just two months behind him, Kennedy saw another threat ahead: the U.S. tax system robbing the private sector of the capital needed to grow the economy. Correcting this was of paramount importance to President Kennedy: "For on the strength of our free economy rests the hope of all free nations."

President Kennedy recognized that shifting funds from the government to the private sector through tax cuts could create a near-term federal budget deficit. However, he contended that it would be a "temporary deficit of transition" that would lead to increased spending and capital formation that would "boost the economy."

President Kennedy believed strongly that a short-term reduction of revenues for the federal government (through tax cuts that would leave resources in the private sector) would almost certainly lead to higher tax collections to support government in the future. It was a counterintuitive political strategy, but Kennedy saw the underlying truth: "In short, it is a paradoxical truth that tax rates are too high today and tax revenues are too low and the soundest way to raise the revenues in the long run is to cut the rates now."

Although John Kennedy had no direct life experience in entrepreneurship and business activities, he was a student of economics and government. He also grew up in an affluent family headed by a father, Joseph P. Kennedy Sr., who was deeply involved in business and commercial activities throughout his life. It was perhaps this combination that led President Kennedy to recognize and advocate this "paradoxical truth": shift funds out of government to grow the future revenues of government.

The history of Discovery Communications proves President Kennedy's "paradoxical truth" that investment funds left in the private sector ultimately lead to more tax collections by government. In 1985 and 1986, thirty individuals and seven companies used a portion of their after-tax earnings to make a risk investment in the start-up of the Discovery Channel. This $25 million private sector investment fully funded the creation of not only a new business enterprise that created more than 4,000 new jobs in the world, but also a company that, to date, has paid more than $900 million in taxes to the federal government.

And Discovery's annual tax payments to support U.S., state, and foreign governments are increasing. In 2011, Discovery paid $253 million in U.S. federal taxes, $38 million in state and local taxes, and $109 million in foreign taxes. Remarkably, this total of $400 million in taxes is only part of the tax benefits enjoyed by government through Discovery's operations. Our 4,000 employees also pay tens of millions of dollars in personal income taxes, as do the many suppliers and vendors that share Discovery's annual cost expenditures—which, in 2011, had climbed to more than $2.4 billion. Thus Discovery Communications is a vibrant contributor of billions of dollars to government and to the U.S. and global economies.

President Kennedy and President Clinton understood how government can unleash the investment power of the private sector to empower entrepreneurs, innovation, and economic growth. Their thoughtful leadership in crafting policies that recognized and exploited the strengths of the free enterprise system was a triumph of statesmanship over politics.

The future of entrepreneurship depends on educated citizens who elect enlightened politicians who act out of wisdom and goodwill, rather than acrimony and political expediency.

Part Four

New Daydreams

Chapter 29

Planet School

Education is learning what you didn't even know you didn't know.

—DANIEL BOORSTIN

If we're lucky, we get a chance once in our life to thank someone whose writings had a significant influence on who we are.

In December 1992, I got that chance. I was part of the Madison Council, a group of individuals recruited by James Billington, the librarian of Congress, to support the work of the Library of Congress, the world's largest repository of knowledge. The occasion was a ceremony to celebrate the twenty-fifth anniversary of the founding of the library's Center for the Book.

There, I finally met Daniel Boorstin.

Boorstin had created the Center for the Book in 1977 while serving as the previous librarian of Congress. Over the course of his remarkable career, Boorstin had been a lawyer, a faculty member at the University of Chicago, and a Pulitzer Prize–winning author of numerous books, most notably a trilogy on world intellectual history.

In the few minutes I had with Boorstin, I thanked him for *The Discoverers*, the first book of the trilogy, an epic chronicle of humans on their many quests of discovery through the ages. He was pleased when I told him that the Discovery Channel was influenced by his book. He told me to look for *The Creators*, his history of artists, which he was then finishing up for publication. Later, in 1998, six years before his death, Boorstin would publish *The Seekers*, his history of religion and science.

Of all the world's technological advances, Boorstin always maintained that the book was the greatest. He also cautioned that learning is a process that is never completed, saying: "Education is learning what you didn't even know you didn't know." That is one of my favorite Boorstin quotes, along with this one: "The greatest obstacle to discovery is not ignorance—it is the illusion of knowledge."

Those two quotes have animated my career. And that's why that day I thanked him.

Daniel Boorstin recognized that the pursuit of absolute knowledge is a fool's errand. The truly educated humbly realize all that they don't know. My father taught me that the more you know, the more you realize all that you don't know. In *The Ascent of Man*, Jacob Bronowski revealed the horrors wrought by those truly ignorant individuals who believed they had obtained "absolute knowledge."

All three were teaching the same lesson. Education fosters intellectual humility, and this humility contributes to an attitude of tolerance that is impervious to notions about superiority and inferiority in race, religion, and politics. It stands to reason, then, that global education will contribute to the ultimate goal of human civilization: a world at peace. Until that goal is reached, however, we will continue to witness the destructive power of ignorance.

Flight 93

There is probably no better illustration of the horrors wrought by truly ignorant individuals than the tragic events of 9/11. At Discovery, we bore witness to the senseless violence caused by humans who simply were not part of the educated world.

Stepping on board United Airlines Flight 93 with her fellow passengers that morning in Newark was a twenty-seven-year-old rising star at Discovery, Elizabeth Wainio. Recently promoted to head up all Discovery Channel stores in the New York area, Liz Wainio had eagerly set off for a meeting with her colleagues outside San Francisco to make plans for our national retail effort for the year-end holiday season. Bright, energetic, and cheerful, Liz was obviously in love with life and with all those around her. Like the crew members and her fellow passengers on Flight 93, Liz represented the very best of humanity and its peaceful aspirations.

The passengers and crew members aboard Flight 93 had the momentary gifts of time and connection. As their hijacked aircraft turned southward with the bright eastern sunlight streaming through the left windows, the men and women of Flight 93 reached out to make vital connections to those they loved. In those precious telephone conversations, they gained critical knowledge about the horrible fate of the other hijacked planes that morning and the resulting tremendous loss of life on the ground in symbolic buildings filled with thousands of innocent lives. And here they were, heading south, most likely bound for buildings in the nation's capital that represented and symbolized democracy, freedom, and liberty. The citizens aboard Flight 93 found themselves aboard a deadly missile apparently aimed at the very heart of a nation and the hearts of thousands of innocent lives.

In those somber and anxious moments when the ominous knowledge of their fate spread through the cabin, the passengers aboard Flight 93 had to make life-impacting choices. They had to overcome every instinct for self-preservation that must have genetically commanded them to just sit still, don't call attention to yourself, and hope for the best. But they continued to reach out through their telephones to learn and to connect with loved ones they had left behind. And they made a plan.

Liz Wainio reached her stepmother in Baltimore. In addition to learning more about the fate of the other hijackings that morning, Liz had the precious opportunity to share her message of love for her mother, her family members, and her coworkers. And she and her stepmother had a brief but profound quiet time together on the phone, sharing a gaze at the same brilliant blue sky that covered and embraced them both. And then Liz broke the silence by saying, "I have to go. They're breaking into the cockpit. I love you."

Instead of accepting a fate in control by the darkest forces of humanity, these citizens rose in defiance from their seats to directly confront and combat a vicious element of the unthinkable terrorism that had struck their nation that day in September. Although every one of their lives were lost in the fight for control of the cockpit, that plane, with its nearly full load of fuel, never reached the target selected by the terrorists. This we know. Others are surely alive today because a bold group of Americans rose from their seats.

So that the brave actions of the passengers and crew of Flight 93 are never forgotten, Maureen and I have joined with former presidents Bill Clinton and George W. Bush and others who have led the effort to fund the Flight 93 National Memorial in Shanksville, Pennsylvania.

At Discovery, our loss of Elizabeth Wainio reminds us that a world without education is a world at risk.

Assets for Global Education

According to the U.S. Census Bureau, there were, in 2012, just over 7 billion people living on the planet. These 7 billion humans live in 1.8 billion households, according to the International Tele-communications Union (ITU). The ITU estimates that 1.4 billion of the world's 1.8 billion households now have television. It also estimates that 650 million households now have cable or satellite TV; computers are now present in 600 million households; and 500 million households now have access to the Internet. Business Wire has reported that at the end of 2011, 439 million households worldwide had installed home Wi-Fi networks.

Discovery Communications currently reaches 415 million global households that have cable and satellite TV service. Although I am grateful for our penetration into nearly a fourth of the world's households, I remain troubled by the millions of households devoid of educational technologies. In a world where an estimated 20 per-cent of our fellow humans still live in dwellings without electricity, it should be no surprise that television and the wonders of modern communications are simply not part of the experience of 1.4 billion people living on planet earth.

In thinking about the power of television to uplift, inspire, and educate, I recall a very special letter I received in 1998. Every day at Discovery, we receive letters from viewers all over the world who tell us, in different ways, how a show or series has affected them. The sheer quantity of mail prevents any one of us at Discovery from reading all of the letters. However, our Viewer Relations staff dutifully categorizes these comments, and we receive regular re-ports on the input provided by our fans.

But every now and then, a viewer letter makes it up to me, often because someone along the way has decided it is too important to merely file away.

In 1997, my assistant, Heidi Schwab, gave me one such letter, from a single mom who lived in Sacramento. It was a rather long handwritten letter on the occasion of her son's acceptance into college. I paused when she wrote that her son had found his passion for science and nature from watching the Discovery Channel every day after school since the time he was in first grade. It only then struck me that we had been telecasting for more than twelve years—time enough for a kid to pass from first grade all the way to college. Because she was raising her son alone, she worried about the potential of juvenile delinquency. Instead of this fate, she wrote, the Discovery Channel had opened her son's eyes to the wonders outside the neighborhood. Our television programs had connected him to the worlds of science and nature, and his innate curiosity had been fully engaged.

That letter really resonated with me. Just as Cronkite's *Twentieth Century* series had broken through the bounds of geography to inspire me in Alabama, the Discovery Channel had penetrated into the living room of a curious boy in Sacramento. Today, as Discovery reaches into more than 215 countries, I find it hard to imagine just how much impact we are having out there beyond just the viewership numbers. I hope that it is profound and positive; at least that's what we've struggled to do. But we will never really know: in the end, the anecdotal information, like that letter, is about all we have to remind us that our work really matters.

Dreaming Forward

What do you do after your dream comes true?

Bringing educational content to television was my dream as a young man; building a company to do so was that of my early adulthood. The realization of that dream was Discovery Communications—and it has become the world's largest provider of nonfiction television, a global corporation employing more than 4,000 people and valued at $23 billion. In leading Discovery to this achievement, I have also had the opportunity to meet some of the most interesting, powerful, and famous people in the world—and even shaken hands with many of my childhood heroes. And, it goes without saying, all of this has had its financial rewards.

Now that many of my wildest dreams have come true, the question is, *What do I do now?*

The answer is the only one I know, the only one that has worked for me to date: follow my daydreams.

Many times in this book I have written about the power and consequence of daydreams. As I'll explain later, one of the key distinguishing traits of entrepreneurs is their willingness to pay close attention to their daydreams. Daydreams offer clues to what really interests us in life and persistent daydreams often unlock pathways toward the creation of something new in the world.

And in recent years, just such a daydream has begun to fill my idle thoughts. It has two parts, but both revolve around a single theme—and that is to *expand the original Discovery vision from impacting millions to billions.*

By that, I mean:

1. How do we—using both the massive archives we've already created plus the latest technology tools and platforms—address the enormous challenge of improving the education of all humans regardless of where they live on the planet? I will look at a potential solution to that challenge in this chapter.

2. How do we—using technology, original content, and new teaching techniques—expand that audience for curiosity-based television from that endemic 25 percent to include the rest of the population? I will use

the concluding pages of this book to look at one possible solution, one that combines the digital world of television with the "analog" world of nature.

So, join me for a while in my daydream.

The GET Plan

The signals of satellite-delivered television now reach all corners of the globe. We take that for granted these days—and yet it represents a major turning point in human history.

Satellite signals now strike every exposed speck of dirt on the African continent—as they do on other places on the planet that still lack the fruits of the information age. Imagine if the world's communications satellite infrastructure could be harnessed to reach children and parents who have never seen the world outside their village. Imagine if programs on world history, science, technology, medicine, and language studies could become part of the everyday life of every single human on the planet.

A decade ago, the idea was impossible. In my daydream, it is already real.

The Village Hub

How would it be done? How do you bring an educational television service—what I call the Global Educational Television Network (or GET Network)—to the 400 million global households who currently lack electricity? The answer, I believe, is to take one step up from homes and focus instead upon the smallest community: the village. And, in particular, the *school* within that village.

Suddenly, we have a more reasonable number: 1.14 million village schools in the developing world, in Africa, South America, and Asia, each serving, on average, 350 families. Equipping a million schools with a satellite-delivered educational television system suddenly becomes an achievable goal. Moreover, with the school educational content being delivered through the day, the evenings could be used for community viewing.

My research tells me that there are just eight components in creating such a hub:

1. Universal global satellite television reach (done!);
2. Electricity, portable generator, or solar power system;
3. Satellite dish;
4. GET Network, consisting of a daily schedule of video content on history, science, technology, medicine, and language studies grouped into daily segments for elementary school, middle school, and high school education;
5. Television screen;
6. Two-thousand-hour DVR;
7. Participating village school; and
8. Trained teacher.

That's not much, is it? Now, here's a surprise: compared to other global activities, such a system would also be inexpensive to implement.

For example, I estimate that the annual operating cost of that commercial-free GET Network would be $50 million. This sum is adequate to pay for all network personnel, content development, and satellite transmission costs.

To this we add the onetime capital expenses needed to purchase all of the equipment on our list. Assuming no available electricity, it totals $5,500. With an electrical service, it is just $1,500.

Now, for planning purposes, let's estimate that, of the million village schools without television service, approximately 60 percent also lack electricity. Using these assumptions, an international effort to enable the world's village schools to receive the Global Educational Television Network would cost only $4.45 billion.

Investing Wisely

I can't imagine a better use that could be made of $4.5 billion in global development funds than implementing such a Global Educational Television Network. We simply cannot leave the rest of the world behind. Children growing up in poverty-stricken regions of Africa and other continents must have a way to envision another life, a more fulfilling and complete life that begins with education. And the rewards would be staggering: imagine the increase in global commerce, in the world's total intellectual capital and innovation, and the improved global health that would come from adding a billion educated new consumers and entrepreneurs to humanity's great Global Conversation.

The Cost of Reality

It's doable and it's affordable—those are the same two factors that guided my decision to create Discovery. So what keeps it from happening?

Organization and politics. Remember, such a program would be transnational, bringing educational programming to more than one hundred nations—each with its own distinct government, educational ministry, and rules regarding pedagogic content. There is no way you can just ship this equipment across borders and then start transmitting educational television—some nations might readily accept it, but others may actively block it.

The solution, I believe—with the knowledge that it won't work everywhere—is to enlist interested nations in participating in the empowerment of their own citizenry, especially the children, with education. And this will require that they put their own skin in the game—with governments, foundations, and global corporations undertaking the financial commitment necessary to open a new world of possibilities to children locked in poverty and illiteracy, children who are currently vulnerable to the worst consequences of ignorance.

As for those nations that refuse to participate? I can only hope that they will soon recognize the cost of being left behind.

In practice, this Global Educational Television partnership could bring together interested nations and their governmental agencies as well as foundations and global corporations in an effort to fund the $4.5 billion in capital costs of equipping those million schools. Perhaps 90 percent of the funding could come from thirty contributing nations in the developing world who might each provide an average appropriation of $135 million to the cause. The balance of $450 million might then be contributed by a consortium of one hundred leading corporations and foundations at $4.5 million each.

Operating costs of the GET Network ($50 million annually) could be funded in the same ratio as the capital costs: 90 percent by appropriations from developing countries and 10 percent by corporations and foundations. Individuals and corporations would, of course, be the primary funders of the entire effort, as the contributions from governments would have been initially sourced from tax collections on corporate earnings and individual incomes. A consortium of educational content providers, including Discovery Communications, would be invited to contribute educational programming at no cost.

A twenty-four-hour schedule of content would be broadcast every day and captured by the target schools utilizing their two-thousand-hour DVRs. Because classroom-length video segments average twelve minutes in length, a two-thousand-hour DVR could index and store up to ten thousand educational videos for immediate retrieval and use. Teachers would play the content at times of their choosing in providing instruction and enlightenment for children at all grade levels. Parents and other adults would be invited to experience television in the evening hours at the school facilities.

Roadblocks

Sound ambitious? It is. But in terms of cost and technology, it is actually less ambitious in many ways than the creation of Discovery Communications.

In fact, thanks to Discovery, we are already partway there. For example, in 1997, we created the Discovery Channel Global Education Partnership (DCGEP) to equip African schools with educational television using a similar funding strategy. Now expanded to South America, the partnership funds the purchase of TV sets and DVDs—as well as teacher training and supplementary study guides.

Through DCGEP, we have witnessed entire African villages turning out to experience television for the first time. Students and their parents sat entranced by a view of the world, and universe, beyond anything they had ever imagined. School attendance dramatically increased and learning improved.

The effectiveness of DCGEP in accelerating learning and in

changing student perspectives has resulted in multimillion-dollar funding commitments by the Coca-Cola Africa Foundation, Chevron, Shell, USAID, and Discovery Communications. To date, more than 480 of these Video Learning Centers have been established in Angola, Brazil, Egypt, Ghana, Kenya, Mexico, Morocco, Namibia, Nigeria, Peru, Romania, South Africa, Uganda, Venezuela, and Zimbabwe. These Video Learning Centers have to date served more than 1 million students, more than 3 million community members, and almost 18,000 teachers.

Impressive numbers, but compared to the overall challenge it is only a tiny start. Still, the model has now been proven, and the corporate and foundation world has shown that it is willing to step up to the challenge. Now it is time for governments to recognize their own stake in making this universal.

In this regard, there is hope. On September 26, 2012, I was in attendance at the United Nations headquarters building in New York when Secretary-General Ban Ki-moon announced Education First, a worldwide initiative to get every child educated. The secretary-general appointed Gordon Brown, former prime minister of the United Kingdom, as his Special Envoy for Global Education. Prior to the UN event, Gordon Brown had phoned me to invite me to join with other corporate leaders on the Global Business Coalition for Education (GBCE). Chaired by Gordon Brown, GBCE will assist in the effort to create the global financial structure needed for global education.

Will all of this happen tomorrow? Hardly. But I learned long ago that the path from daydream to reality can be long and twisty, and filled with roadblocks. But if you refuse to give up; if you are both patient and ready to strike when the moment is right; and if you work smart, daydreams can become more real than you ever imagined. And it helps to have partners in the mission.

Chapter 30

Gateway to Curiosity

Curiosity is lying in wait for every secret.

—Ralph Waldo Emerson

The other side of my daydream takes me in a very different direction—not to the other side of the world, but into my own life and past in search of answers.

I began my journey to the canyons of western Colorado when I was five years old—though it would take nearly forty years before I reached them.

As I mentioned earlier, as a boy I was captivated by my father's old road maps of Colorado and Utah, which he had collected on his own wanderings out west during the 1920s and 1930s. These maps, a little worn but still sporting their colorful illustrations of the joys of traveling the nation by car, worked their magic on me. I longed to see the majestic snow-covered Rockies, the deep canyons cut by raging rivers, and desert vistas so wide that you could see for a hundred miles.

Many evenings after my dad came home from work, I would jump behind the wheel of his 1952 Plymouth Cranbrook and, armed with a Sinclair Oil map of Colorado or Utah, set off on a great imaginary drive to far off Provo, Grand Junction, Rifle, and

Zion. Adding to the wonder of each journey were the illustrated dinosaurs on the map covers that whispered I was traveling to the land of *Tyrannosaurus rex*. And, along the way—that is, until my mother called me for dinner—I always made a point of stopping by the Great Salt Lake.

One of my greatest regrets in life is that I never got to explore the West with my dad; perhaps in part because of that, I cherish the fact that he instilled in me a powerful curiosity about the planet and its wonders.

I also never forgot that he often told me that there was a particular place out west he thought the most beautiful and grand: the canyon country southwest of Grand Junction, Colorado. It had captured his heart the moment he saw it—my mother told me of a train journey in 1945 when our family was returning to West Virginia from Portland, Oregon, following my father's work in the shipyards during the war. I was not yet born, but my older sister and brother, then toddlers, were along for the trip. When the train stopped in Grand Junction my father tried his best to convince my mother to have the family stay a few days and consider living there.

Even before that, in the mid-1920s, my father and his older brother Robert explored the West (hence the maps) by traveling from state to state working ranches for three years. Apparently they had worked on a ranch southwest of Grand Junction—leading to that moment at the train station twenty years later; my father's pitch hadn't been as spontaneous as it seemed.

But my mother longed to be with her friends and family in West Virginia. So the little family reboarded the train, and my father never saw Grand Junction again.

Perhaps it was in the blood. I fell in love with the West on my first visit in 1974, just after I graduated from college. I toured the front range of Colorado from Pike's Peak north to the Rocky

Mountain National Park, where I made an exhilarating and life-changing climb of Longs Peak. Ever since that June day I have relished every opportunity to explore and hike and ski the wondrous landscapes of Utah, Idaho, Colorado, Arizona, and New Mexico.

Our Exotic Backyard

In 1989, I found myself in Kenya around an evening campfire alongside the Mara River with a BBC natural history film crew there to film a joint Discovery/BBC documentary. Knowing the crew members were world travelers, I asked them to identify the most dramatic landscape they had seen.

I had expected them to list exotic locations in Nepal or New Zealand, but to a person they said "the American Southwest." I was only a little surprised: there is really no place on earth possessing such grand contrasts. And after Maureen and I returned to the States we set out in search of a place out west.

We found many beautiful locations. And each new discovery only deepened our desire for a permanent place where we could retreat, reflect, and enrich our lives amid an unspoiled natural landscape. We began to spend time in the summers in Idaho, and in winter we skied the Wasatch Mountains of Utah, where our children developed their own passions for the West.

Maureen is a quilt artist and collector, and so she was naturally drawn to Santa Fe. In early 1995, we discovered a ranch in northern New Mexico that seemed ideal. And after meeting with a realtor, we decided to go for it. I was scheduled to make one last visit prior to making an offer—and then, on the day before my trip, I stumbled across a real estate ad in the *Wall Street Journal*: "Ranch for sale in the spectacular red rock canyon country southwest of Grand Junction, Colorado."

Those words reached places deep inside me that I didn't know existed. I quickly changed my Santa Fe trip plans to include a stop in Grand Junction.

The Realtor was also a pilot. After a sixteen-minute flight in his yellow Cessna 185, we began to circle an area where magnificent red rock canyons converged at the confluence of West Creek and the Dolores River. As we descended into the canyons, a dirt landing strip appeared just ahead of the most stunning red rock landform I had ever seen, glowing in the morning light. "It's called the Palisade," said the Realtor-pilot as he banked us toward the landing strip.

We purchased the West Creek Ranch a few weeks later.

In the years that followed, other large ranch tracts in that scenic region of western Mesa County, Colorado, became available for sale. Fearing purchase by developers for subdivision sales, and anxious to save both the vistas and the wildlife habitats, Maureen and I steadily acquired property outside the little settlement of Gateway, once a thriving mining town.

After acquiring the large Sky Mesa Ranch we placed more than four thousand acres in a permanent conservation easement with the Nature Conservancy in order to protect the ranch's unspoiled wildlife habitat of North Cottonwood Canyon.

In 2001, I met with officials of Mesa County. They too wanted to protect the scenic riches of the canyon country; but they also wanted to revitalize Gateway, which had never recovered from the closing of its mines. Included in our purchase of the Sky Mesa Ranch were parcels in Gateway that engineering studies showed to be the only viable sites for a desperately needed new wastewater treatment facility.

Our family donated the land and construction funds for the treatment plant as part of a "smart planning" program for the community. We also dedicated land we owned within an approximate one-mile perimeter of the Gateway U.S. post office for future commercial development. This would keep new residences and new economic activity confined to where it had historically been located—and that would in turn preserve the surrounding open space.

Now this corner of Colorado would be preserved as nature had created it.

The Oldest Story

As you stare up 2,500 feet of canyon walls to the top of the colossal red rock landform of the Palisade, a full 300 million years of the planet's history is arrayed before you. The colorful geological layers of sandstone preserve each era of the earth's past, even back to a time before the age of dinosaurs. Here the planet seems to open up to tell its story.

In 2004, I began to wonder if this could also become a place where the curiosity of others could come to play. Like Discovery before, the idea captured my imagination and began to consume my every free moment. It wasn't long before I had devised Gateway Canyons, a destination resort devoted to "curiosity adventures."

Today, Gateway Canyons Resort isn't just a chance for guests to get away into some of the most spectacular landscapes on the planet; they can also attend informal lectures and field trips, exploring topics in science and technology, world history, the arts, geology, astronomy, Native American culture, and self-improvement. Needless to say, Gateway Canyons also offers an intimate fifty-six-seat HD theater to watch Discovery video treasures any time of the day.

Teaching the Rest

Gateway Canyons led me to a curious discovery: Like Oprah, I am, at heart, a teacher. It is my destiny in life. And now my passion for helping people explore their world "vicariously" through media has come full circle to helping people to actually "touch" the real world they live in—and thus to integrate the digital and natural worlds in a new and more powerful way.

Perhaps that is the key to reaching that elusive other 75 percent who have never seen television as a medium for learning—the three-quarters of mankind whom I've spent my entire career staying away from. I can't think of a better way to spend the rest of my life than building a bridge to them, and then teaching them how to cross it.

As I write this, I have one granddaughter and another grandchild on the way. Riley Grace Hendricks, one year old, has reddish brown hair and big brown eyes that look at the world around her with a boundless and enviable curiosity. Nothing is more satisfying in my life than walking with her and exploring a universe that is filled with endless novelty. For her, just touching the bark of a tree is an epiphany. In those precious moments, I am her grandfather, her teacher, and personal storyteller.

The vision with which I began this story, the one that defined my life and career, was of the 25 percent of adults who remain endlessly curious. But with children, that figure is 100 percent. Something is lost on the passage to adulthood, as the world of work and responsibility severs our connection with the natural world.

That hasn't always been true. And, in a few weeks after writing this book, I'll be in Tanzania spending time with the Hadza people, the last true hunter-gatherer tribe in Africa. Now numbering only about 1,200 individuals, the Hadza owe their remarkable survival over eons of time to their intense primal curiosity about every aspect of their natural habitat. They chronicle their past in stories told in a language few understand and they share with one another in a way the world has forgotten.

There in the hills to the west of Yaida Valley, sitting at a campfire and staring up at the stars; at home watching Riley discover her own version of the four o'clock flowers; and wherever else my curiosity leads me, I intend to find my way through to the three-quarters of mankind that haven't been part of my daydreams until now.

And I plan to spend the rest of my life in that search.

The Entrepreneur Inside

Whether you think that you can or you can't, you're right.

—HENRY FORD

When I was in high school I fantasized about going to Harvard. It was not to be. I did, nonetheless, finally get a chance to visit the Harvard campus some twenty years later as a guest lecturer.

I am seldom stumped by inquiries about Discovery, but the question I received after my lecture that day in 1991 at the Harvard Business School still sticks in my mind.

It came from a confident young man at the reception following my speech. He asked: "So why were you the one that created the Discovery Channel? What was it about you personally that made it happen?"

I replied in perhaps a too-flippant manner, "Well, I probably had confidence that I really didn't deserve. Since I came as an outsider into the television business, I really wasn't burdened with detailed industry knowledge of all the reasons why Discovery would not work."

I could tell that my answer was not at all satisfying to this person, who I then learned had real dreams about starting a business.

Then he said something revealing: "I guess I just wonder if I would give up."

I thought to myself at that moment that I never, ever even contemplated the possibility of giving up—never, *ever.* This kid already had the dreaded thought before he had even taken the first step in creating a new venture. I assured him that the more he researched his idea the better he'd be able to determine his true level of confidence.

What is it that is inside great entrepreneurs—like Amazon's Jeff Bezos, Silicon Graphics' Jim Clark, or FedEx's Fred Smith—that enables them to do what they do? I'm fascinated by entrepreneurs and, through the years, I've tried to discover some of their common "inside" traits. I have come to believe that there are seven "inside" traits shared by entrepreneurs. Not all of them have these seven in equal measure—I certainly don't—but they are almost always present.

Let's look at each in turn:

1. An intense, driving curiosity

I would like to say that all people have what it takes to be an entrepreneur, but it isn't true. New business ventures can only be started by people who have a fundamental curiosity about the world and are powerfully driven by their curiosity to find solutions and solve puzzles. That is about one-quarter of the population.

2. A willingness to really "listen" to daydreams

Persistent daydreams are often the key precursor to a burning passion to create something new in the world. When you find that your thoughts consistently drift toward an activity or idea or puzzle, this is a clue that there is something worth investigating and exploring in your life. Daydreams offer a path to discover what really engages our curiosity and passions in life.

3. A burning passion that leads to periods of creative obsession

Passion is responsible for the stamina and perseverance needed to "stay on task" until the target is in sight. Yet often that target is in sight but frustratingly just out of reach for months or years. Obsession becomes responsible for that last great human effort to create something new in the world.

In his Menlo Park laboratory, Thomas Edison labored for years to find just the right filament that would bring sustainable light into the darkness. Director James Cameron is perpetually obsessed with creating new special effects technologies that are destined to enchant the world. And who can deny that we owe the incredible iPad and the tablet revolution to the passionate obsession of Steve Jobs? Curiosity-fueled passion and creative obsession underlie most of the world's great entrepreneurial ventures, inventions, scientific breakthroughs, and works of art.

4. An ability to visualize success

There are many activities in a young person's life through which a visualization of a successful effort or project becomes the groundwork for confidence and optimism. Planning a science project, a debate performance, or a well-researched term paper all involve "seeing" the activity before it is actually accomplished. If someone has never experienced the process of visualizing success in advance and seeing that visualization come true, I believe they are poorly prepared to create something new and risky in the world. There is a world full of doubters who stand ready to discourage and kill the dreams of those lacking a confident vision. You need to visualize past them.

5. Optimism and confidence that defy logic

Like that young man at Harvard Business School, if you really think you cannot accomplish something, you won't. If you really think you can accomplish something, you will. Pessimists never become great entrepreneurs. Optimism, even when it is against all odds, is the prerequisite for success. In business, "logical" is only what has been proven to work in the past. Prove your vision, and you will be the new "logical."

6. Self-reliance and an eagerness to undertake the risks of creating one's own destiny

Some people are self-reliant, and some people are dependent. Others fall somewhere in between. It is difficult to know how much of "self-reliance" is inherited behavior and how much is due to life experience. Either way, self-reliance is a vital trait for entrepreneurs, especially at the beginning, because no one will buy into your dreams until you begin to make them real.

7. Purpose

An entire book could be written about this trait. In fact, a friend of mine, the advertising guru Roy Spence, wrote just such a book, titled *It's Not What You Sell, It's What You Stand For*. Like me, Roy believes that no one can build a valuable company without the fundamental ingredient of "purpose." Of the seven traits I have listed, it is "purpose" that most singularly holds the secret to entrepreneurial success.

When many pondered their fates during the recession that swept the world in 2008, Roy wrote:

> When the ashes clear from this economic Armageddon, the only organizations left standing will be the ones that actually stand for something. Without a Purpose that improves people's lives and contributes to the greater good, organizations will struggle.

A person who creates a success story in business is on a mission.

Perhaps like that ancient human who could not rest until he or she found a better, more reliable way to carry fire from one camp to the next, the modern entrepreneur passionately wants to accomplish something for the tribe. Purpose gives life meaning. It provides a drive that is unstoppable.

Purpose provides endurance for the long run that lies ahead.

Business Creation

The ladder of success is best climbed by stepping on the rungs of opportunity.

—Ayn Rand

What is it like to be an entrepreneur in America? What are the key ingredients for creating and sustaining a business concept through research, planning, financing, product development, marketing, and operations? What are the lessons learned in the spirit-testing crucible of the competitive free enterprise system?

Here are the lessons from my career:

1. Listen to, carefully evaluate, and confidently share the persistent daydream.

Every great business that impacts the world has its origin in an individual who listened carefully to a persistent daydream about providing a new service or product that will improve the human condition by making life a little more efficient, more productive, or more enjoyable.

Many entrepreneurial daydreams are fleeting and deservedly so. However, some ideas seem not to go away—even after they pass every internal thought test we can muster.

When you become entranced by a persistent entrepreneurial daydream, outside observers—a work colleague, a spouse, or a friend—may begin to notice your distraction. How you handle the initial sharing of your persistent daydream with others is a critical step—which must be taken carefully.

2. Gain confidence through research.

Before sharing an idea that is half-baked—and thus risking the doubt of others—arm yourself with research focused on every aspect of your business concept. Be tireless. Become an expert. Only after exhaustively researching every conceivable pitfall and convincing yourself you are still on the right path, begin drafting your initial business plan.

3. Convert your mental obsession into a comprehensive written business plan.

Now channel the energy of your obsession into drafting your business plan. Prepare for some hard work. You will not mind it, though. By this point, you should be truly obsessed in a positive and constructive way. If you are not obsessed, go no further; the road ahead cannot be traveled by the weak in spirit and attitude. It is indeed a road less traveled for a reason.

One of my favorite stories of an individual who turned an obsession into an empire is that of Reed Hastings, a businessman made furious by the late fees charged by video rental outlets.

Like many of us, Hastings forgot to return a rented DVD, in his case a copy of *Apollo 13*. In fact, he was actually six weeks late in returning the video rental—and owed a whopping forty dollars. He was embarrassed to even tell his wife that he owed much more in late fees than the actual DVD purchase price.

As often happens to a curious mind when challenged by an

unfairness or deficiency in the marketplace, Hastings began to daydream about a better way to manage and distribute video rentals.

It was on the way to the gym one day that one of Reed's daydreams unexpectedly landed on the solution: use the postal service in a distribution and return system in which customers could rent and return DVDs at their leisure.

Eventually, after the postal delivery model proved wildly successful, Reed also realized that for much less than the cost of that one egregious late fee, forty dollars, he could provide numerous great movie experiences to monthly video streaming subscribers via a new Internet distribution system that completely eliminated the need for hard-copy video returns.

And thus was born Netflix, one of the most successful new media delivery companies of our time. And Reed had the ultimate satisfaction of destroying the entire store-based video rental industry that had made his life miserable. Now no one would ever have to pay late fees on DVDs again.

Reed Hastings turned a personal annoyance that he had experienced in the marketplace into a driving passion to solve a distribution puzzle in a fashion that would delight consumers. In solving that puzzle, Reed Hastings created the Netflix empire that is today worth billions of dollars. The lesson to be learned is that consumers benefit when someone among us, like a Reed Hastings, gets annoyed with the status quo and develops a passion that leads to obsession and—in the most important step—converts that obsession into an actual plan to solve that marketplace disappointment.

In starting the process of writing your business plan, don't be discouraged if you do not have a formal business education. There are a number of good books and online guides available to help you write a compelling business plan. Writing your business plan will serve as your first experience in the discipline you'll need to succeed.

You will likely not be starting out with the money you'll need to launch and sustain a business. Until you reach break-even you'll need either loans or investment funds to finance your venture. All who contemplate backing your idea will carefully assess your personal attributes and your vision as outlined in your business plan. Thus your business plan must contain the following essential elements:

business mission;

financial objectives;

assessment of the market environment;

identification of risk factors;

product development plan;

marketing plan;

operations plan;

financing plan;

organizational and staffing plan;

a "pro forma" of the expected revenue, expenses, and estimated profit and losses over five years;

a revenue or sales outlook over ten years.

4. Make the decision to go "all in"—or drop out of the game.

The most significant decision every successful business creator has had to make is whether to go "all in" and to fully assume the risk of failure. There are no half steps in becoming an entrepreneur.

It is at this point that most individuals begin to tremble over the emotional and financial consequences of failure and choose to drop out of the game.

The decision to proceed in spite of the enormous risks involved is truly the defining moment that distinguishes the entrepreneur from those in other walks of life. There is no such thing as a partial decision in these matters. One's current means of employment is no longer a priority. Nor can there be a fear of assuming personal debt at a level that can be repaid only through achieving success in the new enterprise.

Without being "all in" on the risks of your entrepreneurial venture, it is difficult—even unethical—to convince others to leave the security of their jobs to join your dream. If any venture capitalist senses that you have any lingering doubts, you can be sure that those potential investment dollars will not come your way.

5. Recruit key executives and employees who complete your business knowledge.

It is now time to meet with potential investors or lenders. They will no doubt be impressed by your personal passion and the particular skill sets that you bring to the table. However, there are very few individuals who can do it all to launch a new enterprise.

So, you will need a number of key consultants, allies, and executives to round out your planned management team. With some of these individuals you will secure contingent commitments to join you as soon as financing is secured. Others will be so captivated by your idea that they will freely leave their current jobs and assume risk alongside you. These special "believers" should especially be rewarded with stock options, founders' stock, or a share in a profit-sharing plan so that they too can reap the rewards of the successful enterprise they helped to create.

6. Secure financing that will fund operations until your new business reaches profitability.

Unless your dream is to start a small local business (such as a gift store or bake shop) that can be financed out of personal savings or loans from family members, you will need to enter the world of venture capital.

As an "all in" entrepreneur, you will likely pursue all local bank financing you can. This will be comforting to the venture capital-ists that you will eventually approach. Your local banker will only provide a loan if it is secured by collateral, most likely the equity you have in your home. Venture capitalists will view your personal borrowings as evidence that you harbor no secret thoughts or worries about a fatal flaw in your business plan.

In your quest for financing, you will need a securities lawyer and an investment bank to help you navigate the process of securing the funds to implement your business plan. Although their legal advice and introductions will be key elements in your journey, your success in fund-raising will ultimately depend on the quality of your personal presentation of the business plan.

7. Be emotionally prepared for rejection.

After all my financing rounds had closed and I had successfully raised $25 million, I took a moment in the summer of 1986 to reflect on the number of times I heard "no." I counted 211 rejections from potential corporate investors before I received the collective and enthusiastic "yes" from my seven major financial backers.

I wish that I could tell you that most entrepreneurs don't have to endure this level of rejection. I walked away from meetings with a total of 211 potential investors who thought my idea was not worth funding. However, I have learned from my fellow entrepreneurial travelers that my capital fund-raising experience was far from unusual.

What this means is that successful entrepreneurs are endowed with, or quickly develop, an emotional immunity from rejection. And that immunity, I believe, stems from optimism and confidence.

During the most depressing periods of my fund-raising, I could always buck myself up by recalling the comprehensive and careful nature of my market research and business planning. True or not, I could console myself that I simply knew more about the business sector I planned to enter than did those who predicted my failure.

8. Define your business mission in a way that separates it from what may be a fleeting means of distribution or delivery technology.

If your goal is to create an enduring enterprise that survives for decades you must think very carefully and deliberately about how you define your business to your employees. They must fully comprehend all avenues of growth and opportunity.

Don't limit your growth opportunities by defining your business with a current technology. We live in an age of constant and rapid change, punctuated by major technological revolutions. If you tie your enterprise's fate to today's technology, you risk becoming obsolete tomorrow.

Instead, define your mission by the experiences you will deliver to your customers, whatever the underlying technology—and then inculcate that mission into the minds of your employees. After all, it is they who will carry the torch of your vision long after you are gone.

9. Don't be intimidated by not being a current player in the business sector you are targeting.

I had a distinct advantage in starting the Discovery Channel by not having any experience whatsoever in the television business. I simply did not know all the reasons why the Discovery Channel could fail. Launching a business outside your career experience sounds like a bad idea, but there are also real advantages.

For example, it can be advantageous to not be enmeshed in a static corporate culture that has obviously not seized on the opportunity that you have uncovered. Also, viewed from outside an industry, consumer trends can often be much clearer since they are not obscured by the challenging grind of daily operations within existing industry players.

That said, you must be a serious student of the industry you want to enter. If you can become an A student, you will be well armed to successfully compete with the dinosaur thinking that may have plagued your target industry for decades.

10. Identify long-term consumer trends that form the basis of your growth vision.

It sounds simple, but it is very hard to identify with any certainty major consumer behavior trends that are just now emerging but will define the future of your business.

These are your bedrock assessments of how consumers behave now and how they will behave in the future. And the only way to obtain this knowledge is to get out there in the world and *watch and listen*. Read everything you can, from trade journals to pop culture magazines. When you have the money, commission surveys and focus groups. And never, ever become complacent, or convinced that you know what people are thinking.

Once you have identified and researched these major trends,

you must have the confidence to invest in creating new products and services that will address them. Once again, you may find yourself having to bet the store—and that decision is a lot more difficult when you have a store to bet.

Lesson of Lessons

These ten lessons reflect my experience in creating a business that has passed the test of time for thirty years, and in more than 215 countries. While these lessons are mostly relevant to starting up and sustaining a corporation that operates on the national or international stage, these ten lessons should be applicable to anyone, anywhere who dreams of one day starting their own business.

Acknowledgments

This book project came to life because Gail Ross decided to pay me a visit in late 2010 after she read about my plans for a new Discovery series called *Curiosity*. As a literary agent, Gail had been intrigued to learn in our first meeting that "curiosity" was not only the name of our new landmark television series. It was also the singular, driving force behind the creation of Discovery Channel and our global enterprise. We discussed my belief that all successful new ventures and innovations are due to passionate curiosities that sometime fuel rather obsessive behavior by entrepreneurs and inventors. Afterward, Gail encouraged me to write the story of Discovery Communications in that context.

After I agreed to take on the book challenge, Gail then introduced me to Hollis Heimbouch, Vice President and Publisher of Harper Business at HarperCollins Publishers, and David Hirshey, Senior Vice President and Executive Editor at HarperCollins Publishers. Armed with the intelligent insights of Hollis Heimbouch and the experienced guidance of David Hirshey, I eagerly began to write. I owe a great deal of thanks to Gail, Hollis, and David for their wisdom and support throughout the project. It was also through their introduction that I met the talented Michael Malone, who skillfully edited my final draft while promoting his wonderful new book on memory, *The Guardian of All Things*.

I was very fortunate to have the assistance of a very overqualified proofreader, who took the time to read my drafts and offer suggestions for improvement. I heeded her good advice. For her thoughtful input on my drafts, I owe special thanks to Tia Cudahy, Executive Vice President and General Counsel at Hendricks Investment Holdings LLC (HIH).

My daughter, Elizabeth Hendricks North, honed her writing skills at Princeton and put those talents to excellent use in editing the very best draft that her dad could produce. Elizabeth repaired my confusingly long sentences, offered suggestions to improve the flow of the content, and made the book much more readable. I am very grateful for the time that Elizabeth devoted to my book project.

David Leavy, Chief Communications Officer and Senior Executive Vice President, Corporate Marketing & Affairs at Discovery Communications, cheerfully took on the burdensome task of "fact-checking" the business items in the book. I greatly appreciate his diligent efforts as well as the valuable assistance of Michelle Russo in his department.

My two assistants, Caroline LaMotte at Discovery and Casey Sage at HIH, took charge of managing my schedule, allowing me adequate time to work on the book. Caroline and Casey also helped in certain topic and photo research, as did Suzanne Pilet. Carrie Hurlburt of HIH contributed many creative ideas for the book project. I am grateful to them all.

There would be no Discovery story to tell without the precious chain of people who advanced my initial idea for the company in 1982. These critical steps led to the closing of my final round of venture funding in 1986. The story of the founding of Discovery was made possible by each of these valuable human links in a four-year chain of business formation events: Maureen Hendricks, Richard Ford, Tom Newman, John McCarthy, Harry Hagerty, Lew Meyer, Richard Crooks, Thalia Crooks, Herbert Allen, Walter Cronkite,

David Glickstein, Irv Culpepper, Harlan Rosenzweig, Bill Baker, Dan Moore, Paul Gould, John Malone, John Sie, Robert Miron, James Robbins, Ajit Dalvi, Gene Schneider, Nimrod Kovacs, and Fred Vierra. An entrepreneur forever remembers the people who first believed.

John Malone, Robert Miron, and Paul Gould remain on my board to this day and I am deeply grateful for their continued leadership. Their advice helps to guide Discovery through a very competitive and rapidly evolving media landscape. Joining the four of us "pioneers" on Discovery's board of directors is David Zaslav, Steve Miron, Robert Bennett, Robert Beck, David Wargo, LaVoy Robison, and Decker Anstrom. All bring an enormous wealth of experience to every issue we face. Steve Newhouse also contributes regularly to our board discussions and I appreciate his keen insights and ideas. Until just recently, we enjoyed the journalistic knowledge and digital skills of Larry Kramer. He served on our board until he accepted his new post in May 2012 as president and publisher of *USA Today*.

I am grateful for the four thousand employees of Discovery, who continue to inspire me by their brilliant work to help satisfy the curiosity of viewers and digital consumers around the world. On a daily basis, I have the enormous pleasure of working with the company leaders who manage the innovative and successful activities described in this book. I want to thank them all for their ongoing contributions to the story of Discovery, beginning with my true partner, David Zaslav, our President and Chief Executive Officer. David is responsible for the remarkable new wave of growth and innovation that the company has experienced since his fortuitous arrival in January 2007. The marvelously talented leadership team that is creating new Discovery success stories every day includes: Mark Hollinger, President and CEO, Discovery Networks International; Joe

Abruzzese, President, Advertising Sales; Bill Goodwyn, President, Global Distribution and CEO, Discovery Education; Adria Alpert Romm, Senior Executive Vice President, Human Resources; Bruce Campbell, Chief Development Officer and General Counsel; Andrew Warren, Senior Executive Vice President and Chief Financial Officer; Jean-Briac (J. B.) Perrette, Chief Digital Officer; and David Leavy, Chief Communications Officer and Senior Executive Vice President, Corporate Marketing and Affairs. The Discovery brands, about which I write extensively in this book, are under the able leadership of these individuals whom I must acknowledge as the true authors of the Discovery programming story: Eileen O'Neill, Group President, Discovery and TLC Networks; Marjorie Kaplan, President, Animal Planet and Science Networks; Henry Schleiff, President and GM, Investigation Discovery, Destination America and Military Channel; Deborah Myers, Executive Vice President and GM, Science Channel; Tom Cosgrove, President and CEO, 3net; Margaret Loesch, President and CEO, The Hub. Responsible for the amazing Discovery global distribution story are these executives who all work under the leadership of Mark Hollinger: John Honeycutt, Executive Vice President and Chief Operating Officer, Discovery Networks International; Luis Silberwasser, Executive Vice President and Chief Content Officer, Discovery Networks International; Dee Forbes, President and Managing Director, Discovery Networks Western Europe; Tom Keaveny, President and Managing Director, Discovery Networks Asia-Pacific; Kasia Kieli, President and Managing Director, Discovery Networks, Central & Eastern Europe, Middle East and Africa; and Enrique Martinez, President and Managing Director, Discovery Networks, Latin America/U.S. Hispanic.

You may have noted at the beginning that I dedicate this work to my wife, Maureen, and to our children, Elizabeth and Andrew.

It is hard to express enough gratitude to Maureen for her encouragement and advice. Right from the time that I first uttered aloud the idea of the Discovery Channel, Maureen has lovingly supported my dreams. I am forever thankful for her belief in my vision. One cannot undertake an endeavor like Discovery without huge sacrifices to personal and family life. It is not a nine-to-five job. Luckily, Maureen was always there to do a complete and dedicated job in raising our children when I was away on business.

Even the greatest entrepreneurial success cannot produce rewards that can match the joy of having children who, in so many ways, make life worthwhile. Now in their late twenties, Elizabeth and Andrew still give meaning and motivation to my life.

From the time she was a child, Elizabeth has stirred my imagination with her story creations and her love of writing. Our musings together on the latest plot lines in her novel give me great joy and stimulate my own writing. Her thoughtful perspectives on government, economics, education reform, and politics are inspiring to me.

Andrew's entrepreneurial enthusiasm is a delight for me to watch. His passionate curiosity to find ways that we can more fully enjoy the machines that move us confirms the basic premise of this book. Andrew's new off-road venture, Driven Experiences, is just the latest improvement in the way we humans can enjoy the ancient invention of the wheel.

Index

Note: Abbreviations "DC" and "JH" refer to Discovery Channel and John Samuel Hendricks, respectively.

About the Author

JOHN S. HENDRICKS is the founder of Discovery Communications, the world's number one nonfiction media company, and serves as chairman of the Board of Directors. Hendricks has been the driving force behind the company's dramatic growth, including the expansion of Discovery Communications from its core property, Discovery Channel, to current global operations in more than 215 countries with 150 networks, among them TLC, Animal Planet, and Science. He lives in Maryland.